Jack Huberman grew up in Montreal. After graduating in architecture from McGill University he moved to New York, where he pursued a dizzying succession of careers as a cartoonist, illustrator, graduate student, magazine writer, freelance book editor, newspaper reporter and stock trader. He has written, with Adam Gopnik, *Voila Careme! The Gastronomic Adventures of History's Greatest Chef*. He continues to write while working towards his license as a curmudgeon.

The **Bush-Hater's** *Handbook*

An A–Z Guide to

the Most Appalling Presidency

of the Past 100 Years

JACK HUBERMAN

Granta Books
London

Granta Publications, 2/3 Hanover Yard, Noel Road, London N1 8BE

First published in Great Britain by Granta Books 2004
First published in the US by Nation Books 2003

A CIP catalogue record for this book
is available from the British Library.

1 3 5 7 9 10 8 6 4 2

Printed and bound in Great Britain
by Bookmarque Ltd, Croydon, Surrey

Contents

INTRODUCTION

"Almost every day brings fresh evidence that Bush and his crew believe they can get away with just about anything—no matter how shocking, offensive, corrupt, underhanded or in-your-face the transgression."

—Arianna Huffington, 2002

Around the time this book's first edition went to press in the United States, in September 2003, the topic of Bush-hatred began appearing all over the U.S. media. A strange new psychological disorder, bemused conservative commentators seemed to suggest, was afflicting millions of Americans. Symptoms included angry outbursts, chronic depression, loss of appetite, an urgent need to change the TV channel the moment "W." came on. What could have given rise to this epidemic of irrationality? Some foreign infection? Something in our meat supply, perhaps?

What had broken out rather suddenly was a rash of liberal and left-wing anti-Bush books. Indeed, I worried that, although mine had been in the works for well over a year, I might now appear merely to be trying to cash in on the Bush-hatred boom. I hope to leave the reader in no doubt as to the sincerity and depth of my Bush-hatred, or that this spate of books is an expression—not just an exploitation—of a Bush-hatred which, if less prevalent in America than abroad, is nonetheless widespread[1] and well-founded. As a *Washington Post* columnist wrote, this "weird psychological affliction" is "nothing of the sort. It is a rational response to getting burned." Bush-haters are simply "biting the hand that slapped them in the face."[2]

Let me also assure those troubled by the word "hatred" that we are of course not speaking, primarily, about personal hatred of Bush—who may be, unlikely as it seems, a wonderful man—but about his politics and policies.

Bush, who ran on the promise of bringing honor and integrity back into the White House, used lie after lie to sell the Iraq war to the American people as an urgently necessary part of the "war on terrorism"—as a "preemptive" war to defend the greatest military power in history against imminent attack by a tin-pot dictatorship with a military less than one-three-hundredth the size of ours. Since September 11, 2001, Bush & Co. have used the "war on terror" to entrench and expand their own power and further the rest of their agenda—their war, if you will, on the economic interests of the majority of Americans; on the already inadequate regulations that protect the environment, workers, and consumers; on programs that help the unemployed, the poor and the elderly; a war on Democrats; on labor unions; and on constitutional principles

1 One U.S. pollster called Bush hatred "as strong as anything I've experienced in 25 years now of polling." A conservative columnist described it as a "hatred . . . that I have never seen in 44 years of campaign watching." (Bush, who ran as a "uniter" but whose policies have divided America more deeply than it has been since Vietnam, recently warned against a return to "the old policies and the old divisions." They don't call this White House "Orwellian" for nothing. See **BushSpeak**.)
2 E.J. Dionne, ". . . Or a Rational Response?" *The Washington Post*, 12/31/03

and international agreements that have guided and protected us for decades; a program of radical, reactionary change that no majority or even plurality of Americans voted for or wanted—in effect, a revolution from above.

This book catalogs the Bush administration's abysmal record of deception and hypocrisy, relentless rollbacks of progress of every kind, tireless devotion to the interests of big business and the wealthy, and confederacy with the programs and prejudices of right-wing and religious zealots. It addresses the effect of Bush policies on global peace and stability—for example, the Pandora's box that could be opened by the doctrine of preemptive war. But I write above all as an American who believes Bush's policies will leave America more isolated, more hated, and less secure, its public finances crippled, its people less secure financially and less healthy, its children more poorly educated, its scientific progress blunted, its culture coarser and stupider, its wealth concentrated in fewer hands, its news media likewise, its courts packed with partisan right-wing judges, and its corporations more free to escape taxes, pollute the air and water, ravage the landscape, and lie to consumers—all for decades to come.

But let's also give the more personal aspects of Bush-hatred their due. One journalist (who began his article with admirable simplicity: "I hate President George W. Bush.") referred to Bush-haters who "have a viscerally hostile reaction to the sound of his voice or describe his existence as a constant oppressive force in their daily psyche."[3] My sentiments exactly. Such was my response, from the start, to

3 Jonathan Chait, "Mad About You," *The New Republic*, 9/29/03

Bush's famous smirk; his ridiculous, gunfighter stance and strut; not just his voice but, with apologies to good Texans, his accent, which, strangely, bore not a trace of his Connecticut childhood or his expensive Andover (Massachusetts) and Yale (Connecticut) education; his (il)literacy and knowledge of the world, which likewise bore not a trace of that or any other education; and not least, the fact that, throughout his life, none of his personal shortcomings, his outstanding mediocrity and seemingly willful ignorance, had hampered his rise, in business and politics, by "virtue" of his family name and connections. Bush truly embodied the American dream—that any kid in America who has a former president for a father, plenty of corporate fat-cat buddies and backers, and the biggest campaign war chest in history can become president of the United States.

Reviewing Kevin Phillips's book *American Dynasty: Aristocracy, Fortune and the Politics of Deceit in the House of Bush*, Joan Walsh of *Salon* noted how the Bush family "was able to use its vast web of shadowy and sun-shiny connections again to 'restore' the Bush dynasty in the White House—'a turn that would have surprised and presumably appalled the founding fathers,' [Phillips] writes." Now, "we have a second George Bush running the country and advancing his family's perverse agenda: serving the rich domestically, increasing the dominance of the energy industry, enlarging the security state, and pursuing a bumbling foreign policy that's clearly made the world less safe, from Afghanistan to Iraq to the Middle East."[4]

4 Joan Walsh, "The Bush Dynasty's Dark Magic," *Salon.com*, 1/27/04

In 1999, Walsh had written that Bush "stands for the open defense of inherited status and power, of the rights of people like us to run the world because people like us have always run it... The next election could be a plebiscite on the notion of dynasty vs. meritocracy."[5] Today, one might more aptly say "dynasty vs. republican *democracy*," for that is what appears to be at stake. U.S. voter turnout has been dropping alarmingly for years; but following 9/11, Americans' interest in democracy in *any* sense seemed to be at an all-time low. It was not just the broad public acceptance, at first, of that sweeping and ominous presidential power-grab and rollback of **civil liberties**,[6] the USA Patriot Act of October 2001. If some pollster had ventured to ask, I suspect we'd have been shocked by how many Americans would, at that point, have been indifferent to even more draconian police measures, the dissolution of Congress, the disappearance of the Democratic party, and the abolition of term limits on the presidency. We appeared to want a *king*. (When Benjamin Franklin was asked what form of government the Founding Fathers had given the new country, he famously replied,"A republic, if you can keep it.") Those acutest of observers, the cartoonists, have taken to depicting Bush wearing a crown. Commentators have likened him, with his supposed metamorphosis from youthful wastrel to great war leader, to Henry V. And indeed, our George II, who has laid hold of more power than any previous U.S. president, probably has

5 Joan Walsh, "The Mediocrity that Roared," *Salon.com*, 11/23/99
6 Throughout this book, bold type indicates a cross-reference to a separate section.

xii *Introduction*

more power than any British monarch since George II, if not since Charles I. Moreover, public criticism of the royal family is far more permissible in Britain than criticism of Bush has been in America through much of his first three years.

The idea of a loyal opposition is alive in America, but not well. Republicans in the White House, Congress, and the mostly pro-Republican U.S. media have openly equated Democratic opposition to Bush and his policies with disloyalty to the country. Congressional Republican leaders have altered the very legislative process to shut the Democrats out, redrawn the electoral map to eliminate Democratic seats, and helped Bush pack the federal courts with rightwing judges (who can, as we have seen, decide elections). "One of the operating political assumptions of the Bush administration," a former Clinton aide wrote, "is that the checks and balances have essentially been checked. Every Democratic effort to launch an inquiry in the Senate into the Bush administration's actions, from its abuse of intelligence about WMD in Iraq to its energy policy, has been suppressed. The watchdog press has been kenneled."[7] There is growing, and well-founded, fear of America becoming, for all practical purposes, a one-party state.[8]

The shockingly dumb **Bushisms**; the cowboy act; the smirk and the swagger; Bush's election, or as some prefer to say, "selection" by the Republican-appointed Supreme

7 Sidney Blumenthal, "He Cannot Tell a Lie," *Salon.com*, 1/15/04
8 See, e.g., Robert Kuttner, "America as a One-Party State," *The American Prospect*, 2/1/04

Court justices; his invocations of God and Jesus at every pandering opportunity; the blind loyalty of his followers, many of whom openly proclaim, as Bush himself has all but done, that his presidency is divinely ordained (see **God and Bush**); the vast private and corporate wealth behind his rise; the great-leader cult woven around him by his party and the right-wing media; the Bushies' relentless dishonesty, ferocious partisanship, and determination to achieve a permanent stranglehold on power—all this is bad enough. But it is what Bush and his party seek to use their power *for*—the further enrichment of their corporate and wealthy clientele, the reversal of social progress on all fronts (see **Abortion**, **Environment**, **Gay Rights**, etc.), and the pursuit of various personal obsessions (see **Iraq** and **Missile Defense**)—that makes this regime such a complete scandal.

What we have, above all, is government of, by, and for corporate special interests and the economic elite. Throughout the administration, Bush filled top positions with executives, lawyers, and lobbyists from the very industries they are now charged with overseeing on the public's behalf. As noted in *The New Republic*, "the Bush administration official assuring the country about the safety of the nation's beef supply last week was none other than a former beef-industry lobbyist. And that's just one example of how far Bush has moved politics to the right. Undermining **Social Security** to finance tax cuts for the wealthy, turning **Medicare** into a voucher program, subjecting regulations to cost-benefit analyses that favor industry—these ideas were all dismissed as radically conservative when 1990s House Speaker and GOP leader Newt Gingrich included them in the

Contract With America. Now they are law or on the way to becoming it."[9]

One area of federal government after another is being reconfigured to benefit the private sector. Bush has increased, not cut, federal spending, even while enacting enormous tax cuts, always disproportionately benefiting the wealthiest few, and driving up federal deficits. I suspect, as many do, that the deficits are part of a deliberate Republican strategy to eventually force drastic cuts in, if not elimination of, the "entitlement programs"—principally Medicare, **Medicaid**, and Social Security—hated by the right. For now, however, the draconian cuts in spending and services, such as schools, are being made mostly by deficit-plagued **state and local governments**, to which the Bush administration has increasingly shifted the burdens and costs of government without providing the necessary funding.[10]

But as federal spending increases, it is increasingly funneled into private, corporate coffers, as the Bushies seek to privatize every square foot, literally and figuratively, of the public domain, from Medicare and Social Security to **education**, environmental regulation, and vast tracts of public land—even military, national security and intelligence functions. (Perhaps the only thing more alarming than government spying on its citizens is private government contractors doing it.)

9 Jonathan Cohn, "The Case for Howard Dean," *The New Republic*, 1/19/04
10 Favorite headline: "States Putting Inmates on Diets to Trim Budgets . . . Inmates lose 300 calories a day; Texas gains $6 million."—*The New York Times*, 9/30/03. The cuts left many inmates 300 calories a day below federal health guidelines.

And while all this has gone on, what has the country been preoccupied with for the past two years? **Iraq**—Bush's "weapon of mass distraction."

The reader will know all too well about the damage done to America's international relations, image, and prestige by Bush, by the Iraq war, and more generally, by the Bushies' famous disdain for international agreements and bodies such as the United Nations and the world court—and more generally still, by the Bushies' embodiment of everything many foreigners find most disagreeable about America: as Hans Magnus Enzensberger summarized it, "a fair supply of double standards [in foreign affairs], a curious mix of ruthless self-interest and missionary rhetoric, and, at home, a bizarre gun cult and a relish for the death penalty . . . Think of a place where cigarettes are perceived as more of a threat to human health than machine guns . . . where almost everyone believes in some god or other and where the outside world, unless it intrudes with bombs, is largely ignored!"[11]

As an American critic noted, "Defenders of the Bush administration point out that it isn't the president's job to please the French or Brazilians,[12] but first and foremost to protect the United States. This is true as far as it goes, but it ignores one crucial insight: We are safer when fewer people hate us."[13] Wealthier, too, to the great extent that America

---

11 *Granta*, Spring 2002

12 Reflecting the new Bush ethos, a *New York Post* columnist remarked that any U.S. president who *does* please the Europeans probably isn't doing his job.

13 Robert Lane Greene, "Commanding Presence," *The New Republic*, 1.13.04

depends on its cultural exports, which, broadly speaking, include the brand names on its manufactures, restaurant chains, etc.

Of course, to Bush-haters at home and abroad, it is not Bush-hatred but Bush's abiding popularity among Americans—exaggerated though it is by our media—that defies comprehension. Or does it? While momentous stories like Michael Jackson's alleged pedophilia can dominate TV network news for weeks and months on end, outrage after Bush outrage, scandal after scandal goes unreported or else plays for a few days or weeks, perhaps even appears to spell serious trouble for the Bushies—but then just evaporates, or vanishes down the black hole of the left-wing media to live on subterraneously.

And make no mistake, the Bushies' rate of outrage production is stupendous. Consider some highlights from just the few months after this book first went to press—beginning with FOREIGN POLICY, IRAQ, AND THE "WAR ON TERRORISM":

- Upon resigning in January 2004, the chief weapons inspector in Iraq, David Kay, said he was convinced Iraq had had no significant chemical weapons stockpiles since the mid-1990s, no large-scale production of biological weapons, and a nuclear weapons program that remained rudimentary at best. In an exhaustive report, *The Washington Post* concluded that Iraq had scarcely a WDM *program*, let alone actual weapons, since the early 1990s.
- A report from the Carnegie Endowment for International Peace concluded there was no evidence of a prewar connection between Saddam Hussein and Al

Qaeda, and condemned the Bush administration for deliberately exaggerating the threat from Iraq and pressuring intelligence analysts to conform.

- The inspectors *had*, Bush proclaimed, found "weapons of mass destruction-related program activities." So *that* was what we'd gone to war over—"program *activities*". . .
- Pressed during an interview about the existence of actual weapons vs. "the *possibility* that [Saddam] could move to acquire those weapons," Bush replied, "So what's the difference?" (Somewhat like a police officer explaining that he shot a man because he looked like he was thinking about buying a gun.)
- In a new book, former Bush treasury secretary Paul O'Neill, who was fired in December 2002 for questioning some of the Bush tax cuts and not being enough of a "team player," said the Bush White House had been focused on an invasion of Iraq from its first week in office—belying the Bush claim that it was in response to Sept. 11.
- Saddam Hussein was captured—and more Americans were killed and wounded in the four weeks after than in the four weeks before. In January 2004, attacks on occupation forces were running at about one and a half dozen a day, not including those against Iraqi security forces or civilians.
- The Pentagon warned the media that filming or photographing coffins carrying U.S. war dead home from Iraq is forbidden. Bush meanwhile was not attending soldiers' funerals, apparently to avoid TV coverage of them.

- A report published by the U.S. Army War College said the war in Iraq was a "detour" that undermined the war on terrorism.
- Libyan leader Muammar el-Qaddafi agreed to dismantle his WMD programs, which Bush credited to the example he had made of Iraq. But a former member of Bush's own National Security Council wrote that Bush "misrepresents the real lesson of the Libyan case," which was that years of economic sanctions and secret diplomacy begun under Clinton had paid off.[14]
- The White House finally agreed to provide classified intelligence reports to the commission investigating the **September 11** attacks—but only on condition the White House be allowed to "edit" them and determine which portions are "relevant." Bush officials acknowledged that "intelligence reports Mr. Bush received in the weeks before 9/11 might be construed to suggest the White House failed to respond to evidence suggesting Al Qaeda was planning a catastrophic attack."[15]
- Federal appeals courts ruled that the indefinite imprisonment of 660 terrorism suspects at Guantanamo Bay, Cuba violated both the U.S. Constitution and international law, and that Bush lacked the authority to define a U.S. citizen arrested in the U.S.

14 Flynt Leverett, "Why Libya Gave Up on the Bomb," *The New York Times*, 1/23/04

15 "Deal on 9/11 Briefings Lets White House Edit Papers," *The New York Times*, 11/14/03

as an "enemy combatant" (as had been done in at least one case) and to deny him or her due process.

OTHER GLOBAL ISSUES:

- A study published in *Nature* warned that one-third of all animal and plant species could become extinct by 2050 due to **global warming**—whose link to fossil fuels, indeed, whose very existence, the Bush administration still refused to acknowledge. Meanwhile, the administration, which had abandoned the Kyoto Protocol on climate change, "continues to bad-mouth the treaty at every opportunity."[16]
- While his fundraising speeches trumpeted the commitment of "this great, compassionate land" to "bringing the healing power of medicine to millions ... now suffering from AIDS," Bush put off for several years the fulfillment of his funding pledges to fight **AIDS** and poverty in the third world, cutting the $550 million Congress allocated to the Global Fund to Fight AIDS, Tuberculosis and Malaria down to $200 million, among other cutbacks.

ENVIRONMENTAL AND **ENERGY POLICY:**

- After promising not to, the Bushies abandoned the Environmental Protection Administration's (EPA) years-long, nearly complete investigations of

16 *The New York Times* editorial, 12/4/03

violations by more than fifty power plants'—of Clean Air Act **air pollution** rules—which the Bushies were in the process of dismantling.

- Two more top EPA enforcement officials resigned, citing the administration's chumminess with industry groups and hostility to environmental enforcement. "The direction the agency was going . . . was contrary to everything that I had worked for," one of them said.[17]

- The administration moved to legalize the environmentally catastrophic coal strip-mining technique called "mountaintop removal," which had already devastated large areas and killed countless streams in Appalachia. The coal industry had lobbied hard for the change.

- The administration removed anti-logging legal protection from the Tongass National Forest in Alaska, the nation's only temperate rain **forest**, where, before the Clinton administration imposed the "roadless rule," clear-cutting had already destroyed a half million acres of old-growth trees. The rule was under assault all over the country by the Bushies and the timber industry.

HEALTH, CONSUMER, AND WORKPLACE PROTECTIONS:

- To ensure the subordination of **science** and **health** policy-making to Bush political aims and (same thing) business interests, the White House Office of

17 Amanda Griscom, "Jumping Ship at the EPA," *Grist*, 1/8/04

Management and Budget (OMB) was put in charge of "reviewing" the scientific accuracy of any government-issued warnings related to public heath, safety, and the environment, for which, a former OMB official said, "the agency is completely lacking in the personnel, expertise, and knowledge necessary to be that sort of judge and jury ... It's an extraordinary act of hubris."[18] (Also see **Deregulation**.)

- Continuing the administration's support for U.S. junk-food manufacturers, the U.S. Department of Health and Human Services issued a 28-page, line-by-line attack on a U.N. Food and Agriculture Organization diet and nutrition report urging people to limit their sugar consumption. "Although the department framed the critique as a principled defense of scientific integrity," wrote two public health experts, "much evidence argues for another interpretation—blatant pandering to American food companies that produce much of the world's high-calorie, high-profit sodas and snacks."[19] (And contribute much to Republican coffers.)

- A new study concluded that the supposed explosion in the economic costs of class-action lawsuits against corporations by consumers, employees, etc.—on which the Bush administration based its relentless drive for "**tort reform**"—was nonexistent.[20]

18 Amanda Griscom, "The Green Elephant in the Room," *Grist*, 1/15/04
19 Kelly D. Brownell and Marion Nestle, "The Sweet and Lowdown on Sugar," *The New York Times*, 1/23/04
20 Jonathan D. Glater, "Study Disputes View of Costly Surge in Class-Action Suits," *The New York Times*, 1/14/04

LABOR ISSUES:

- Bush proposed legalizing millions of undocumented workers under a guest-worker program. "The stated goal is improving the lives of immigrants and improving relations with Mexico. But the actual target audience is corporate employers seeking low-wage, docile employees, and Hispanic voters ... Imagine what will happen to Americans and foreigners with green cards making a too-low seven or eight dollars an hour when there's a whole new force of 'guest-workers' willing to work for five dollars."[21]

- An exhaustive *New York Times* report found that, out of 2,197 workplace deaths caused by employers' willful violations of safety laws over the past twenty years, the federal Occupational Safety and Health Administration (OSHA) declined to seek criminal charges in 93 percent of cases; only 81 cases ended in convictions and only 16 in jail sentences. Even repeat violators and cases involving multiple deaths were rarely prosecuted. Presented with the report, OSHA's administrator—regarded as one of the least anti-Labor of Bush's Labor Department appointees—confirmed the numbers, yet "made it clear that he saw no need to change either the law or OSHA's handling of these worst cases of death on the job."[22]

21 Robert Kuttner, "Look Closely," *The American Prospect*, 1/25/04
22 David Barstow, "U.S. Rarely Seeks Charges For Deaths in Workplace," *The New York Times*, 12/22/03

BUDGET, TAXES AND THE **ECONOMY:**

- The International Monetary Fund (IMF), whose business is to monitor fiscally irresponsible and debt-ridden governments, warned that U.S. deficits were spiraling out of control, threatening to create a currency crisis and imperiling the U.S. and global economies. The IMF warned that Washington's fiscal recklessness would undermine the two pillars of America's social safety net, **Social Security** and **Medicare** (as though that weren't the Republicans' intent) and said the Bush tax cuts were deliberately designed to mask their true fiscal impact.

- A year after predicting the end of the federal deficit by 2007 and an accumulated *surplus* of $1.3 trillion by 2013, the Congressional Budget Office said that it now expected total deficits of nearly $2 trillion over the next decade, and more than $4 trillion[23] if Bush's further tax cut proposals were enacted.

- Bush proposed another cut in taxes on investment income (stock dividends, interest and capital gains) that would effectively abolish all remaining taxes on such income, most of which is "earned" by the rich. (Of Bush's previous cuts in these taxes, 72 percent of the benefits went to the richest 5 percent.[24]) Under this champion of traditional values, "work," a critic noted, "has become a distinctly inferior kind of

23 Not including an additional $1 trillion in added interest costs.
24 Based on analysis by Citizens for Tax Justice, Fall 2003.

income. Bush tax policy rewards investment and inheritance. Relying on work for your income, by contrast, turns you into a second-class citizen."[25] (See **Estate Tax**; **Tax Evasion**.)

- After the loss of 3 million jobs since 2001, the White House boasted of some 278,000 new jobs created in the second half of 2003. Bush's Council of Economic Advisers had predicted nearly two million, including 510,000 as a result of the Bushies' 2003 round of tax cuts for the rich—or as they call them, "jobs measures." By subsidizing job growth in Asia rather than in the U.S., Bush tax policy was also helping to depress wages at home, where real wages fell in the fourth quarter of 2003.

SOCIAL, CULTURAL, RELIGIOUS, AND RACIAL ISSUES:

- Amid pressing social needs on all sides, Bush found $1.5 billion for a new program to promote marriage among poor people on **welfare**. Critics doubted (based on a previous experiment) that it would succeed in promoting marriage; worried that the government would pressure poor women into staying in bad relationships; and/or argued that it would do nothing to help people lacking jobs, skills, and hope; but most agreed it would appease Bush's core religious-right voters.

25 Harold Meyerson, "Second-Class Citizens," *The American Prospect Online*, 1/15/04

- Bush also doubled spending on encouraging sexual abstinence by teens and pledged $23 million for schools—to buy books or make badly needed repairs? No, to investigate students for drug use. As journalist Andrew Sullivan observed, "There's barely a speech by President Bush that doesn't cite the glories of human freedom ... But there's a strange exception to this Bush doctrine. It ends when you reach America's shores ... The government, Bush clearly believes, has a right to be involved in many personal decisions you make—punishing some, encouraging others ..." Other examples: Funneling public money to religious groups for "social work" under Bush's "faith-based initiative" (see **Church and State**); tripling funding for "character education" to, as Bush said, "teach our children ... right from wrong" (as the Right sees it); spending hundreds of millions on anti-drug propaganda; and sending federal agents to bust users of medical marijuana (see **Drugs, war on**). "It's the nanny state with more cash. Your cash, that is. Their morals."[26]

- Bush signed a bill banning so-called "partial-birth **abortions**," with no exceptions for protecting a mother's health. The bill, *The New York Times* reported, "strikes at the heart of *Roe v. Wade* [the 1973 Supreme Court decision legalizing **abortion** in the U.S.]" A priceless news photo showed Bush signing the bill as its Congressional sponsors—ten mostly

26 Andrew Sullivan, "The Nanny in Chief," *Time*, 2/2/04

elderly white men, and only men—looked on. Failing to plant a few women in the shot was a rare slip-up by the White House "communications" team.

- Bush said he would support a constitutional amendment banning gay marriage or even, possibly, same-sex "civil unions" and domestic partnerships. (See **Gay Rights**.) On this issue as well as abortion, medical marijuana, and others, Bush would let the federal government overrule state laws. States' rights, traditionally sacred to conservatives, "are well and good—as long as the states don't do things that some Republicans disapprove of."[27]

- Taking Bush's "faith-based" war on **church-state** separation to the great outdoors, the National Park Service placed plaques bearing biblical verses in Grand Canyon National Park and approved selling a book there that suggests the canyon was created in six days several thousand years ago. Bush political appointees in top Park Service positions were reportedly acting in cahoots with religious-right groups.

- Bush and Defense Secretary Donald Rumsfeld refused to criticize remarks made by Gen. William Boykin—the nation's top uniformed intelligence officer and the man charged with pursuing Saddam Hussein and Osama bin Laden—who told evangelical Christian audiences that these foes "will only be defeated if we come against them in the name of Jesus"; that Islamists hate the U.S. "because we're a

27 Ibid

Christian nation, because our foundation and our roots are Judeo-Christian . . . and the enemy is a guy named Satan"; that when battling a Muslim warlord in Somalia, "I knew my God was bigger than his. I knew that my God was a real God and his was an idol".

- Using the Congressional recess to bypass Senate approval, Bush appointed one of the most "controversial" of all his far-right-wing **judicial nominees**, Charles Pickering of Mississippi, to a Court of Appeals judgeship. The Senate Judiciary Committee had rejected Pickering over concerns about his record of support for racial segregation and leniency toward racial and gender discrimination and hate crimes.

BUSH AND THE **MEDIA**, POLITICS VS. POLICY, BUSH'S PERMANENT ELECTION CAMPAIGN, AND THE REPUBLICAN DRIVE FOR PERMANENT POWER:

- Securing his reputation as the most insulated and out-of-touch U.S. president ever, Bush admitted he rarely reads news stories; "the best way to get the news is from objective sources, and the most objective sources I have are people on my staff who tell me what's happening in the world." In his first three years, Bush had given only eleven press conferences, vs. around seventy by most of his recent predecessors in their first three years.
- Along with his candor about Iraq, former treasury secretary O'Neill said Bush was "disengaged" at cabinet meetings and had little or nothing to say; that there

was little or no debate on policy—he described Bush as a "blind man in a roomful of deaf people"; and that in this White House, politics—surprise, surprise—took precedence over policy.

- Bush called for new manned missions to the moon and eventually to Mars, which would provide little or no scientific advantage over unmanned space exploration yet cost far more—this at a time when already tight public school budgets were being cut, 40-60 million Americans lacked health insurance, poverty was on the rise, and the federal deficit was nearing $500 billion a year. The initiative would, however, pump money into aerospace-defense corporations and into some key electoral districts around Cape Canaveral, *Florida*, and lend Bush, in an election year, that elusive thing his father used to call "the vision thing" while diverting attention away from certain terrestrial debacles. An expensive way to get a photo of himself in a space suit, comedians cracked.

- On a wreath-laying visit to Martin Luther King, Jr.'s tomb in Atlanta to observe King's birthday, Bush was loudly booed by protesters (who are usually kept far out of his and the cameras' sight and earshot). "Bush's policies contradict everything Dr. King stood for," one protester said. On King's birthday the previous year, a former colleague noted, Bush had "initiated plans to gut affirmative action."

- The three largest manufacturers of the touch-screen voting machines being installed around the country were Republican Party contributors. The head of the largest, Ohio-based Diebold Inc., declared in a GOP fund-raising letter that he was "committed to helping Ohio deliver its electoral votes to the president [Bush] next year." Moreover, it was learned that some of these manufacturers' own programmers regarded the machines as so unreliable and full of security flaws that an election could easily be rigged.

- Eighty-nine Republican members of the House of Representatives cosponsored a bill to replace Franklin D. Roosevelt's portrait on the U.S. dime with Ronald Reagan's. Even Nancy Reagan objected. (No news on an effort to add Reagan's head to Mt. Rushmore; perhaps the Republicans would now rather save the space for George W. Bush.)

- Bush's annual State of the Union address in January 2004 omitted certain aspects of the state of the union, such as America's loss, on his watch, of some three million jobs, health insurance coverage for millions, key environmental protections, a projected $5 trillion budget surplus (which had turned into a $5 trillion *deficit*), international prestige and good-will, and our leaders' credibility on national security matters. Nor did the speech mention that Bush policies had forced every state *in* the union to make drastic cuts to everything from health care and schools to police and prisons.

A book like this is bound to age quickly, as fresh outrages flow from the White House almost daily and new twists develop in older ones. Some obsolescences are inevitable, and I apologize for them. On the other hand, my purpose was to catalog the Bushies' policies, aims, and priorities as much as their actual achievements—and their policies, aims, and priorities were apparent, all too apparent, from the start.

Equally inevitable are various omissions. Exactly which outrages deserved to be included is, I suppose, partly in the eye of the Bush-hater. After all, what is utter abomination to one of us is mere heinousness to another. But for any truly unforgivable omissions, I apologize.

Finally, as it may seem odd at first, I should note that I wrote the book entirely in the past tense, or what might be called the "past hopeful," in the ardent hope that the Bush administration will in fact have passed into the past tense while this book is still being read, and, meanwhile, to help conjure up the day when Bush & Co. are, indeed, history.

ABORTION, BIRTH CONTROL, AND REPRODUCTIVE HEALTH

According to an ABC News-*Washington Post* poll released in January 2001, 59 percent of Americans supported a woman's right to choose abortion in all or most cases; 46 percent of Republicans supported that right; and only 14 percent of Americans thought abortion should be illegal in all cases.

On Monday, January 22, 2001—President Bush's first working day in office—he issued an executive memorandum blocking U.S. federal funding for international organizations that perform abortions or provide abortion counseling or services overseas. The announcement coincided with the anniversary of *Roe v. Wade*, the 1973 Supreme Court ruling that legalized abortion across the U.S.

Bush v. family planning. Since 1973, U.S. law had prohibited the use of federal foreign assistance funds to perform abortions. Bush's action prohibited recipients of federal funds even from providing abortion counseling or information regarding the availability of abortions using non-U.S. government funds. It revoked the Clinton administration population assistance policy and reinstated President Reagan's "Mexico City" policy—a.k.a. the "global gag rule"—first announced in 1984 at the Second UN International Conference on Population in Mexico City.

Bush's move drew immediate criticism from women's rights groups and government officials around the world. If applied to organizations within the U.S., critics noted, the same measure would be deemed an unconstitutional restriction on free speech. Family-planning organizations and development experts argued that placing these restrictions on family-planning assistance in developing countries would lead to an increase in the number of unintended pregnancies and abortions, in direct contradiction of Bush's stated goal.

Organizations that lost funding as a result of Bush's action were active in distributing condoms and providing **AIDS** education. The International Planned Parenthood Foundation (IPPF) lost around $20 million in cash and supplies—more than 20 percent of its budget. The Family Guidance Association of Ethiopia—where abortions were only permitted to protect the health of the mother, maternal mortality rates were among the world's highest, and more than 4 million people were infected with HIV—lost 60 percent of its annual budget. Bush's action "translates to clinics closed, contraceptives not available" and AIDS programs curtailed, IPPF's director-general said, adding, "There is a clear and direct relationship between women's ability to control their fertility and their ability to escape poverty."[1] The European Union's Social Affairs Commissioner called Bush's announcement, simply, "a step backwards." The chairwoman of Republicans For Choice remarked, "He's supposed to be measuring for drapes on his first day, not interfering with women's rights."[2]

The move was but the opening shot in a broad assault on abortion rights and birth control. In the next two years, Bush also froze U.S. funding for the World Health Organization's reproductive health program and used UN conferences to push a "pro-life" agenda. In January 2002, he eliminated U.S. funding for the United Nations Population Fund (UNFPA) under the pretense that the program may fund or advocate abortion. In fact, the UNFPA *prevented* abortions and saved lives by providing family planning services in 156 countries; it also aided in HIV and sexual violence prevention, maternal care, emergency disaster relief (notably in post-Taliban Afghanistan), and taught women literacy and income-earning skills. UN officials estimated the loss of funding from the U.S. would undermine their ability to prevent 800,000 abortions and could result in the deaths of 4,700 women and 77,000 children. "The upshot is that women and babies are dying in Africa because of Mr. Bush's idealism," wrote Nicholas Kristof in *The New York Times*.[3]

The sole form of birth control the Bushies *were* willing to support was abstinence. Bush's 2003 budget increased funding for abstinence programs by one-third, to $135 million; it was the largest percentage increase for any area outside of defense. The funding passed through the Department of Health and Human Services (HSS), whose secretary, TOMMY THOMPSON, was, like just about every other Bush official, an outspoken opponent of abortion rights. There was, to date, no evidence that abstinence programs were effective. Bush also diverted $300 million from **welfare** funding to promote marriage for welfare mothers.

In November 2003, Bush signed a bill banning certain late-term, so-called "partial-birth abortions." The bill, *The New York Times* reported, "strikes at the heart of Roe v. Wade by criminalizing many midterm abortions and omitting exceptions for a mother's health." Judges in several states immediately issued restraining orders blocking enforcement of the new law on the grounds that it could be unconstitutional and could threaten mothers' health.

Sinking SCHIP. In January 2002, in a move of awesome cynicism, HSS Secretary Thompson announced that henceforth, a fetus would be defined as a "child" for the purpose of entitling poor women to get prenatal care under the federal Children's Health Insurance Program (SCHIP). Actually, SCHIP already had mechanisms in place to provide prenatal care. What it didn't have was *funding*. The program was running out of money—and no new funding was provided for this "expansion." Indeed, it was estimated that budget cuts would result in at least 600,000 children *losing* SCHIP coverage by 2007 and joining the 8 million American children with no health insurance coverage.[4] (See **Medicaid**.) There would be precious little left in federal budgets for poor women, children *or* fetuses after Bush's $2 trillion in tax cuts for the rich.

The abortion–breast cancer canard. In December 2002, the Bushies, pressured by antiabortion members of Congress, altered a fact sheet on the National Cancer Institute (NCI) website to suggest that abortion could cause breast cancer, a pet scare tactic of anti-abortion activists. The doctored fact sheet referred to studies on the supposed link between abortion and breast cancer as "inconsistent," when the scientific evidence overwhelmingly denied any such link, as the fact sheet previously stated. It was one of many instances in which the Bushies censored or distorted scientific or health information in the interests of politics and ideology. (See **AIDS; Health and safety regulations; Science policy.**)

Rx for women's health problems: Prayer. In October 2002, Bush named W. DAVID HAGER to chair the powerful Reproductive Health Drugs Advisory Committee of the Food and Drug Administration (FDA), which evaluated the safety and effectiveness of drugs used in obstetrics, gynecology, and related specialties. (Because this committee had not met once in the nearly two years since Bush came to office, its charter lapsed, leaving Bush free to fill all eleven positions.) Hager, an obstetrician-gynecologist whom the Bushies had already appointed to two other federal women's health advisory committees, wasn't just vehemently opposed to abortion rights. He was best known as the author of *As Jesus Cared for Women: Restoring Women Then and Now* and *The Reproduction Revolution: A Christian Appraisal of Sexuality, Reproductive Technologies and the Family*, which endorsed the medically inaccurate claim that the birth control pill causes abortion.[5] Women who suffer from premenstrual syndrome, postpartum depression, and eating disorders, Hager suggested, should seek help from reading the Bible and praying. He had spoken out against the use of the pill and condoms outside of marriage, and he called for the FDA to reverse its approval of the RU-486 "abortion pill," saying it endangered the lives and health of women. The FDA determined in October 2000 that the drug was safe and effective.

AIDS

In his State of the Union address in January 2003, Bush surprised and pleased most of his audience by announcing a

$15 billion initiative for the prevention and treatment of AIDS in twelve African countries, plus Haiti and Guyana. To the more cynical, the move seemed designed to offset the less humane-sounding part of the speech—the part in which Bush again made clear his intention to make war on Iraq. Indeed, nothing in Bush's prior record on AIDS inspired confidence that his new initiative was for real:

- He had failed to make good on a previous commitment of $500 million to prevent mother-to-child AIDS transmission.
- During Bush's second month in office, his chief of staff, Andrew Card, announced that the White House office on AIDS would be shut down (along with the office on race relations). In the ensuing furor, the White House backed down, insisting Card had been mistaken.
- In August 2002, Bush blocked a spending bill that included $200 million for global AIDS programs.
- Bush consistently put the wishes and biases of the Christian right ahead of AIDS prevention and other health needs. This lobby was uninterested in any AIDS-prevention or birth-control methods other than abstinence and had prevailed on Bush in January 2002 to eliminate funding for the United Nations Population Fund (UNFPA) under the pretense that the program, which provides HIV prevention, family planning, and other services around the world, may fund or advocate **abortion**.
- The administration shut down a Centers for Disease Control and Prevention (CDC) web page that advised

teens to practice safe sex. It also revised a CDC online fact sheet on prevention of sexually transmitted diseases, removing information on effective condom use and censoring out references to studies showing that teaching teens about condoms did not encourage adolescent sexual activity, but in fact tended to delay the onset of intercourse. Ignoring the scientific evidence, the Bush delegation claimed at a UN population conference in 2002 that promoting condom use, even in HIV prevention programs, would encourage adolescent sexual behavior.

- The administration gave scant support to the Global Fund to Fight AIDS, TB and Malaria, set up by UN Secretary General Kofi Annan in 2001. The fund's needs were estimated at $10–15 billion per year. Bush's 2004 budget froze U.S. funding at $200 million.

Blocking generic drug exports. Bush's new promise to provide generic AIDS drugs to poor countries conflicted directly with Bush trade policies aimed at protecting **pharmaceutical** companies from generic competition. The vast majority of the more than 22 million deaths from AIDS so far had occurred in poor countries, where drug companies had long refused to lower the prices of AIDS drugs and opposed importation of generics,[6] and where treatment therefore remained largely unaffordable. Only two months before Bush announced his plan, the administration urged the World Trade Organization (WTO) to ban exports of generics. Drug companies holding AIDS drug patents were among the GOP's biggest contributors.

In Brazil, government-supported labs had become

leading manufacturers of generic AIDS drugs, free distribution of which had cut annual deaths from AIDS in Brazil in half. Worse (from the U.S. drug industry's point of view) than just producing its own drugs, Brazil offered assistance to other countries seeking to set up similar programs. So, in Bush's second month in office, the U.S. filed a complaint with the WTO alleging Brazil was violating the WTO's Trade-Related Aspects of Intellectual Property Rights (TRIPS) Agreement. A month later, thirty-nine major pharmaceutical companies, with strong U.S. backing, sued the South African government under TRIPS for permitting the manufacture and importation of generic AIDS drugs. The U.S. threatened trade sanctions against other poor countries that imported generics.

The Bush AIDS plan: Far less than met the eye, or the need. Globally, 8,500 people—roughly three times the September 11 death toll—are dying of AIDS every day. Of the 30 million people in Africa with AIDS, only around 30,000 (or one in a thousand) are receiving treatment. By 2010, there will be 20 million AIDS orphans in Africa alone. The problem threatens not only the lives and health of millions, but the economies and the social and political stability of entire regions.

The plan Bush announced so dramatically in January 2003, critics said, fell far short of being a realistic and adequate response, either in the level of funding or the way it was to be spent. The promised $15 billion over five years might be compared with the $75 billion Bush requested two months later as a down payment on the Iraq war, or his $48 billion defense budget *increase* for 2003, or his more than $2 trillion in tax cuts. Moreover:

- Of the "$15 billion commitment," $10 billion was new money—$5 billion had already been allocated for AIDS relief—and only $450 million would be spent in the first year.
- Twelve African countries were included under Bush's plan; thirty-six, including some the continent's most AIDS-ravaged, such as Malawi and Zimbabwe, were not. "[The plan] can't be successful because borders are porous [to AIDS]," said Salih Booker of Africa Action.
- Most of the money would go to no fewer than twelve U.S. government agencies, that were instructed to create a national working group on HIV/AIDS, which would in turn recommend how the money would be used—in short, the very sort of wasteful, bloated, bureaucratic morass Republicans loved to disparage. It might be years before Bush's "initiative" actually produced any international treatment programs for AIDS.
- Much of the money would likely go to the U.S. Agency for International Development (USAID), whose AIDS programs were notorious for focusing on abstinence-based prevention while almost entirely excluding treatment.

AIR POLLUTION

Bush wasted little time rewarding some of his and his party's biggest contributors—energy and power companies—by undermining the Clean Air Act, the country's most important air-pollution law, which was enacted in the 1970s (under Nixon) to limit harmful emissions from power plants, oil refineries, and other industrial facilities. Even by Bush standards, the assault on the Clean Air Act represented a shocking disregard for public health and a selling out of the public interest for corporate and political benefit.

In early 2001, the Bushies used the **California energy crisis** as a pretext to attack environmental rules. They argued that the cost of complying with those rules discouraged power companies from expanding or building urgently needed plants. A year later, the stock prices of the biggest power producers and marketers—El Paso Corp., Williams Companies, Dynergy, Reliant Energy, Mirant, not to mention **Enron**—had been decimated because of slack demand and *over*capacity; and the California "crisis" was revealed to have been manufactured by those same companies in order to drive up prices and profits. Curiously enough, four of the six above-named companies were based in Texas and were major Bush and GOP contributors.

How the administration undermined Clean Air enforcement. The Bushies' first target was the Clean Air Act provision called NEW SOURCE REVIEW (NSR), which required the oldest and dirtiest power plants to install pollution-reducing equipment to meet current air-quality standards if and when the plants are expanded. For decades, many companies evaded that expense by calling their major expansions "maintenance" or "life extension projects." As a result, by the '90s, dozens of such plants were spewing out pollutants such as sulfur dioxide and nitrogen dioxide in quantities that far exceeded the current legal limits. Much of this pollution got blown from aging plants in the Midwest to the Northeast and caused severe and widespread health problems, including asthma, pneumonia, bronchitis, emphysema, heart attacks, strokes, and lung cancer, along with environmental damage such as acid rain.

Under Clinton the Environmental Protection Agency (EPA) sued thirteen utilities for expansions of fifty-one plants without the required permits or pollution controls, and reached settlements with four of them. Collectively, these companies emitted a quarter of the entire country's sulfur dioxide emissions and 2 million tons of nitrogen dioxide each year—causing, the EPA estimated, some 10,800 premature deaths, 5,400 cases of chronic bronchitis, and 5,000 hospital emergency visits annually. Settlements of the pending cases would have reduced emissions by millions of tons, not to mention reductions from other companies with whom the EPA was still negotiating.

Then the Bushies came to town and pulled the rug out from under the EPA's own enforcement efforts. In May 2001, Bush called for a ninety-day "review" of the NSR rules—which was still in effect nine months later. This precluded any new enforcement actions. Bush also instructed the Justice Department to review the ongoing lawsuits and determine whether they should continue. Meanwhile, the Bushies cut the EPA's enforcement staff by more than 100—leaving it heavily outgunned by corporate defendants—and leaked their plans to scrap NSR. Power companies now had no incentive to agree to settlements based on those rules. Even the companies that had already come to agreements now refused to sign them. Others walked away from ongoing negotiations.

The fact that Bush's EPA administrator, Christie Whitman, didn't resign until May 2003 seemed remarkable, given the endless abuses and betrayals she, her agency, and environmental interests suffered under Bush. One senior EPA official, Eric Schaeffer, director of the Office of Regulatory Enforcement, resigned in February 2002 after twelve years at the agency, citing frustrations with a pro-industry administration bent on weakening environmental laws and undermining EPA enforcement actions.

"Clear Skies": "A gift for polluters." In February 2002, the White House unveiled a bold new air pollution plan— bold in the shameless way it gutted the Clean Air Act, lowered pollutant reduction targets, and pushed back target dates. In classic **BushSpeak,** the scheme—which Sen. John Edwards (D-NC) called "a gift for polluters"—was named the "CLEAR SKIES INITIATIVE."

Comparing it to the Clean Air Act, the Bush plan:[7]

- Permitted twice as much SULFUR DIOXIDE emissions up to 2018 and 50 percent more after 2018. Sulfur dioxide (SO_2) causes acid rain and thousands of premature deaths from respiratory disease.
- Permitted 50 percent more NITROGEN OXIDE up to 2018 and 33 percent more after 2018. Nitrogen oxide (NO) causes lung-damaging ozone smog.
- Permitted five times as much MERCURY up to 2018 and three times as much after 2018. Mercury emitted by coal-fired power plants causes brain, lung, and kidney damage and reproductive problems. In 2002 at least 6 million women of childbearing age in the U.S. had mercury levels in their bodies that exceeded those considered safe by the EPA.
- Broke a Bush campaign pledge by including no new

controls for CARBON DIOXIDE, the main contributor to global warming.

- Permitted "POLLUTION TRADING": Even Bush's lowered targets would likely never be reached because instead of making polluters reduce emissions to comply with legal standards, his plan allowed them to simply buy "rights" to pollute from cleaner industries. The result might well be no net pollution reductions, perhaps even increases. The new rules (with some modifications) took effect in December 2003. The Bushies had indicated they would continue to act against violations of the old Clean Air rules, but in November 2003, they entirely abandoned the EPA's now nearly complete investigations of such violations at more than fifty power plants.

See **Deregulation; Energy; Environment; Global warming.**

ASHCROFT

In early 2001, in a victory for and reward to the far right, Bush put a quick end to any hopes for moderation by naming former Missouri governor and senator John Ashcroft as attorney general (AG). For this crucial post, Bush had chosen a hard-right ideologue and religious fundamentalist widely considered the most right-wing member of the Senate, known for his hostility to civil rights, reproductive rights, **gun control**, regulation of business, and the constitutional separation of **church and state**. Ashcroft was aptly described as a "religious warrior with politics more appropriate to 17th-century Salem, Mass.—or late-1990s Kandahar—than to [a] secular democracy."[8]

AS MISSOURI ATTORNEY GENERAL (1976–84) AND GOVERNOR (1984–93), Ashcroft vigorously opposed court-ordered desegregation of the St. Louis and Kansas City public schools. In two separate cases that dragged on for decades, federal courts eventually concluded that students attending public schools in those cities were being denied their constitutional rights to an equal education. In his 2001 Senate confirmation hearings, Ashcroft said Missouri had never been found guilty of wrongdoing and that he had "followed the [court desegregation] order, both as attorney general and governor." In fact, Missouri had tried to appeal the orders and was repeatedly rebuffed by the U.S. Supreme Court; a U.S. District Court in 1981 had threatened to hold Ashcroft in contempt for "continual failure to comply"; and court documents named Missouri a "primary constitutional wrongdoer" in maintaining segregated and unequal schools. As U.S. AG, Ashcroft would have power over federal enforcement of desegregation laws that he himself had fought tooth and nail.

AS MISSOURI SENATOR (1994–2000), Ashcroft:

- Gave an interview in 1998 to pro-Confederate *Southern Partisan* magazine in which he praised the magazine for "defending Southern patriots like [Robert E.] Lee, [Stonewall] Jackson and [Jefferson] Davis." A 1995 article in this magazine said "neither 'slavery' nor 'racism' as an institution is a sin" and "there is no indication that slavery is contrary to Christian ethics."[9] The magazine regularly praised Klan leaders and celebrated the assassination of Abraham Lincoln.[10]

- Blocked Clinton's appointment of black Missouri Supreme Court Justice Ronnie White to the federal bench.
- Voted against funding for minority-owned businesses.
- Sponsored the "Charitable Choice" clause in the 1996 Welfare Reform Act, opening a wide crack in church-state separation and creating the wedge for the Bush White House's "Faith-based Initiatives."

The Christian right's reward. Ashcroft's nomination was payback to Christian-right leaders for backing Bush in 2000 and helping him defeat Sen. John McCain in the critical South Carolina primary, and for the role of the Florida Christian Coalition in supporting Bush during the vote recount dispute.[11] Ashcroft's longtime backers included many of the leading figures on the Christian right, including televangelist PAT ROBERTSON, political strategist RALPH REED, activist PAUL WEYRICH, and financier RICHARD MELLON SCAIFE. Also instrumental was the **Federalist Society**, a powerful network of right-wing lawyers and jurists. The "movement," these folks stated clearly, was especially concerned with the AG's position because it would be so important in determining Bush's **judicial nominations**.[12]

Defender of freedom. After 9/11, Ashcroft began to outrage and frighten even lifelong, through-and-through conservatives. Consider: A few years earlier, he had declared that citizens "armed with both the right to possess firearms and to speak freely" are "less likely to fall victim to a tyrannical government" than if "disarmed from criticizing government or defending themselves." This same man, after 9/11, led the Bush administration's assault on **civil liberties**—its creation of secret military tribunals, secret detentions, etc.— and accused critics of these measures of "trying to scare peace-loving people," saying their "tactics only aid terrorists . . . erode our national unity [and] give ammunition to America's enemies." Ashcroft also:[13]

- Rounded up thousands of terrorism suspects after 9/11 who were detained in secret and without charges. The roundup produced no 9/11-related arrests and, officials said, "little usable intelligence about terrorism."
- Found time in the immediate aftermath of 9/11 to order a crackdown on doctors in California and Oregon who, under state laws, prescribed marijuana to ease pain of dying patients. "If this were almost any other issue— enforcement of gun regulations or environmental laws or equal-employment rules—Ashcroft would have been in court fighting this federal seizure of power as an assault not just against the states but against the express wishes of voters."[14] (See **Drugs, war on**.)
- Tried to kill the huge federal lawsuit against the **tobacco industry**.
- Did little or nothing to address a U.S. Commission on Civil Rights finding of widespread disfranchisement of black voters in Florida in **Election 2000**.
- Said he would shut down former AG Janet Reno's task force to prevent violence against **abortion** clinics and

delayed providing federal marshals to protect an abortion clinic doctor who had already been shot.

- Refused to halt executions while he studied the causes of racial disparity in federal **death penalty** prosecutions—indeed, he ordered prosecutors to seek the death penalty in more cases.

- Refused to support legislation mandating a national study of racial profiling by police unless a loophole permitted local police departments to opt out.

- Indicated he did not favor civil suits against police departments that habitually violate citizens' rights. Such suits had been authorized by federal law since the 1992 Rodney King beating by Los Angeles police.

- In his own words, ordered federal prosecutors, "[i]n virtually all cases, [to] bring the toughest charges available, yielding the toughest penalities under the sentencing guidelines," and to plea bargain only under extremely limited circumstances.

AXIS OF EVIL

The Axis consisted of **Iraq**, Iran, and North Korea, according to Bush, who revealed its existence to the world in his 2002 State of the Union address. His purpose was to rally public support for an expansion of the war beyond Afghanistan and Al Qaeda to a broader range of enemies and to other regions; to inflate the significance of his planned victory over Iraq; and to help justify his grossly expanded military budget. The comparison to the World War II Axis—indeed, the notion that

Iraq, Iran, and North Korea were in any sense an "axis"—was almost too absurd to bother picking apart. Germany, Italy, and Japan had a formal alliance and compatible ideologies, and were each bent on—and in Germany and Japan's case, more than capable of—conquering an empire. Iran and Iraq were traditional enemies who slaughtered hundreds of thousands of each other's people in an extraordinarily long and bloody war in the 1980s. Iraq in 2002 was far weaker than it had been in 1991, when its forces were routed in short order with barely an Allied casualty. North Korea, to quote columnist Robert Scheer, "is a tottering relic of a state whose nuclear operation was about to be bought off under the skilled leadership of the South Korean government when Bush jettisoned the deal."[15] Some said Bush threw North Korea into his axis because he didn't want to appear to be targeting only Muslim countries, or that he used the threat of a North Korean attack on the U.S. as a rationale for building a **missile defense** shield. Meanwhile, Saudi Arabia, which produced fifteen of the nineteen 9/11 hijackers, plus Osama bin Laden, and provided most of Al Qaeda's funding, was "inexplicably," Scheer noted, "excluded from the new enemies list." (See **Oil**. Also see **God, Bush, Good and Evil; War on terrorism.**)

BIOLOGICAL WEAPONS

The threat of biological weapons attacks became real and terrifying after September 11, 2001, and the anthrax-letter attacks that followed a few weeks later. In 1972, 143 nations, led by the

U.S., ratified the BIOLOGICAL AND TOXIN WEAPONS CONVENTION, which banned the development, production, or possession of biological weapons. But in July 2001, Bush effectively killed an international agreement to enforce the 1972 treaty by establishing verification measures. In rejecting the agreement—the product of eight years of negotiations—the Bushies claimed the proposed monitoring system would not work and, on the other hand, would work too well because it would give foreigners too much access to U.S. biodefense installations and pharmaceutical plants. (The **pharmaceutical industry,** jealously guarding its trade secrets, had objected.)

The decision was announced the same week that the Bushies—this time bowing to the National Rifle Association—rejected an international treaty to regulate the smallarms exports that feed terrorists and civil wars, soon after their rejection of the Kyoto protocol on **global warming**, and just before they were to junk the Anti-Ballistic Missile Treaty. The move told the world (1) the Bush administration was indifferent or hostile to international agreements; and (2) the U.S., despite having ratified the 1972 treaty, was still working on biological weapons projects—and if they can do it, others might well say, why can't we? China, Pakistan, India, and Iran were all reportedly looking for just such an excuse.

BUDGET AND TAXES:
ROBIN HOODS IN REVERSE

In the Bush White House, the worship of tax cuts for the wealthy wasn't just preached but practiced, daily and devoutly.

This was one area in which Bush delivered (and delivered) on his campaign promises—although few average Americans could have realized how little they themselves would benefit, how much of the loot would go to the richest few, or the impact on federal finances, vital social needs, and the economy.

The all-weather politics of tax cuts. Tax cuts—always overwhelmingly benefiting the rich—seemed to be Bush's answer to all economic conditions; only the packaging changed. In 1999–2000, with the economy still booming and the federal budget in surplus, candidate Bush announced his amazing discovery that tax revenues are actually the taxpayers' money, so the government should give it back. When the "Clinton recession," as the right liked to call it, set in during Bush's first months in office (why *wouldn't* the economy feel depressed?), he renamed his tax-cut plan "economic stimulus." After September 11, 2001, the same plan became a vital part of the country's "economic security." The Bushies literally wrapped their 2003 budget in the American flag—printing it on the cover of the budget plan. (See **War on terrorism**.)

Clearly, Bush was going to have his tax cuts come surpluses, deficits, lean years, fat years, war, peace, hell or high water—because his tax cuts had little to do with economics or job creation (much less with national security) and everything to do with buying and rewarding political support, especially from fat-cat contributors—even at the cost of crippling the federal budget (or was that the intent?), bequeathing a mountain of public debt to future generations, and weakening the economy.[16]

"A new kind of conservative." But any old politician could procure support by recklessly cutting taxes. The

Bushies' game was much slicker: It set out to reap the political benefits of tax cuts *without* really reducing taxes for most Americans, but only *shifting* the tax burden—from the federal to state and local governments and from higher- to middle- and lower-income Americans.

Columnist Lars Erik Nelson nailed Bush's budget and tax policy even before the 2000 election: "Bush and Cheney are a new kind of conservative. Traditional conservatives wanted to reduce, even eliminate, government and cut taxes. These new conservatives want the government to continue to collect taxes—but turn the proceeds over to private industry. Here is the common thread of Bush's major proposals: Government collects Social Security taxes—but gives a chunk of the money to Wall Street. Government collects school taxes—but gives the money out in vouchers that can be used in private schools. Government collects Medicare taxes—but gives the money to private insurers who will provide health coverage. . . . [Using] the government's coercive powers of taxation and legislation to funnel public wealth to the private sector [is] what made Bush and Cheney rich."[17]

The Bushies also sought to:

- Eliminate taxes on investment income, such as dividends and capital gains, which are overwhelmingly paid by the wealthy. The administration wanted to "have only people who earn wages pay taxes," a Nobel economist concluded.[18]
- Ultimately eliminate income tax entirely and replace it with a consumption or sales tax—a goal Bush first revealed openly in February 2003. This portended a huge tax increase for the poor and the elderly, who

typically spend more than they earn. This—combined with the previous measure—would do away with one of the pillars of American democracy, a progressive tax system, and put middle- and lower-income Americans into, in effect, higher tax brackets than the rich.

- Use tax cuts to drive up federal deficits, crippling government's ability to fund social programs hated by the right, like **Social Security** and **Medicare,** and adding pressure to privitization efforts. As Bush adviser GROVER NORQUIST famously said, "My goal is to get [government] down to the size where we can drown it in the bathtub."

A tax cut for the rich every year. By mid-2003, the Bushies had passed three huge rounds of tax cuts in three years at a total cost to the Treasury of at least $2.4 trillion over ten years, and more likely double that amount. In round one—the $1.3 trillion tax cut of June 2001—38 percent of the benefits went to the richest 1 percent of taxpayers.[19] Overall, this group—which paid about 25 percent of federal taxes and owned 40 percent of the nation's wealth—got benefits averaging $100,000 a year, while the bottom half (and after 2005, three-quarters) of all households were to get less than $100.

Even the famous $300 rebate went disproportionately to the well-off. For the top 10 percent, the average rebate was $559; among the bottom 60 percent, it was $185, and 42 percent got none at all. "Like the rest of the Bush tax plan," the director of Citizens for Tax Justice remarked, "the rebates have been carefully designed to give as little as possible to those who need the money, and as much as possible to those who don't."[20]

Stripping the cupboard bare. By early 2003, the $5.6 trillion projected budget surplus left by Clinton—which included $2.5 trillion in Social Security surpluses that Bush had vowed to leave alone—was gone, replaced by a projected deficit of over $4 trillion—a $10 trillion reversal of fortune. Annual deficits exceeding $500 billion stretched into the future as far as the eye could see. This from a president who had vowed not to run deficits—not to "pass along our problems to other Congresses, to other presidents and other generations"—and to *eliminate* the federal debt.

Former Secretary of Commerce, Federal Reserve Bank of New York chairman, and lifelong Republican Peter G. Peterson wrote that his party had abandoned "the bedrock principles" it had always stood for, including "the principle of fiscal stewardship." Coming into power, the Bush administration "faced a choice between tax cuts and providing genuine financing for the future of Social Security . . . They chose tax cuts. After 9/11, they faced a choice between tax cuts and getting serious about the extensive measures needed to protect this nation against further terrorist attacks. They chose tax cuts. . . . Again and again, they chose tax cuts." It "has evolved into a religion, indeed a tax-cut theology that simply discards any objective evidence that violates the tenets of the faith."[21]

Cooking the books. The Bushies hid the true cost of their tax cuts with, in the words of former Clinton economic adviser Laura D'Andrea Tyson, "accounting gimmicks breathtaking in their audacity and duplicity." For example, they:

- Assumed (or rather, pretended) large budget

surpluses would continue for years to come, ignoring the weak economy and stock market, which everyone knew would mean a steep drop in tax revenues.

- Ignored the fact that the tax cut would reduce (in fact, halt) the paydown of the federal debt, thus increasing interest payments by around $300 billion a year. By early 2003, interest on the debt had become the second-largest item in the federal budget, after defense.

- Set aside barely half the cost of the bare-bones **Medicare** prescription-drug benefit proposed in Congress—and praised by Bush.

- Projected spending cuts they knew Congress would override. "When Congress inevitably surpasses Bush's spending targets . . . he has a ready scapegoat for the ensuing red ink."[22]

- Assumed a wildly optimistic 70 percent increase in corporate profits by 2005 in an attempt to show that their deficits would be short-lived.

- Ignored the estimated $292 billion cost of modifying the alternative minimum tax (AMT), to which tens of millions of middle-class Americans would become subject as a result of Bush's tax cut.

Hitting the "trifecta." Just in case Americans couldn't see the humor in a $5.6 trillion surplus becoming a $4 trillion deficit, Bush added a joke to his standard stump speech after 9/11: He claimed to have promised not to run deficits except in the event of recession, war, or national emergency. "Lucky me," he said. "I hit the trifecta." (He said he had laid out those provisos during a campaign stop in Chicago in 2000, but this—which became known as "the Chicago line"—was denied by reporters who were present. Also see **Hypocrisy and deception.**)

Redefining "increase." When Democrats called for postponing or rolling back some of the not-yet-implemented tax cuts, the Bushies promptly added a term to the **BushSpeak** glossary, labeling any postponement or reduction an "increase."

"Operation Enduring Avarice." Within hours, it seemed, of their massive 2001 tax cut, the Bushies were hungry for more. September 11 was a pretext not to be wasted. The Bushies' response was a "stimulus" plan—dubbed by Arianna Huffington "Operation Enduring Avarice"—that would accelerate the $1.3 trillion, ten-year tax-cut package, make the cuts permanent, and add $750 billion in new cuts. The plan would abolish the **estate tax**—paid only by the richest two percent—and give retroactive tax cuts to corporations (which got 92 percent of the package), some of which had not paid any taxes in years, including Enron, which stood to get $254 million. No corporate crooks or fat cats were going to have to help pay for the war on terrorism.

Absurdly titled (**BushSpeak** alert) the "Economic Recovery and Assistance for American Workers Act," the plan's sole provision for workers was a thirteen-week extension of benefits for a narrowly limited segment of the unemployed—which the Democrats succeeded in including against the wishes of Republicans, who said it would encourage people not to try to find new jobs. ("I haven't heard that kind of compelling logic since [Reagan] Attorney General Ed Meese said homeless people enjoyed it," columnist Mark

Shields commented.) In an especially nice touch, $11 billion in aid to the unemployed was to come out of already inadequate funding for the State Children's Health Insurance Program (SCHIP), which covered poor children (see **Medicaid**).[23]

For business, on the other hand, the package contained, among many other goodies, a depreciation tax cut worth $97 billion—seven times the amount provided for the unemployed. Airline companies got a $5 billion bailout. Tens of thousands of laid-off airline employees got nothing.

"Voodoo economics" redux. The plan's rationale was the hoary Republican notion, or assertion, that cutting taxes on business and the rich will encourage them to invest in job-creating enterprises. But most economists acknowledged that, while the rich could just sit on their money, middle- and lower-income people were far more likely to spend their tax savings and thus stimulate the economy. In the twenty-two-plus years since George Bush Sr. called Reagan's "trickle-down" theory "voodoo economics," little had trickled down; while the top 20 percent enjoyed a 50 percent increase in real after-tax income and the top 1 percent had seen a 157 percent increase, average income for the bottom 20 percent had stagnated at around $11,000.

All other needs (but military) shortchanged. In polls, large majorities consistently favored rolling back the Bush tax cuts if it made more money available for increased education funding, a prescription drug benefit for seniors, environmental protection, and other domestic needs. Instead, to help pay for their tax cuts, the Bushies cut back or underfunded almost every area of domestic spending: Unemployment insurance, job training, child care, children's health insurance, **Medicaid** and **Medicare** services, workplace safety, medical research, public transportation, highway spending, funding for police and fire departments. Even border protection and other vital aspects of **homeland security** were persistently shortchanged.[24]

Bush's policies only added to the **state and local governments'** woes. Federal spending cuts shifted burdens to the states, while Bush's repeal of the federal estate tax, rollback of tax on stock dividends, and cut in corporate taxes directly reduced state revenues, as state taxes were tied to these federal taxes. With state spending already slashed to the bone, these lost revenues would have to be replaced by state and local tax increases. Talk about passing the buck.

Bush's spending cuts—which hurt middle- and lower-income Americans most—came just *when* they hurt most. In Bush's first year as president, the number of unemployed in the U.S. rose 40 percent, to 8.3 million. In his first two years, the U.S. **economy** lost 3 million jobs. By the end of 2001, 33 million Americans—11.7 percent of the population—including 11.6 million children, were officially living in poverty, following the first increase in poverty in (what do you know) eight years. At least 40 million Americans lacked **health insurance**. Doctors were turning away elderly Medicare patients because of cuts in reimbursements.

Obviously, what was needed was another huge tax cut for the rich.

The "Leave No Millionaire Behind Act." Bush's January 2003 "stimulus plan" consisted of another $674 billion in tax cuts, of which 70 percent went to the richest 5 percent. Just the top 226,000 tax filers—those with income over $1 million—would receive *as much as the bottom 125 million taxpayers combined.* Nobel economist Joseph Stiglitz called the plan—which critics dubbed the "Leave No Millionaire Behind Act"—astounding in the magnitude of its inequality." He was among ten Nobelists who, along with 400 other economists, signed a statement condemning the Bush plan for being, as one said, "both *grossly* unequal *and* ineffective" as economic stimulus. What it *would* do, they said, is make the rich richer, raise interest rates, increase borrowing from abroad, worsen the balance of payments, and weaken the economy.[25]

Dividends "double taxation." The plan's centerpiece was the elimination of individual income tax on stock dividends, ending the evil of so-called "double taxation." This measure would cost $300 billion over ten years while benefiting the richest 1 percent of taxpayers—those who earned more than $300,000 per year—*more than the bottom 95 percent combined.* Millionaires would receive an average of $27,100 over ten years; the average taxpayer earning $30,000–$40,000 would save $42.

Tax on dividends was dubbed "double taxation" because—in theory—corporations first pay corporate taxes on their profits, then pay out part of those profits as dividends to shareholders, who in effect pay tax on the same profits again. But in fact, corporations had become so adept at exploiting tax loopholes that fewer and fewer paid tax at all—and some, such as **Enron**, paid no tax for years; despite declaring hefty profits (real or fraudulent), Enron received tax rebates. (An Enron official told investigators the company regarded its tax department as a "profit center.") So, far from being "double taxation," tax on dividends was barely *half*-taxation. Meanwhile, the economy was full of actual double and even triple taxation: income and payroll tax, sales tax, tax on Social Security benefits; but those weighed heaviest on lower-income taxpayers. With dividend taxes eliminated, wealthy individuals who got most of their income from investments would often end up paying lower tax rates than ordinary, working people.

Another thing eliminating "double taxation" was *not*, contrary to GOP claims, economic stimulus. According to Nobel economist Franco Modigliani, it would reduce, not increase, business investment by discouraging companies from retaining and reinvesting earnings. "The Bush plan is bad, the dividend portion is worse than the rest," Modigliani concluded.[26]

Other 2004 budget lowlights:

- $6 billion less for Bush's "No Child Left Behind" **education** act than the $18.5 billion called for by the act, meaning reduced or eliminated funding for rural schools, after-school programs, the Even Start literacy program, and school aid for children of armed forces personnel.
- Elimination of $330 million for hiring of police officers nationwide.
- An increase in fees **veterans** must pay for medical treatment and prescription drugs.
- **Environmental** programs cut by $1.6 billion, including

a 32 percent cut for water treatment projects and a further 100-person reduction in EPA staff.

See **Compassion; Defense; Economy; Tax evasion.**

---

12 million children left behind. The tax bill Bush signed in May 2003 doled out a further $350 billion (on top of around $2 trillion) in tax cuts favoring the wealthy, while saving $3.5 billion by denying 6.5 million minimum-wage families and their 12 million children the $400-per-child increase in the CHILD TAX CREDIT that higher-income taxpayers received. Eight million mostly low-income taxpayers received no benefit at all from Bush's law. Those earning more than $500,000 got an average saving of $17,000; those earning $40,000 averaged $320.

BUSH'S BUSINESS CAREER

"The Bushes' shadowy business partners come straight out of the world in which the CIA thrives—the netherworld of secret wars and covert operators, drug runners, mafiosi and crooked entrepreneurs out to make a fast buck. What Bush family members lack in business acumen, they make up for by cashing in on their blood ties to the former Director of Central Intelligence who became president [George Bush Sr.]. In return for throwing business their way, the Bushes give their partners political access, legitimacy, and perhaps protection. The big loser in the deal is the democratic process."

—Jack Colhoun, *Covert Action Quarterly*, Summer 1992

"When actually in private business for himself, Bush was a perennial loser. His profits came chiefly from investors who gave him money because of government tax breaks for the oil industry...In these self-proclaimed conservative candidates [Bush and Cheney], we see two of the nation's prime beneficiaries of a government practice widely known as corporate welfare, or socialism for the rich. Both owe virtually every dime they have earned to the help of government."

—Lars Erik Nelson, *New York Daily News*, October 11, 2001

The awl bidniz: Bath, bin Ladens, and BCCI connections. Bush's career as an oilman was a peculiar mixture of repeated failures as an oilman and successes as, well, a Bush.

Much the way George Bush Sr.'s oil company was initially financed by his family, in 1978, W., after running for Congress and losing, used $17,000 from his education trust fund to start his oil and gas company, Arbusto Energy ("arbusto" means "bush" in Spanish). Another $50,000 investment came from JAMES BATH of Houston, a close Bush family friend said to have CIA connections, and the sole U.S. business representative for SALEM BIN LADEN, head of the bin Laden family and one of Osama's seventeen brothers. There has been much speculation that Bush's Arbusto investment came directly from Salem. Bath also had ties to Saudi banker KHALID BIN MAHFOUZ and other major players in the notorious BANK OF COMMERCE AND CREDIT INTERNATIONAL (BCCI), which in the 1980s defrauded depositors of $10 billion—the largest bank fraud in history.[27] Some of Bath's BCCI connections (including bin Mahfouz, whose sister was one of Osama bin Laden's wives) attempted to funnel millions of dollars to Osama in the late 1990s, according to *USA Today* and *ABC News*. (Mahfouz was among the defendants in a trillion-dollar lawsuit filed in 2002 by families of 9/11 victims, who accused members of the Saudi royal family, their banks, and "charities" of financing Al Qaeda.) Bath came under FBI investigation in 1992 for his Saudi business relationships; he was accused of funneling Saudi money through Houston to influence the foreign policies of the Reagan and Bush I administrations.

Spectrum 7. Arbusto, meanwhile, was soon being called "El-Busto." Bush in fact renamed it "Bush Exploration Company," and secured a rescue/buyout by Spectrum 7 Energy Corp., owned by wealthy investors WILLIAM DEWITT and MERCER REYNOLDS. (In 2001, Bush appointed Reynolds ambassador to Switzerland after he and DeWitt raised nearly $1 million for the Bush 2000 campaign.) Bush was named CEO and director of Spectrum at a salary of $75,000 a year plus a 15 percent share of equity in the merged company.

Harken: Shades of Enron. In 1986, with oil prices down and Spectrum nearing collapse (despite a successful drilling partnership with **Enron**), Bush negotiated its sale to a bigger Dallas firm, Harken Energy. Bush became a Harken director, at a salary of $120,000 a year and around $600,000 worth of Harken stock. "His name was George Bush," Harken founder Phil Kendrick was quoted as saying. "That was worth the money they paid him."[28]

But beknownst only to insiders, Harken's finances too were precarious. What kept it afloat were Enron-like accounting tricks and investments from Bush political supporters and Mideast business associates. In 1987, JACKSON STEPHENS, the head of an Arkansas investment bank, a large Reagan-Bush campaign contributor in 1980, and later a Bush I and II contributor, arranged for major investments from Union Bank of Switzerland (UBS) and from Saudi tycoon SHEIKH ABDULLAH TAHA BAKHSH, who joined Harken's board. Stephens, UBS, and Bakhsh all had ties to BCCI. Bakhsh's banker in Saudi Arabia was BCCI partner Khalid bin Mahfouz, the alleged Osama bin Laden financier, and Bakhsh was a business partner of GAITH PHARAON, BCCI's front man in a Houston bank. *The Wall Street Journal* concluded in 1991, "The number of BCCI-connected people who had dealings with Harken—all since George W. Bush came on board—raises the question of whether they mask an effort to cozy up to a presidential son."[29]

Within weeks of Bush Sr. becoming president in 1988, Harken, a relatively small company that had never drilled a well offshore or abroad, beat out giant Amoco to obtain exclusive rights to gas and oil off the coast of Bahrain in the Persian Gulf. Helping to finance the venture were the BASS BROTHERS, Texas billionaire oilmen/investors who were later among Bush Jr.'s top campaign contributors.

In June 1990, Bush sold two-thirds of his Harken stock for a $318,430 profit, a week before Harken announced a $23 million loss, which caused the stock to lose 60 percent of its value over the next six months. Not long before, financial advisers told a Harken committee on which Bush sat that "only drastic action could save Harken." *U.S. News and World Report* reported, "There is substantial evidence to suggest that Bush knew Harken was in dire straits in the weeks before he sold [his stock]."[30] Moreover, instead of notifying the Securities and Exchange Commission of the sale immediately, as required by law, Bush filed eight months late. An investigation by the SEC (under the authority of the Bush I administration) concluded there was no evidence of insider selling. Handling the "investigation" was SEC general counsel James Doty, who previously served as W.'s personal lawyer in his Texas Rangers purchase (see below), and who neglected to interview any Harken directors.

Stealing home: Bush and baseball. In 1989, Bush helped assemble a group of investors who purchased the Texas Rangers baseball team. Bush became part owner of the team and one of its two managing general partners. By threatening to move the team from its home in Arlington, Texas, the new owners persuaded the city to build a new stadium at a cost of $135 million—financed by a sales tax hike on local citizens. Through a public authority set up for the purpose, the team owners were able to buy land for the stadium—and large tracts around it—at below-market prices; if the owners refused to sell, the city simply condemned the land. As a *Harper's* exposé put it, "Never before had a municipal authority in Texas been given license to seize the property of a private citizen for the benefit of other private citizens."[31] ("The idea of making a land play, absolutely . . . that's kind of always been the strategy," Bush let slip to the *Fort Worth Star-Telegram*.) Finally, the Rangers got a rent-to-buy agreement, paying $60 million over time for a state-of-the-art stadium that cost more than twice as much to build. This tripled the team's value. When it was sold in 1998 for $250 million, then-Governor Bush's initial $600,000 investment yielded $15 million—"the direct result of government intervention on his behalf."[32]

"Bushwater." There was much, much more; Bush's dealings with such tycoons as RICHARD RAINWATER and THOMAS HICKS—friends, business associates, major Bush contributors (see **Campaign finance**), and beneficiaries of Bush actions as governor—could fill a volume. Comparing Bush's affairs to Clinton's Whitewater deal, *Arkansas Democrat-Gazette* columnist Gene Lyons wrote, "If Arkansas is 'incestuous,' it's hard to think what adjective describes Texas, where public and private fortunes are commingled to a degree unknown in other states, and GOP leaders have helped themselves to public-sector capital while lecturing the poor on the virtues of hard work and self-reliance. Under laws enacted at Bush's behest, rich Republicans have used billions in state funds to finance leveraged corporate buyouts and other risky investments to benefit themselves and their friends. If you didn't know better, you'd think [it was a story about] Indonesia or Saudi Arabia."[33] And you could be forgiven for feeling that the White House was not the federal facility Bush belonged in.

BUSH'S PERSONALITY AND SENSE OF HUMOR

As Marilyn Quayle bitterly told The Arizona Republic, 'the caricature they made of Dan [Quayle] in '88 is George W. It's him. It wasn't true about Dan. But it is him . . . A guy that never accomplished anything . . . Everything he got, Daddy took care of." [34]

In the summer of 2002, Bush, taking a shot at Bill and Hillary

Clinton's holiday habits, said, "most Americans don't sit in Martha's Vineyard, swilling white wine." He could have added that most Americans didn't own a ranch, or have a family compound in Kennebunkport, Maine, where they once did plenty of "swilling" themselves; most Americans (decidedly *including* Bill Clinton) weren't born into wealth and power, didn't have a president for a father, or an endless supply of connections and sponsors eager to give them a leg up in business and politics, regardless of personal merit. Well, as was often said of Dubya, "He was born on third base and thinks he hit a triple."

A spoiled-adolescent cockiness, callousness, and puerility revealed itself in Bush's sense of humor. Let us skip over the one where, prior to a 1998 trip to Israel, Bush told a group of reporters that the first thing he would tell Israeli Jews was that they were all "going to hell,"[35] and proceed straight to his famous 1999 *Talk* magazine interview with conservative journalist Tucker Carlson. Describing for Carlson a Larry King interview with Texas death row inmate Karla Faye Tucker, whose plea for clemency Bush had denied, then-Governor Bush performed an amusing little imitation of a woman begging for her life, whimpering, "Please, don't kill me." (Nothing like the exchange Bush described had taken place.) "Ridiculing the pleas of a condemned prisoner who has since been executed seems odd and cruel, even for someone as militantly anticrime as Bush," wrote Carlson, a Bush fan. He thought Bush was angry at Tucker for accusing him on *Larry King Live* of playing politics with her life. "Bush never forgot it. He has a long memory for slights."[36]

Also interesting, in light of Bush's Christian goodness

and decency and all, was that in the first three pages of this on-the-record interview, he said "fuck" three times. Noting that Christians were offended by both Bush's swearing and his mocking a condemned woman, Christian intellectual Roberto Rivera told *Salon*, "The Christian right would quickly forgive Bush for cocaine [which Bush had recently admitted to having used]. The problem with Bush is that there's a growing impression that he really isn't a changed man."[37] Conservative writer Richard Brookhiser wrote that "a larger picture of a fairly unpleasant 53-year-old teen-ager looms behind" the *Talk* profile;[38] another conservative, George Will, wrote, "Carlson's profile suggests an atmosphere of adolescence . . . a carelessness, even a recklessness, perhaps born of things having gone a bit too easily so far."[39]

Joan Walsh of *Salon* said much the same. His "gaffes [see **Bushisms**] aren't a symptom of stupidity, but of his rich-kid's luxurious detachment, his frat-boy's 'Whatever, dude!' attitude. He veers weirdly between this fortunate-son insouciance and, when seeking gravitas, a born-again absolutism (the force that helped pull him out of his drunken youth)."[40] The seriousness of Bush's convictions—and the "veer[ing] weirdly" between "insouciance" and "gravitas"—was captured perfectly by his wonderful golf-course remark in August 2002: "I call upon all nations to do everything they can to stop these terrorist killers. Thank you. Now watch this drive."

Brookhiser noted that when asked by Carlson to name his heroes, Bush couldn't think of any. "What will the boys without heroes do to show, if not their manhood, then their potency?" Brookhiser wondered. "We know what Bill Clinton does, and it's a lot worse than frisking with Monica. He lobs the odd cruise missile into Khartoum and Kosovo.

What will President W. do, when he runs out of pardons to withhold?" That was 1999. Today, we know.

(See **Bush's business career; Chickenhawks; Compassion; God, Bush, good and evil.**)

BUSHISMS AND THE BRAINS ISSUE: *DID WE "MISUNDERESTIMATE" HIM?*

Bush Sr.'s bizarre verbal meanderings, non sequiturs, and other spectacular manglings of English filled several published collections of Bushisms—and Jr. appeared to have inherited this genius, along with so much else. Indeed, his remarks attained levels of sublime idiocy that surpassed those of any previous president.

It was difficult to agree with those who said it was merely dyslexia (which Bush once dyslexically denied having). As *Slate* writer Jacob Weisberg remarked in his compendium of horrifyingly stupid Bush comments, *George W. Bushisms* (the source for some of those quoted below), "Under the educational standards Bush has supported in Texas, he'd be doing eighth grade for the thirty-ninth time." Media critic Mark Crispin Miller thought Bush's verbal bumbling betokened bratiness. "Every time he opens his mouth, he demonstrates how casually he treated his expensive education." Moreover, Miller thought it had helped Bush politically; "his propaganda team was very good at spinning his illiteracy as folksy unpretentiousness," and it blended seamlessly with the vapidity of television.[41]

Meanwhile, Bush's image-makers and his GOP and media

acolytes, working to envelop him in an aura of greatness, made sure to heap praise on him for the work of his speech-writers. Sen. John Warner (R-VA) called Bush's post-9/11 speech to Congress "maybe the greatest speech ever given by any president." As noted in *Salon*, "As long as Bush doesn't spew mangled words like a Tourette's sufferer, he is apparently to be regarded as a kind of reincarnated combo pack of Demosthenes, Lincoln and Churchill."[42]

As a candidate in 2000, Bush explained his view of Middle East policy thus: "It's also important to keep strong ties in the Middle East with credible ties . . . .I hope to get a sense of, should I be fortunate enough to be the president, how my administration will react to the Middle East." "It is that kind of dangerous ignorance," said former Clinton aide Paul Begala, "the blind recitation of vapid, vacuous platitudes, that Bush has made his forte. And yet precisely because they know Bush is so intellectually thin, the media grades him on a curve."

On the world stage, Bush's gaffes could indeed be dangerous, as in Japan in February 2002, when his confusion of "deflation" with "devaluation" sent the yen into a tailspin. This man could induce depression in more ways than one. Was there reason to worry that a man who could make the following remarks now occupied the Oval Office? Judge for yourself:

Geography and foreign affairs
- *Deport him to Texas*: "More and more of our imports come from overseas."
- "We have a firm commitment to NATO. We are a part of NATO. We have a firm commitment to Europe. We are a part of Europe." *Hey, maybe* we're *the "new Europe."*

- *Long as it doesn't upset the Turkians*: "Keep good relations with the Grecians."
- *Referring to a meeting with the prime minister of Slovenia:* "The only thing I know about Slovakia is what I learned firsthand from your foreign minister." *Close enough.*
- *To the Brazilian president, home to more blacks than any country outside Africa*: "Do you have blacks, too?"
- "The problem with the French is that they don't have a word for entrepreneur."
- *To Welsh singing star Charlotte Church*: "So what state is Wales in?" "Um, it's a separate country next to England." "Oh, okay." (*Related by Church on BBC TV.*)
- "Border relations between Canada and Mexico have never been better."
- *In Spokane, WA*: "The people who care more about that land are the hard-working farmers and ranchers of your part of the state of Washington, D.C."
- "It's important to think beyond the old days of when we had the concept that if we blew each other up, the world would be safe."
- "These terrorist acts and the responses have got to end in order for us to get the framework—the groundwork, not framework—the groundwork to discuss a framework, to lay the—all right."

Government and politics

- *Missed grade-one civics*: "The legislature's job is to write law. It's the executive branch's job to interpret law."

- "A low voter turnout is an indication of fewer people going to the polls."
- "They want the federal government controlling Social Security like it's some kind of federal program."
- *Read his lips—no more principles*: "If you are sick and tired of the politics of cynicism and polls and principles, come and join this campaign."
- "One word sums up probably the responsibility of any Governor, and that one word is 'to be prepared.'"
- "And so, in my State of the—my State of the Union—or state—my speech to the nation, whatever you want to call it, speech to the nation—I asked Americans to give 4,000 years— 4,000 hours over the next—the rest of your life—of service to America."
- *To the Swedish prime minister*: "It's amazing I won. I was running against peace, prosperity, and incumbency."
- *We're getting there*: "If this were a dictatorship, it would be a heck of a lot easier, just so long as I'm the dictator."

Budget, taxes, and the economy
- *Alert the Nobel committee:* "It's clearly a budget. It's got a lot of numbers in it."
- *Calling Gore's tax plan a terrorist plot?* "It's going to require numerous IRA agents."
- *Breathed too much exhaust?* "I think we need not only to eliminate the tollbooth to the middle class, I think we should knock down the tollbooth."
- "I know how hard it is to for you to put food on your family."

- "It's your money. You paid for it."
- *The "death tax" should be eliminated,* "so that people who build up assets are able to transfer them from one generation to the next, regardless of a person's race."

Science, nature, and the environment

- "I know the human being and fish can coexist peacefully."
- "It isn't pollution that's harming the environment. It's the impurities in our air and water that are doing it."
- "For NASA, space is still a high priority."
- *Earth to Bush:* "[It's] time for the human race to enter the solar system."
- *After saying an "arbolist" would be identifying the trees on his ranch:* "I don't know, maybe I made it up. Anyway, it's an arbo-tree-ist, somebody who knows about trees."

Education and literacy

- "Rarely is the question asked: Is our children learning?"
- "You teach a child to read, and he or her will be able to pass a literacy test."
- *Don't brag about it:* "I don't read what's handed to me."
- "One of the great things about books is sometimes there are some fantastic pictures."
- *Your connection has been lost:* "It's important for us to explain . . . that life is important. It's not only life of babies, but it's life of children living in, you know, the dark dungeons of the Internet."
- "Will the highways on the Internet become more few?"

Himself

- *Supreme confidence:* "I have made good judgments in the past. I have made good judgments in the future."
- *Just the problem:* "I stand by all the misstatements that I've made."
- "They misunderestimated me." *Later, attempting to poke fun at himself, he misquoted himself:* "I've coined new words, like, 'misunderstanding.'"
- "They said, 'You know, this issue doesn't seem to resignate with the people.' And I said, 'You know something? Whether it resignates or not doesn't matter to me.'" *(Sure wish he'd resignate.)*
- *Asked, had he ever used Marijuana? Cocaine?* "I'm not going to talk about what I did as a child."
- *We know:* "It was inebriating what Midland [Texas] was all about then."
- *Hmm:* "The most important job is not to be governor, or first lady in my case."
- *Hmmmm:* "My mother was president. No, I mean my father. Yes, he was, but no longer. How true that is."

Morals, ethics, and values

- *Just as we suspected:* "Well, I think if you say you're going to do something and don't do it, that's trustworthiness."
- "Families is where our nation finds hope, where wings take dream." *(What was he taking?)*
- "You've got to love your neighbor like you like to be loved yourself."

Various issues

- "If affirmative action means what I just described, what I'm for, then I'm for it. I am against hard quotas, quotas they basically delineate based upon whatever. However they delineate, quotas, I think vulcanize society."
- "Those of us who have spent some time in the agricultural sector and in the heartland understand how unfair the death penalty is—uh, the death tax is—and we need to get rid of it. [*Pause.*] I don't want to get rid of the death penalty. Just the death tax."
- *12 and older?* "I think we ought to raise the age at which juveniles can have a gun."
- "I am here to make an announcement that this Thursday, ticket counters and airplanes will fly out of Ronald Reagan Airport."

History

- "I think we agree, the past is over." *Unfortunately, no, it's* back.
- "That's a chapter, the last chapter of the twentieth, .twentieth, twenty-first century that most of us would rather forget. The last chapter of the twentieth century. This is the first chapter of the twenty-first century."—*Our very own Winston Churchill.*
- "The Holocaust was an obscene period in our nation's history. I mean in this century's history. But we all lived in this century. I didn't live in this century." *We wish.*

All-around wisdom

- "I hope the ambitious realize that they are more likely

to succeed with success as opposed to failure." And, "If we don't succeed, we run the risk of failure."

- "Our nation must come together to unite."
- "There's an old saying in Tennessee—I know it's in Texas, probably in Tennessee—that says, fool me once, shame on—shame on you. Fool me—you can't get fooled again." *We can but pray.*

BUSHSPEAK

Among the most consistently outrageous, insulting, and sinister Bush administration practices was the brazen and systematic use of Orwellian speech and nomenclature to conceal the character and purposes of their policies— indeed, to suggest quite opposite ones—or to vilify opponents or their views. A sampling:

- **"Axis of evil"**: Identified by Bush as consisting of **Iraq,** Iran, and North Korea. Unlike most other evil Axes, these three countries lacked any formal or informal alliance (or even good relations), compatible ideology, genocidal dream, or means or intention of conquering empires.
- **"Class warfare"**: What you were accused of waging if you dared point out that Bush **budget and tax** policies disproportionately favored the rich. *Pursuing* such policies was called "job creation," "economic stimulus," etc.
- **"Clear Skies Initiative"**: A program to gut the

Clean Air Act and substitute weaker anti-pollution regulations.

- **"Clinton recession"**: The recession that began in 2001 under Bush and continued for at least the next two years. See **Economy**.
- **"Compassionate conservatism"**: The liberal-sounding cloak beneath which the Bushies smuggled themselves and their hard-right agenda into the White House.
- **"Double taxation"**: The right's war cry for abolishing taxes on dividends and on estates. In practice, neither taxation was "double," and tax on dividends was barely half-taxation. See **Budget and taxes** and **Estate tax**.
- **"Economic stimulus"**: Massive tax cuts for corporations and the rich that failed, in theory and practice, to stimulate.
- **"Energy security"**: The barely lessened dependence on Mideast oil to be achieved by drilling in U.S. national parks and wilderness preserves.
- **"Free speech"**: 1) The constitutional right of **pharmaceutical** and other companies to make exaggerated or false advertising claims for their products; 2) the right to raise and spend as much **campaign** money as you want, in any way you want.
- **"Healthy Forests Initiative"**: A policy of blaming forest fires on tree-hugging environmentalists and letting logging companies cut down the **forests** to save them.
- **"Politicians"**: Democrats in Congress.
- **"Reform" of**: A euphemism for attack on, destruction of, privatization of—as in "reform of" public

education, Medicare, Social Security, etc. (as embodied in Bush's "Commission to *Strengthen* Social Security"—i.e., *privatize* it)

- **"Sound science"**: The kind that shows that the "economic" costs (to corporations) of health, safety, and environmental regulations outweigh the benefits to the public. (See **Science policy**.)

- **"Special interests"**: Unions and environmentalists. (But not, say, the oil, gas, or coal industry, HMOs, the gun lobby, or right-wing Protestant fundamentalists.)

- **Tort "reform"**: Making it harder for citizens to sue corporate wrongdoers for harm they've caused.

- **Welfare "reform"**: Raising work requirements to force states to throw more people off welfare. In the midst of the worst job slump in decades, and while cutting funding for job training, Bush called for (BushSpeak italicized): "*Empowering* states to seek new and innovative *solutions* to help welfare recipients achieve *independence*." He announced the plan standing before a backdrop emblazoned with slogans like "Opportunity," "Work," "Family," "Responsibility," and "Working toward independence"—whose hollowness elevated them, too, to the exalted realm of BushSpeak.

Those creepy backdrops were indeed among the most Orwellian creations of the Bush "communications" machine. Placed behind the Leader during his televised speeches, bearing slogans like "Protecting the homeland," "Strengthening the economy," and "Helping Workers," according to the theme du jour—repeating like wallpaper designs, true to the propaganda princple of simplicity and hypnotic repetition—they evoked nothing more than the banners that once festooned the Red Squares and Karl-Marx-Platzes of the world. (See **Media, manipulation of**.)

CALIFORNIA ENERGY CRISIS: HOW THE BUSHIES LET THEIR ENERGY INDUSTRY BUDDIES STEAL $30 BILLION FROM A DEMOCRATIC STATE

Between May 2000 and May 2001, power shortages in California, Oregon, and Washington caused frequent blackouts and brownouts, staggering electricity price increases, and economic and political chaos. The handful of electricity wholesalers that supplied the bulk of California's power— half of them Texas-based companies with close ties to Bush and Cheney—and their Republican political pals blamed environmental regulations, which they said had discouraged the construction of needed power plants. "The California crunch," Bush explained, "really is the result of not enough power-generating plants and then not enough power to power the power [*sic*] of generating plants." That explanation (talk about outages) turned out to be a lie.

By September 2002, the California Public Utilities Commission had confirmed what state officials and economists had alleged all along—that most of the blackouts took place because the major power wholesalers deliberately kept much of their capacity off line. Federal investigators found that Houston-based **Enron** Corp.—the biggest player in the California crisis, and Bush's biggest backer—had created and profited from shortages by, for example, deliberately overbooking transmission lines at choke points, then seeking multimillion-dollar payouts for relieving the congestion. Enron traders gave the schemes names like "Death Star," "Get Shorty," and "Ricochet."

FEDERAL ENERGY REGULATORY COMMISSION (FERC) judges ruled that El Paso Electric Co., another major Bush contributor, had exploited its control over a key pipeline to create an artificial shortage of natural gas used to fuel electric plants. Williams Companies deliberately shut down power plants to drive up prices; AES, Mirant, and Reliant Energy withheld power from California; and all these companies, along with Dynergy, Duke, and CMS Energy, admitted to engaging in "round-trip" or "wash" trades in which no energy actually changed hands but which increased revenues.

Under California's **deregulation** of wholesale electricity in 1996—which Enron pushed for and indeed helped design—the state's utilities had sold off all their power plants, mostly to the aforementioned, out-of-state companies. And in 2000, after intensive Enron lobbying, Congress passed a bill exempting energy trading from regulatory oversight. All this was supposed to create competition and lower prices. But from May 2000 to early 2001, California's wholesale electricity prices increased by as much as *3,700 percent*—during which time Enron's stock price rose 89 percent and Dynergy's profits tripled.

The Bushies refused to intervene. The day after a private meeting with Enron CEO and Bush pal "Kenny boy" Lay in April 2001, Cheney announced he would not support electricity price caps, which Enron was seeking to block. Instead, Bush & Co. continued to blame environmentalists for the "shortage" of generating capacity—and for good measure, they insisted the crisis pointed up the urgency of opening Alaska's ARCTIC NATIONAL WILDLIFE REFUGE to oil drilling (see **energy policy**), which could not have been more irrelevant.

"How could a $30 billion robbery take place in broad daylight?" *The New York Times'* Paul Krugman asked. Perhaps, he suggested, the energy companies believed they had bought protection. (The ten leading suppliers gave $4.1 million to Republican candidates in 2000—more than twice as much as to Democrats—and gave Bush thirteen times as much as Gore. Texas-based Enron, Dynergy, and Reliant gave the Bush-Cheney campaign $1.5 million.) It was noted that the severe power shortages began just after the 2000 election and ended when Democrats gained control of the Senate in May 2001. A week later, FERC imposed limited price controls on electricity in California. Throughout, federal regulators "certainly seemed determined to see and hear no evil," Krugman noted, "and above all not to reveal evidence of evil to state officials."[43]

These companies' White House ties went beyond contributions. Williams board member Thomas Cruikshank was Cheney's predecessor as CEO of oil-services giant Halliburton and had personally picked Cheney to succeed him. Cheney reportedly kept in close touch with *his* successor at Halliburton, David Lesar, who was also a board member at Mirant.[44] AES board member Richard Darman worked with Cheney in the first Bush administration, and was a managing director of the CAR-LYLE GROUP, the Washington investment firm headed by Reagan and Bush I alums. Even as the blackouts rolled, these companies' reps were drafting national **energy policy** in closed-door meetings with Cheney. Could the White House have been in the dark about the tricks they were up to in California?

CAMPAIGN FINANCE REFORM:
BUSH'S BOUNTY OF BIG-BUCKS BACKERS

"I heard apparently sane commentators state that since George W. Bush is reading a biography of Teddy Roosevelt, he would speak out against 'the malefactors of great wealth' and possibly even endorse campaign finance reform . . . these folks have absolutely no idea who he is."
—Molly Ivins, syndicated column, February 15, 2002

By the 1990s, the influence of moneyed special interests on government was so manifest and corrosive, even some Republicans regarded it as a cancer that had to be excised. The problem was not only public policy being sold to the highest bidder, but also an ever-shrinking pool of potential candidates, as Arianna Huffington noted: "[O]nly the super rich or those willing to spend their every waking moment raising money from the super rich need apply."[45]

Most notorious was the explosion in "soft money"—unlimited donations by corporations, unions, and other interests that were permitted for party-building activities but in practice were used to get around "hard money" limits and buy candidate-specific advertising. Soft-money donations went from $100,000 in the 1988 election to $86 million in 1992 and nearly $500 million in 2000. But hard money—individuals' contributions limited (then) to $1,000 per candidate—still accounted for more than 80 percent of the funds raised by federal candidates and parties, and came predominantly from the wealthiest 1 percent of the population—Bush's crowd.

Republicans were doing just fine under this system, thank you. In his 2000 campaign, Bush raised far more than any other presidential candidate in history: $100 million in hard money and another $93 million or so in soft—50 percent more than poor Al Gore. Republicans opposed campaign finance reform on the grounds that—as the senator nicknamed "the Darth Vader of Campaign Reform," Mitch McConnell (R-KY), declared on the Senate floor—"spending is [free] speech." In a system of government-for-sale, the Republicans had a powerful advantage as the preferred party of industry lobbies, corporations, their executives and families, and other wealthy individuals. The **energy** industry, for example, contributed $32 million to candidates and parties in the 2000 election cycle, *90 percent* of it to Republicans (including nearly $2 million to Bush, whose top contributor was Houston energy giant **Enron** and its top executives). Democrats enjoyed more union support than Republicans—but in 2000, business out-contributed labor by a 9–1 margin.

And not in vain. Studies showed that the candidate with the bigger war chest won the race around 80 percent of the time. As for legislative results, in March 2002, when the Senate voted 68–32 to remove higher vehicle fuel efficiency standards from an energy bill, the "yeas" had received an average of $18,000 from the car lobby—more than three times the average received by the "nays." (In 2000, Bush got $1,289,747 from the auto industry, or seventeen times as much as the next largest recipient.) As of 1999, around half the members of the House of Representatives had accepted contributions from the National Rifle Association; but nearly four-fifths of it went to Republicans, who overwhelmingly opposed **gun control.** Sen. John McCain (R-AZ) described both parties as "bought and paid for," but with all due respect, one party was far more bought and paid for than the other.

McCain and Sen. Russ Feingold (D-WI) had been trying to pass a campaign finance bill for years; Republicans always succeeded in filibustering it. But in early 2002, corporate/political scandals—particularly Enron—brought the issue to a boil. Republican leaders tried desperately to kill the MCCAIN-FEINGOLD bill up to the last minute. "You guys need to realize this is a life-or-death issue for our party," House Speaker Dennis Hastert (R-IL) told his colleagues. But just enough Republicans broke ranks, and on March 27, Bush signed the bill—now misnamed the Bipartisan Campaign Reform Act (BCRA)—into law. McCain wasn't invited to the signing.

Right afterward, Bush embarked on a fund-raising tour for Republican candidates. Two days later, he named Michael Toner, chief counsel to the Republican National Committee and general counsel to the Bush-Cheney 2000 campaign, to the Federal Election Commission (FEC), the supposedly impartial agency that oversees enforcement of election laws.[46]

THE BCRA'S CORE PROVISION banned national parties and candidates from raising soft money. However, the law raised the limit on hard-money contributions by individuals from $1,000 to $2,000 per candidate per election (and for certain "self-funded" candidates, to $12,000), and raised individuals' total contributions limit from $25,000 to $95,000 per election.

McCain's concern was that his bill "will only thwart the special interests for so long. Twenty years from now, they will have figured out ways to get around it." In fact, they already had—and the chief way around it was *through* it.

The Bush-Cheney 2000 campaign had an army of at least 538 "Pioneers"—an assortment of billionaire tycoons, corporate executives, and industry lobbyists, each committed to raising at least $100,000 in $1,000 hard-money donations from family members, friends, and associates—a process called "bundling." Each Pioneer's total was carefully tracked so that they, their donors, and the corporation or industry they represented could later be rewarded accordingly. This information was obtained by public-interest groups who challenged the hard-money increases in the McCain-Feingold bill in court. "Bundlers," they noted, would now be able to double, or more, the amount of hard money they raised from wealthy donors; indeed, the 2004 Bush campaign expected to double its 2000 haul. "[E]lite donors such as the Bush Pioneers will achieve a stranglehold over the electoral process and ordinary voters will be locked out," said the director of the National Voting Rights Institute.[47]

The reform law gets FECked over. "The FEDERAL ELECTION COMMISSION (FEC) has earned a well-deserved reputation for refusing to enforce the campaign finance laws," wrote former FEC attorneys Lawrence Noble of the Center for Responsive Politics and Paul Sanford of FEC Watch. "The commission also has a long tradition of creating loopholes in the laws Congress has directed it to enforce"—including, they noted, the soft-money loophole the new law sought to close.[48] Indeed, just three months after McCain-Feingold was passed, the FEC took the axe to it and reopened that very loophole, effectively removing the ban on soft money with a series of rules that said:

- State and local parties could raise and spend unlimited soft money in federal campaigns.
- National parties could set up "independent committees," which could be staffed by former party activists and allies; could raise and spend unlimited soft money; and would not have to disclose where their money came from.
- Federal officeholders and candidates could help organize or speak at soft money fundraisers as long as they did not directly and personally ask for the donations.

The FEC "must have been asleep when they took their oath of office to uphold the law," *The New York Times* editorialized.[49] Both parties rushed to take advantage of the new loopholes, setting up "independent committees" by the dozens. A record $500 million in soft money was raised for the 2002 midterm elections.

Bush's backers. Bush's greatness—as a fund-raiser—was evident from the start, beginning in **Bush's business career,** when deep-pocketed backers and sweet deals seemed always at hand—as though his name itself exerted some mysterious pull on money. So too from the start of his political career. In his 1998 gubernatorial campaign, Bush broke all state records, raising $25 million. In the 2000 election, he broke the fundraising record for a presidential candidate even before the end of 1999, raising more than Clinton and Dole combined in the entire 1996 campaign. His final tally, from all sources, was over $193 million.

The Bushies boasted of how "grassroots" his support

was—the zillions of small donations he received. But as Andrew Wheat of Multinational Monitor revealed, "It is large corporations that are powering Bush's unprecedented political money machine."[50] This had also been the case in his two gubernatorial races, when more than half of the $41 million Bush raised came from donors of at least $5,000, and Bush got more than $2.5 million "from just 23 tycoons, who chipped in between $100,000 and $175,000 apiece."[51] Some of the biggest donors had been partners and investors in Bush's oil and baseball ventures.

In 2000, despite the hard-money limits, Bush's "Pioneers" raised a record-smashing $100 million in "bundled" $1,000 checks. The Pioneers were modeled after Bush Sr.'s 1988 fund-raising force, "Team 100"—and included some of the same people, such as Lee Bass of the Texas oil billionaire Bass brothers, and Bush's former oil and baseball partners DeWitt and Reynolds, who came in first with $605,000. Bush later appointed Reynolds ambassador to Switzerland (and, not surprisingly, made him his 2004 campaign finance chairman). In second place was Michigan businessman Ronald Weiser, subsequently appointed ambassador to Slovakia. The bronze went to the team of Howard Leach and Kristen Hueter. Leach became ambassador to France. In all, nineteen Pioneers were subsequently appointed ambassadors.

The Pioneers included at least forty-four top energy executives and a host of other corporate chiefs, each with a unique lobbying agenda. They included the chairman of ConocoPhillips; the heads of the American Petroleum Institute, the Chemical Manufacturers Association, and the Food Marketing Institute; the CEOs of credit-card giant MBNA and hospital chain Tenet Healthcare; and Lonnie Pilgrim of Pilgrim's Pride, the fourth largest U.S. poultry producer, who once gave out $10,000 checks on the floor of the Texas Senate while lobbying lawmakers to gut workers' compensation legislation[52]—and who clearly understood that politically, Bush's Washington was Austin writ large.

The Bush campaign long refused to disclose the identities of any Pioneers, despite the fact, Wheat noted, that Bush was "on record favoring better campaign disclosures, rather than contribution limits, as the solution to what ails the U.S. political system." But the Bushies made sure to know just who their contributors were; they assigned special tracking numbers to be written on all checks—to "ensure that our industry is credited," as explained on a fund-raising letter sent out by Pioneer Thomas Kuhn, head of the Edison Electric Institute, a lobby group representing utilities.

White House "For Rent" again. Republicans had a field day bashing Clinton for letting friends and campaign contributors sleep in the White House's Lincoln Bedroom, calling it everything from a "disgrace" to a possible criminal violation. No sooner had Bush moved into the White House than the Rooms for Rent sign went back up. In his first eighteen months, Bush hosted over 160 White House sleepover guests, including Pioneers—individuals who donated at least $100,000 to his campaign. Republicans as a whole were silent on the matter.

CHENEY AND HALLIBURTON

As with **Bush's business career**, Dick Cheney's was all about political connections—domestic and international. Indeed, he epitomized the corporate-government revolving door whereby former administration officials—sometimes, as in Cheney's case, with no business experience—were hired by corporations for their government connections, then later were appointed to the Bush administration with lots of hype about their supposed private-sector expertise. Typically, the corporations they served, far from embodying the genius of free enterprise, lived off of government contacts and contracts.

It was largely the foreign contacts Cheney made as secretary of defense under Bush I that got him hired to run the Houston-based oil services giant Halliburton in 1995. But he had also sent a lot of business the company's way. In 1991, right after the Gulf War—in a preplay of what was to happen after the 2003 Iraq war—Cheney hired Halliburton to put out oil fires in Kuwait and awarded contracts to rebuild Kuwaiti infrastructure to Brown & Root (B&R), Halliburton's construction and engineering subsidiary. B&R, according to *Texas Monthly* magazine, "had long been a de facto arm of the U.S. military," receiving huge Pentagon contracts for construction of military bases, airports and port facilities in Vietnam. By the time Cheney left office in 1993, he had carried out the largest peacetime *reduction* of U.S. military forces in history—the key to which was the "outsourcing" of traditional military functions to companies like B&R. Cheney's Pentagon first paid B&R $8.9 million for studies on how to do this, then gave it an exclusive worldwide contract to provide everything from food, laundry service, and toilets to runways—the first such contract ever given to a civilian enterprise. In 1993, B&R's U.S. Army support group in Somalia briefly became Africa's biggest employer.

When Cheney took the helm at Halliburton in 1995, he simply moved from the giving to the receiving end of the system: In the next few years, B&R received nearly $2 billion in Pentagon contracts. Meanwhile, to keep the wheels of the military-industrial complex well greased, Cheney doubled Halliburton's contributions to (Republican) federal political campaigns to $1.2 million.

Halliburton didn't only benefit from the U.S. government. More than 40 percent of its revenues came from overseas, much of it from Arab and former Soviet bloc nations. Cheney, had who never run a business before, "would be able to open doors around the world and to have access practically anywhere," the Halliburton chairman who hired him told *Texas Monthly*.[53] Indeed: On Cheney's watch, a Halliburton subsidiary sold $23 million in equipment to Saddam Hussein's **Iraq,** and the company maintained an office in and sold equipment to Iran. Cheney lobbied against sanctions on Iran until he joined Bush's presidential ticket.

Also on Cheney's watch, dubious accounting practices at Halliburton—inflating revenue by including unpaid bills, and failing to disclose the accounting change—led to an SEC investigation and a lawsuit for defrauding shareholders of billions of dollars. By 2002, Halliburton's stock had lost 80 percent of its value, devastating ordinary shareholders. But—true to the pattern of corporate scandals then roiling the markets—the top executive made out just fine. When Cheney bailed out of Halliburton in 2000 to join the Bush ticket, he was paid $20 million, not counting $18 million in stock options, which he made "an extraordinarily serendipitous decision to sell," *The New Republic* noted, "in August 2000—just two months before the company publicly revealed how poorly it was performing, sending its stock price into a nosedive."[54] Cheney and his wife reported more than $36 million in income for 2000, of which some $34 million came from Halliburton stock options and other perks.

CHICKENHAWKS

True to what scientists call the chickenhawk paradox, among current and former federal officials, the leading advocates of caution against going to war in **Iraq** tended to be former military officers and decorated combat veterans—including Senators John Kerry and Chuck Hagel, retired generals Wesley Clark, Colin Powell and Norman Schwartzkopf (at least for a while), and Bush I National Security Adviser Brent Scowcroft. Conversely, most of the leading hawks had done no military service and some were conspicuous draft avoiders.

W. in flight: Bush's military record.

> *"I am angry that so many of the sons of the powerful and well-placed . . . managed to wangle slots in Reserve and National Guard units . . . Of the many tragedies of Vietnam, this raw class discrimination strikes me as the most damaging to the ideal that all Americans are created equal."*
>
> —Colin Powell, *My American Journey.*

Bush sure looked great in that flight suit, landing on an

aircraft carrier in May 2003 to declare victory in Iraq. Perhaps the bravest thing about the stunt was reminding people that he'd worn a flight suit before. Bush had also emphasized—and embellished—his fighter-pilot experience to help win his 1994 gubernatorial election. Investigations of Bush's military record by the *Boston Globe* and others showed that Bush's family connections kept him out of Vietnam by getting him into the Texas Air National Guard, and that—according to the records, his commanding officers, and fellow flyers—he didn't show up for duty for a full year.

In 1968, upon graduating from Yale, Bush applied for a coveted position in the Guard, which required only part-time military duties at home. He jumped to the front of 500 other applicants after a friend of his father, then a wealthy Houston congressman, phoned the Speaker of the Texas House, Ben Barnes, who helped place W. in a "champagne unit" (full of sons of the wealthy and well-connected) of the Guard[55]—as Barnes swore under oath in a civil lawsuit in 1999. Both Bushes later denied any knowledge of the intercession. After 18 months of pilot training, Bush began a four-year commitment as a part-time fighter pilot.

AWOL. In his 1999 campaign autobiography—titled *A Charge to Keep*—Bush wrote that "I continued flying with my unit for the next several years." But he actually stopped flying after twenty-two months, in April 1972, when, in order to work on a U.S. Senate campaign in Alabama, he received a transfer (for which he was not eligible) to an Alabama National Guard unit. But Bush never showed up for duty there, according to the Guard records and to the unit's commander and his assistant, who were interviewed by the *Boston Globe*.

Those caught shirking National Guard duty were usually punished by being drafted into the real army—meaning, Vietnam. But, despite more than a year absent from duty, no punishment befell W. In fact, he apparently won early release to attend Harvard Business School in September 1973. He later claimed he was released because his unit was switching to newer planes that he couldn't fly, but the unit's records and commander contradicted this as well. The commander told the *Globe* he would have kept Bush flying, "[b]ut I don't recall him coming back [to the Texas base] at all."[56]

After the *Globe* published the story in the middle of the 2000 presidential campaign, the rest of the media largely ignored it. According to former Clinton aide Paul Begala, there were 13,641 media stories about Clinton's Vietnam-era draft dodging during his first presidential race, versus forty-nine about Bush's military past during his campaign.

AMONG OTHERS in and close to the administration who were of age but avoided service in Vietnam:

John Ashcroft, who got a deferment by claiming his job teaching business education filled a vital national need.

Dick Cheney, who maintained a series of student defer-ments from 1959 through to 1966, when he became exempt from service after his wife became pregnant. In his own words, he "had other priorities."

Tom DeLay (R-TX). Upon graduating from university in 1970, DeLay, the *Houston Press* reported, "chose to enlist in the war on cockroaches, fleas and termites as the owner of an exterminator business." In 1988, when the press was jumping all over Dan Quayle's use of family ties (à la Bush) to get into a national guard unit instead of going to Vietnam—DeLay told reporters that so many minority youths had volunteered for well-paying military positions to escape the ghetto that there was just no room for people like himself and Quayle.

Marc Racicot, Republican National Committee chairman and Bush's close confidante. Like DeLay, Racicot attacked critics of Bush and his war—including wounded and decorated war veterans—as unpatriotic. According to a newspaper from his home state, Montana, Racicot claimed to be "an Army ROTC Graduate" at a college that had no Reserve Officer Training Corps program, and although picked twenty-third out of 366 in the first draft lottery after student deferments were ended, he somehow went on to law school instead.[57]

ALSO Energy Secretary **Spencer Abraham**; National Security Council official and leading Iraq hawk **Elliott Abrams** (bad back); State Department ultra-hawk **John Bolton**; Florida Gov. **Jeb Bush**; White House chief of staff **Andrew Card**; Commerce Secretary **Don Evans**; Solicitor General **Ted Olson**; Defense Policy Board chairman and ur-Iraq hawk **Richard Perle**; former SEC chairman **Harvey Pitt** (Harvard law school); "General" **Karl Rove** (college); Health and Human Services Secretary **Tommy Thompson** (National Guard); drug czar **John Walters**; and Assistant Deputy of Defense and Iraq megahawk **Paul Wolfowitz**.

(See **Veterans' rights**.)

CHURCH AND STATE, UN-SEPARATION OF: *BUSH'S CRUSADE AGAINST CONSTITUTIONAL PRINCIPLES*

> *"[T]he famous saying in the Gospel according to St. Matthew, 'Render unto Caesar what is Caesar's, and render unto God what is God's'. . . . is supposed to be an indication of the separation of the church and state."*
>
> —Ibn Warraq[58]

The belief that religious freedom is safest when religion is left as purely a private matter was the basis of the First Amendment "Establishment Clause" forbidding state-supported religion. The constitutional separation of church and state had been more or less scrupulously maintained for 200 years (and, it was observed, had resulted in the U.S. having the highest proportion of professed religious believers in the industrialized world). This was the tradition Bush set about undermining in his second week in office.

This came as no surprise from one who, as governor, had declared a "Jesus Day" in Texas; who, as a presidential candidate, had named Jesus as his favorite political philosopher; who had all but referred to *himself* as divinely anointed to lead (see **God**); and for whom the political support of the Christian right was, as it were, crucial.[59]

Bush—who by his own account had said in 1993, "Only Christians have a place in heaven"[60]—wasted no time turning the White House itself into what Catholic theologian Jeffrey Siker described as a "quasi-church setting."[61] The invocation at Bush's inauguration was given by evangelist and old Bush buddy Franklin Graham, Billy Graham's son—

who on other occasions called Islam a "very wicked and evil" religion, and proclaimed, "The true God is the God of the Bible, not the Koran." The first words speechwriter David Frum (a Jew) heard in the Bush White House were, "Missed you at Bible study."[62]

"Faith-based Initiatives." One journalistic wit referred to the September 11 attack as a "faith-based initiative." But I refer here to the assault launched by Bush on church-state separation in February 2001, when he set up his new Office of Faith-Based and Community Initiatives in the White House for the purpose of expanding government funding of religious ministries and creating church-state "partnerships."

Under the First Amendment, Americans are—or were—free to decide for themselves whether to support religious ministries. In 1811, President Madison, "Father of the Constitution," vetoed a bill that gave federal sanction to a church that provided aid and education to the poor because, in his words, it "exceeds the rightful authority to which governments are limited by the essential distinction between civil and religious functions." According to Americans United for Separation of Church and State (AU), "Forcing taxpayers to subsidize religious institutions they may or not believe in is no different from forcing them to put money in the collection plates of churches, synagogues and mosques . . . .America's founders would be appalled at the Bush initiative."[63]

The F-B-I's aim was to expand federal funding of "faith-based" programs from aid to the poor, as permitted under the "CHARITABLE CHOICE" provision (sponsored by then-Senator John Ashcroft) of the 1996 welfare act, to job training, juvenile delinquency, drug rehab, and other social services.

How could we be sure these organizations would not use any of their public funding to promote their own religious beliefs? Why, have faith. Bush assured Congress that "Government, of course, cannot fund, and will not fund, religious activities."

Meanwhile, the Bushies quietly assured the religious right of just the opposite. An August 2001 article in the evangelical magazine *World* by former Bush adviser Marvin Olasky (who coined the term "compassionate conservatism") assured evangelicals that White House officials were carefully diverting congressional and press scrutiny away from loopholes and a "stealth provision" in the F-B-I scheme that would permit the use of taxpayer dollars to proselytize. The Justice Department lawyer drafting the rules was "a master of vague language," Olasky assured, quoting a White House "insider" as saying biblical teaching could be "interwoven" into federally funded programs "as long as you do it right and keep separate books"[64]—a uniquely Bushie mix of evangelism and Enronism.

Bibles for job training (and other F-B-I mischief). Piece by piece, the pretense of preserving church-state separation was dropped. *The Boston Globe*, May 8, 2003: "The Bush administration has quietly altered regulations for the nation's leading job training program to allow faith-based organizations to use 'sacred literature,' such as Bibles, in their federally funded programs"—"as historical texts" or "as inspirational stories."

The same day, the House of Representatives approved a change allowing faith-based groups running federally funded job-training programs to discriminate on the basis of religion in their hiring, which had been banned by federal law for two decades. Religious groups were already exempt from nondiscrimination laws in hiring for other purposes. Under Bush's F-B-I, they could now legally discriminate while receiving public dollars. A taxpayer might help pay for a job that he himself would be denied because of his faith (or lack thereof).

Many among the clergy realized that funding religious activity was Bush's real purpose—and were unhappy about it. The leadership of Bush's own United Methodist Church, the country's second-largest Protestant denomination, came out against the F-B-I because, they said, it violated church-state separation, subsidized religious discrimination, and threatened the independence of churches.[65] The door Bush opened between church and state swung both ways: Religious ministering infiltrated publicly funded social services, and government would get involved in—and could end up regulating—religious activity. "I have one piece of advice for church leaders: Say 'no, thank you' to government funds for your religious ministries," a prominent Baptist minister said. "Charitable Choice threatens to make religion the servant of the state, rather than its conscience."[66]

The record in Texas. Every one of these concerns was borne out by the F-B-I Governor Bush set up in Texas—where "it is impossible to demonstrate, after five years of aggressive implementation, a single positive outcome," according to Samantha Smoot, director of the Texas Freedom Network.[67] Thanks to religious providers being exempt from state licensing requirements, Texas became "a refuge" for religious groups with histories of regulatory violations, theological objections to state oversight, and rates of abuse and neglect ten times higher than those of licensed facilities.

The Rovesputin of F-B-I. The head of Bush's Office of Faith-Based Initiatives, John DiIulio, quit in August 2001. In a subsequent interview with *Esquire*,[68] he made clear that the person really in charge of F-B-I was Karl Rove, whose concern was to manipulate F-B-I to please the religious right for the White House's political benefit—and that it was the same on every other issue as well: "[E]verything, and I mean everything, [is] being run by the political arm. It's the reign of the Mayberry Machiavellis."

Unseating the Constitution as guarantor of freedom. Bush's dependence on the Christian right gave their lobby powerful leverage over Bush appointments and policies. According to one analysis, "If the **Ashcroft** nomination [as Attorney General] is payback for anything, it is for the efforts of [televangelist Pat] Robertson and other top leaders of the Christian Right to elect Bush."[69] And in Ashcroft, the fundamentalists got a true Christian soldier. In February 2002, he told a Christian broadcasters' group in effect that God was on our side in the war against terror. The nation's top law-enforcement officer also said, "We are a nation called to defend freedom—*a freedom that is not the grant of any government or document*, but is our endowment from God" (italics added).[70]

In his 2003 State of the Union address, Bush said much the same thing—that the freedom we enjoy as Americans is "God's gift"—a harmless-sounding phrase, but one which Bush repeated again and again in other contexts—and which really meant that for Bush, too, religious beliefs took precedence over the Constitution—implying that Americans' laws and rights, like Iranians' or Saudis', could ultimately depend on what someone informs us is God's will. These guys just didn't get it. Any individual might well regard his or her own religion as "higher" than any man-made laws—*and that was exactly why the state must not.*

Toward religious control over the courts. In June 2002, a California circuit court ruled that reciting the Pledge of Allegiance in public schools is an unconstitutional endorsement of religion because of the words "under God" after "one nation" (which Congress inserted in the Pledge in 1954). In response to the ruling, Bush said, "We need common-sense judges who understand that"—here we go again—"*our rights were derived from God. Those are the kind of judges I intend to put on the bench.*" (Italics added.) Bush clearly intended to exclude nonbelievers from serving on the judiciary—which would be in violation of Article 6 of the Constitution, which states, "No religious Test shall ever be required as a Qualification to any Office." Just such a test appeared to be already in effect, judging by Bush's **judicial nominees.**

Creationism and evolution. In 1998, Pope John Paul II announced that the Roman Catholic Church would no longer oppose the teaching of evolution. That seemed to leave American fundamentalist Protestants—among them, George W. Bush—as *the* most backward segment of humanity (perhaps along with certain mullahs and their followers) in their views on and attitudes toward science.

In February '03—that's *2003*, not *1903* or 1303—a survey found that nearly twice as many Americans believed in creationism and as in evolution, which only 28 percent believed to be a fact. Three times as many believed in the Virgin Birth of Jesus. Bush himself had said, "The jury [was] still out" on evolution and that both evolution and creationism should be taught in schools.

That same month, a Lubbock, Texas, biology professor (and devout Catholic) who insisted that students who wanted recommendations to med school or advanced biology accept the reality of evolution—the central coordinating concept of modern biology—found himself under investigation by the Bush-Ashcroft Justice Department. (See **Abortion; Education; Federalist Society; God; Health; Science.**)

CIVIL LIBERTIES AND PRIVACY: "SEIZING DICTATORIAL POWER"

"There ought to be limits to freedom."

—George W. Bush

While their disdain for Americans' civil liberties and privacy rights was evident before **September 11**, the **war on terrorism** provided the Bushies with a pretext for extraordinary expansions of presidential and law enforcement power as well as extraordinary intrusions upon the democratic rights of Americans, which alarmed liberals and conservatives alike. The weeks after 9/11 saw the hurried enactment of probably the most sweeping expansion of presidential power ever, the USA PATRIOT ACT "anti-terrorism" bill, along with a series of far-reaching curtailments of Americans' freedoms and privacy proclaimed simply by presidential decree. These measures attacked the right to a fair and open trial, the presumption of innocence, lawyer-client confidentiality, and constitutional protections against unreasonable searches and surveillance, secret arrest and detention, seizure of property, summary loss of citizenship, and deportation. Definitions of "terrorism" were expanded to cover almost any conceivable crime, exposing even minor offenders and nonviolent political activists to severe punishments.

The Bushies' appropriations of new powers continued, "under the radar," for the next year and a half, as they prepared a second, even more draconian legislative package dubbed "PATRIOT ACT II," which critics termed "a quantum leap" in executive branch power. Meanwhile, the Pentagon and Homeland Security departments set up computer systems of unprecedented size and power to collect information on Americans' private activities. As for the courts, in March 2003, Supreme Court Justice Antonin Scalia said matter-of-factly that Americans could expect that "protections [of their rights] will be ratcheted down to the constitutional minimum." That proved a gross understatement.

King George hereby decrees: In the first two months after 9/11, in addition to propelling the Patriot Act (details below) through Congress, the White House and/or Justice Department (DOJ) issued several sweeping directives by executive proclamation, several of which violated Constitutional protections upheld by judicial precedent over many decades. They:

- Authorized special, secret MILITARY COURTS to try suspected terrorists, on the president's sole directive, with none of the normal judicial rules and procedures. Trials would be held in secret. No information about them would have to be made public. The accused would have no recourse to appeal in any state, federal, foreign, or international court. Sentences could range up to life imprisonment or execution. To convict would require only a two-thirds majority of the military officers presiding, who would be selected by the secretary of defense. Their identities could be concealed from the public—recalling the hooded army officers of Latin American military courts. And the tribunals would not have to prove guilt beyond a reasonable doubt or follow established rules of evidence— violating the most elementary principles of legal justice that applied even in existing military courts. ("Perhaps Ashcroft learned these techniques of jurisprudence from the abattoir regimes, like those of Chile and Guatemala, that the American right has so long defended," Christopher Hitchens mused in *The Nation*.[71])

- Authorized the monitoring of conversations between lawyers and clients in federal custody, including people detained but not charged with any crime.

- Rounded up at least 1,187 immigrants in the antiterror dragnet (the DOJ thereafter stopped issuing tallies of how many had been rounded up), and refused to disclose their names. Under the new rules, many of these could be held without charges, indefinitely, and all were assumed to have terrorist links until the FBI said otherwise—i.e., they were guilty until proven innocent. In June 2003, a report by the DOJ's inspector general concluded that the roundup "made little attempt to distinguish" between immigrants with possible ties to terrorism and those without, and that many of the latter had been left languishing in jail, subjected to harsh conditions and physical and verbal abuse from guards. The DOJ's response: "We make no apologies . . . "

The military tribunals authorized by Bush in November 2001 may "only" have applied to noncitizens, but the Bill of Rights applied to "persons," not just citizens. (Moreover, historically, the slippery slope of civil rights curtailments had typically started with immigrants.) In authorizing them, the Bushies simply discarded one of the most basic democratic principles of U.S. law, the presumption of innocence. Vice President Cheney said terrorism *suspects* "don't deserve the same guarantees and safeguards that would be used for an American citizen going through the normal judicial process," and that a military tribunal "guarantees that we'll have the kind of treatment of these individuals *that we believe they deserve*" (emphasis added). I.e., *suspects* were now as good as guilty.

USA Patriot Act. The Uniting and Strengthening America by Providing Appropriate Tools Required to Intercept and Obstruct Terrorism Act—a law drafted by Ashcroft and his aides—gave the government broad new police and surveillance powers and eliminated judicial checks and balances, fundamental civil liberties, and privacy safeguards. Yet it was rushed through a panicky Congress in October 2001 after less than six weeks of what could hardly be called debate. (The House passed it in ten days by a 337–79 vote— the Senate in seven days, 99–1.) The White House implied that members who voted against it would be blamed for any further attacks—a tactic that fit one of the act's own broad new definitions of terrorism: to "influence the policy of a government by intimidation or coercion."

Many of the Patriot Act's (PA) provisions had nothing to do with terrorism. Many were long-standing items on law enforcement's wishlist that had previously and repeatedly been rejected by Congress. Provisions included:

Giving the attorney general the unprecedented power to detain noncitizens indefinitely—with no requirement for a trial or hearing—based only on claiming "reasonable grounds to believe" the person endangers national security, rather than "proof beyond reasonable doubt," as in criminal trials, or "clear, convincing, and unequivocal evidence" as required in deportation hearings.

Broadening "terrorism." The PA permitted the secretary of state to designate foreign and domestic groups that have never engaged in violent activities as "terrorist organizations" and created a new crime of "DOMESTIC TERRORISM," defining it so broadly—as "any action that endangers human life that is a violation of any Federal or State law," or "to influence the policy of a government by intimidation or coercion"—that it could easily be applied to environmentalists and other activists. Providing lodging or assistance to such "terrorists" could now result in surveillance, prosecution, and/or deportation; and the authorities could detain or deport noncitizens belonging or donating money to such "terrorist" groups without having to prove they intentionally assisted terrorist activity. (GUILT BY ASSOCIATION is generally forbidden by the First Amendment; most laws based on it had been struck down or discredited by the courts.)

Domestic "Foreign Intelligence" surveillance. Under the PA, rules and procedures that had been created for the gathering of foreign intelligence, and were exempt from key constitutional restrictions on unreasonable searches, could be used widely in ordinary, domestic criminal investigations of Americans. The FBI could secretly search citizens' homes, offices, or records, or conduct electronic surveillance of phone and Internet use, without proving probable cause (i.e., a likelihood of criminal activity or intent) as the Fourth Amendment explicitly required, by obtaining a warrant from the secretive FOREIGN INTELLIGENCE SURVEILLANCE COURT.

The Foreign Intelligence Surveillance Act (FISA) of 1978 established the FISA court to review and authorize secret searches and surveillance aimed at terrorists, spies, or foreign political organizations. Legal standards for obtaining such warrants were much lower than for ordinary criminal investigations, but—in theory—law enforcement agents were expected to show that the subject of the search was a foreign agent or terrorist group, and they could not distribute information they gathered to domestic criminal investigators. FISA could not be used simply because there was insufficient evidence to obtain a conventional warrant.

In practice, however, that is just what increasingly happened. Even before 9/11, the FISA court—which always met behind closed doors—issued around 1,000 warrants a year, exceeding all other federal surveillance warrants. Indeed, since its inception, the court had approved all but one application—proof, civil libertarians said, that the court was just a rubber stamp for the government.

The PA dramatically accelerated this shift. Foreign intelligence gathering no longer had to be the "primary" purpose of a FISA search but only "a significant" purpose. Ashcroft had tried to reduce it down to merely "*a* purpose." Going further, in 2002, Ashcroft issued new procedures allowing free exchange of information between police and spy agencies—completely breaking down the separation the FISA court itself said was essential "to protect the privacy of Americans in these highly intrusive surveillances and searches."

Putting the CIA back in the domestic spying business. As a result of abuses in the 1970s, when the CIA engaged in widespread spying on political dissidents and other Americans, the lead role in gathering foreign intelligence within the U.S. was supposedly given to the Justice Department. The Patriot Act put the CIA back in charge and permitted domestic law enforcement to share information gathered in criminal investigations, including wiretaps and Internet captures, with the CIA, which could in turn share information with other agencies, including foreign governments.

Unrestricted records searches. The PA vastly expanded the government's access to citizens' banking, credit card, medical, Internet, airline, hotel, bookstore purchase, and library loan records—indeed, any records—held by third parties:

- Under loosened FISA rules, the government no longer had to show evidence that the subject of such a search was an "agent of a foreign power." The government no longer had to show that the records were even *related* to criminal activity, much less meet the Fourth Amendment requirement to show probable cause. Now, the feds merely had to say the request was related to a terrorism or foreign intelligence investigation.

- Judges had no authority to reject applications for search warrants, rendering judicial oversight virtually nonexistent.

- Surveillance could result from books that individuals read, Web sites they visited, or letters or articles they may have written—a violation of First Amendment **free speech** rights.

- A third party forced to turn over records was prohibited from disclosing the search to anyone (a free-speech violation), including the surveillance subject, who would never find out his or her personal records had been examined by the government, and who therefore lost the ability to challenge illegitimate searches (a Fourth Amendment violation).[72]

"Sneak and peek" secret searches. The PA amended the Federal Rules of Criminal Procedure to allow the government to conduct searches of homes or offices—whether in terrorism-related *or* normal criminal investigations—without notifying the subjects. Such notice—the "knock and announce" principle—had long been recognized as part of the Fourth Amendment protection against unreasonable searches and as a crucial check on the government's power, because it forced authorities to operate in the open and allowed the subject to verify that the warrant was in order and its scope was not exceeded.

Wiretaps and Internet monitoring. The pre-9/11 law on wiretaps made it much easier for law enforcement to obtain phone numbers used by suspects than to monitor actual conversations. To get a "trap and trace" warrant—named for devices used to capture phone numbers—the FBI did not have to show probable cause or even reasonable suspicion of criminal activity, but merely to certify to a judge that the warrant was "relevant" to an ongoing criminal investigation.[73] The Patriot Act extended the same loophole to Internet monitoring, allowing law enforcement to obtain email headers and website addresses (URLs) visited by Internet users (the FBI promised it would only look at the headers and addresses, not read the messages). Within hours of the PA's passage, the Justice Department said it had already used its new powers to obtain logs from Internet providers.

"Nationwide" warrants. Under the PA, "trap and trace" warrants—for phone *or* computer use—were no longer valid only in the issuing judge's jurisdiction but anywhere in the U.S. Nationwide warrants violated the Fourth Amendment requirement that warrants be written "particularly describing the place to be searched" in order to prevent abuses such as random searches of the homes of innocent persons.

"Roving" wiretaps. The PA expanded authorities' power to wiretap any phone the subject might be near, anywhere, and to listen in on whoever was using it. Federal law first permitted roving wiretaps in 1986, and an amendment by Congress widened the power in 1998. But the PA went much further, allowing roving wiretaps to be authorized by the FISA Court secretly and without proof of probable cause.

Global electronic spying: The PA permitted electronic surveillance by foreign governments to be used against Americans "even if the collection would have violated the Fourth Amendment," in the Justice Department's own words. This would include information gathered by ECHELON, a vast, automated data collection system operated jointly by the U.S., U.K, Canada, Australia, and New Zealand, which allowed those countries' spy agencies to monitor most of the world's electronic communications (including as many as 3 billion phone calls per day and an estimated 90 percent of all global Internet traffic); it was described as the most powerful intelligence gathering organization in the world. There was no way for the public to know whether it was used to spy on private citizens; it operated with little oversight, and the agencies that ran it—the lead one being the U.S. National Security Agency—disclosed little information about its legal guidelines, if any.

"Lust for power": Even right-wingers appalled. Civil-libertarians on the left and right found common cause in opposing the new "domestic security" measures. Paul Weyrich of the conservative Free Congress Foundation—who had helped promote Ashcroft for AG—warned of "serious restrictions on the personal freedoms and civil liberties of all Americans," and said the right feared the new laws "had little to do with catching terrorists but a lot to do with increasing the strength of the government to infiltrate and spy on conservative organizations." (If *they* were worried . . .) "The attorney general doesn't seem to be making any effort to contain the lust for power that these people in the Department of Justice have," then-House Majority Leader Dick Armey, a

right-wing Republican, told *The New Republic*. The DOJ "seems to be running amok and out of control [and] right now is the biggest threat to personal liberty in the country."[74]

Led by Armey, libertarian-minded members of Congress succeeded in blocking some measures Ashcroft tried putting into the Patriot Act, such as a national ID card and, most notoriously, the TERRORISM INFORMATION AND PREVENTION SYSTEM or TIPS program, which would have encouraged delivery employees, meter readers, and other private citizens to spy on their fellow citizens and neighbors and report suspicious activity to the FBI. Most of the public was appalled, Congress wasn't interested—but, as Armey said, "[the Justice Department's] attitude is, 'We're going to do it anyway.'"[75] Also thanks to Armey et al., some of the Patriot Act's provisions were to expire after four years.

Beyond the Patriot Act. Yes, the Patriot Act could have been worse—and it *got* worse. Powers that Ashcroft wasn't given by the PA, he just appropriated. And much more was to come in PATRIOT ACT II.

Freeing the FBI to spy on domestic religious and political organizations. In September 2002, Ashcroft scrapped guidelines that prevented the FBI from spying in mosques or churches even if there was no evidence of any crime. The guidelines were imposed in the 1970s, when it was learned that the FBI, under the "Cointelpro" program, had engaged in widespread domestic surveillance of antiwar protesters, the Black Panthers, Martin Luther King, Jr., and others in efforts to undermine and discredit them. For twenty-five years, those guidelines remained fundamental restraints on the bureau's conduct, making clear that, as the ACLU put it, "advocacy of unpopular ideas or political dissent alone could not serve as the basis for an investigation."[76] Ashcroft's new guidelines allowed just that.

"No Child Unrecruited," ran a *Mother Jones* headline. A little-noticed provision in Bush's much touted "No Child Left Behind Act" **education** bill of 2002 required public high schools to turn over students' names, addresses, and telephone numbers to military recruiters. Schools that did not comply would lose all federal aid. The military had complained that many high schools denied access to recruiters—which some had done on the grounds that the military discriminated against gays and lesbians. Rep. David Vitter (R-LA), who sponsored the new provision, said such schools "demonstrated an anti-military attitude that I thought was offensive."

The "Total Information Awareness" program and Big Brother Poindexter. In August 2002, the Defense Department's Defense Advanced Research Projects Agency (DARPA) began awarding contracts for the creation of a "virtual, centralized, grand database" using "revolutionary technology" to store and analyze data on Americans, allowing everything from employment, medical, and credit card to Internet, EZ Pass, and pay-per-view records, to be collected in "unprecedented," "ultra-large" quantities. Technologies such as face recognition would be developed to identify and track individuals from a distance—all of this ostensibly aimed at detecting terrorist activity prior to an attack.

And who was put at the controls? None other than (retired) Admiral JOHN POINDEXTER—President Reagan's national security adviser, Oliver North's boss, the man who supervised the IRAN-CONTRA operation and was convicted in 1990 of five felony counts of conspiracy, making false statements to Congress, and obstructing congressional inquiries. (The convictions were overturned on appeal on the grounds that he'd been granted immunity in exchange for his testimony to Congress.) So Americans could rest assured that TIA would operate strictly within its mandate and the law. The ever-creative Poindexter was canned in August 2003 for initiating a government-sponsored futures market for betting on future terrorist strikes, assassinations, etc.

Computer Assisted Passenger Pre-Screening System (CAPPS II). As a first step toward deploying it throughout the country, Delta Airlines in March 2003 began a test run of CAPPS II, a system developed by the new Transportation Security Administration to perform electronic background checks—including credit reports, banking, and criminal records—on all passengers who book a ticket. The system would then assign them a threat level—red, yellow, or green—with which authorities would determine if they should be subjected to increased security checks at the airport or refused boarding. The system would store information about those deemed a yellow- or red-level threat for up to fifty years. The information could be shared with government agencies, including intelligence agencies such as the CIA and international agencies and foreign governments, to be used for any conceivable purpose. "This system threatens to create a permanent blacklisted underclass of Americans [with poor or no credit ratings] who cannot travel freely," an ACLU lawyer said.[77]

Patriot Act II: *Be afraid. Be very afraid.* By mid-2003, three states and more than 150 U.S. cities and communities had adopted resolutions protesting the Patriot Act and other invasive federal policies already in effect. But far from backing off from any of them, the Bushies greedily grabbed for still more power. Even while assuring Congress that no new bill was in the works, the Justice Department in January 2003 internally circulated a confidential 120-page draft of the "Domestic Security and Enhancement Act of 2003," which was leaked by a government official to the nonpartisan Center for Public Integrity.

Patriot Act II, as it was nicknamed, would dramatically extend the police-state powers the Bushies seized under PA I. Among many other provisions, it would:

- Remove the five-year sunset (expiration) clause from key sections of PA I.
- Allow the government to secretly and indefinitely detain *U.S. citizens* in connection with a terrorism investigation; not disclose their names or whereabouts; exempt such information from the Freedom of Information Act, and even make it a crime to release it. An American citizen "could simply disappear."[78]
- Allow the attorney general to revoke citizenship of terrorism *suspects* and to prosecute and/or revoke citizenship of those who, intentionally or not, provide "material support" to terrorists.
- Expand crimes punishable by death to include any terrorist act or support for a terrorist act.
- Remove any statute of limitations for "terrorists" (as broadly defined by the PA) or those who support them.

- Repeal court-ordered limits ("consent decrees") on local and state police spying on religious, political, and other non-criminal activities and organizations.
- Set up a national DNA database of "suspected terrorists" and allow the government to collect DNA from anyone the government maintains might assist terror investigations, without their consent and without a court order.
- Permit government access to a citizen's credit reports and library, Internet, and bookstore purchase records without any warrant at all.
- Grant government agents immunity for spying on Americans without a court order, and severely restrict citizens' ability to obtain court injunctions against federal violations of civil rights.
- Destroy whistle-blower protection for federal agents.
- Create "lifetime parole" for a long list of crimes.
- Allow the government to summarily deport legal immigrants, without charges, evidence, court hearing, or review, if the attorney general merely suspects they may be a risk to national security.
- Allow Americans to be extradited, searched, or wire-tapped at the behest of foreign nations, regardless of the nature of their governments and courts, and whether treaties allow it or not.
- Allow the federal government to use wartime martial law powers domestically and internationally without Congress declaring a state of war.
- Provide liability protection for businesses that spy on their customers and violate their privacy agreements by releasing their records to government and law enforcement agencies.

"Alarming as the Patriot Act was," said the director of the Samuelson Law, Technology and Public Policy Clinic, "these provisions are right off the edge."[79] An ACLU report observed, "The bitter irony is that the Patriot Act II could make our nation more vulnerable to terrorism." Given such indiscriminate new powers of arrest and detention for such a wide range of activities, law enforcement could lose the focus on actual terrorists. (The vast majority of the 1,100-plus people rounded up after 9/11 turned out to have no terrorist connections.)

(See **Free speech; War on terrorism.**)

"COMPASSIONATE CONSERVATISM": IF NOT ON A PAR WITH "ARBEIT MACHT FREI," STILL AMONG HISTORY'S HOLLOWEST PROMISES

The Bushies' "compassionate conservative" election strategy deserves to be remembered as perhaps the greatest deception in U.S. presidential history. It was conceived out of a recognition that the American public had moved to the left (as conservative columnist Fred Barnes put it, "Bush is saying, 'I'm not Newt Gingrich'"), but served as a Trojan Horse to smuggle into the White House an army of far-right ideologues and "pro-business" radicals. Examples of the hollowness of this slogan make up much of this book, so I will mention just a few here.

In 1999, candidate Bush criticized Republicans in Congress for trying to "balance the budget on the backs of the poor." President Bush managed to *un*balance the budget on the backs of the poor (see **Budget and taxes**), doling out huge tax cuts for the wealthy while programs to help the poor, the ill, the disabled, and the elderly were under attack at all levels of government. The day after he exhorted the audience at the National Religious Broadcasters convention in Nashville to "rally the armies of compassion" to ease suffering, his administration proposed a rent increase for thousands of poor people receiving HOUSING AID.[80] Bush's 2003 budget eliminated AFTER-SCHOOL PROGRAMS for 500,000 children. The administration cut funding for the SCHOOL LUNCH PROGRAM and tried to remove from it up to a million children, or as many as one in five. Bush proposed cuts in CHILDREN'S HEALTH INSURANCE and a 30-percent cut in grants for CHILDREN'S HOSPITALS; tightened work·requirements for **welfare** recipients in the teeth of the worst job slump in decades—while cutting funding for JOB TRAINING; exempted "workfare" payments from minimum wage requirements; cut funding for the LOW INCOME HOME ENERGY ASSISTANCE PROGRAM, which helped the poor pay for winter heat and electricity; froze funding two years running for the CONGREGATE NUTRITION PROGRAM, meaning 36,000 seniors would be cut from meals-on-wheels programs while another 140,000 remained on waiting lists; and even undermined funding for his own **education** reform program, the "NO CHILD LEFT BEHIND ACT." He proposed a radical restructuring of **Medicaid** that would undermine the states' ability to gurarantee even a minimum level of health care to the poor.

While siding with the "tax cheaters' lobby" to allow patriotic millionaires and corporations flee to offshore tax havens (see **Tax evasion**), the administration singled out the working poor who claim the EARNED INCOME TAX CREDIT for an IRS crackdown. And while doling out another $350 billion (on top of $2 trillion) in tax cuts mostly for the rich, Bush saved $3.5 billion by denying 6.5 million minimum-wage families and their 12 million children the $400-per-child increase in the CHILD TAX CREDIT that higher-income taxpayers received. Among a host of anti-**labor** acts, Bush repealed regulations that helped miners dying from BLACK LUNG DISEASE claim benefits from the mining industry, refused to raise the MINIMUM WAGE, and "deregulated" company PENSION PLANS, reducing benefits especially for older workers. He cut veterans' benefits. He cracked down (Ashcroft, in this case) on the use of MEDICAL MARIJUANA to ease the pain of dying patients. He placed crippling restrictions on human embryonic STEM-CELL RESEARCH, which researchers believe could lead to cures for major diseases. His "compassion" for the **environment** is well known.

After the head of the White House Office of Faith-Based Initiatives, John DiIulio, quit in August 2001, he said there was a "virtual absence" in the administration of "any policy accomplishments that might, to a fair-minded nonpartisan, count as flesh on the bones of so-called compassionate conservatism." All there was, he said, was "on-the-fly policy-making by speechmaking."[81]

Inclement W. A president has the power to grant executive clemency for federal offenses—to reduce (by commutation) or eliminate (by pardon) the punishment. As of July 31, 2002, Bush had granted *no* clemency requests since taking office. He had denied 508 pardon petitions and 1,346 commutation requests. In total, President Clinton issued 395 pardons (not *all* of them admirable) and sixty-one commutations. Bush

Sr. granted clemency seventy-seven times. As governor of Texas, inclement W. issued fewer pardons for state offenses than any Texas governor since the 1940s: sixteen up to January 2000, as opposed to seventy for his predecessor Ann Richards, 822 for well-named governor Bill Clements, and 1048 for John Connally. Under Bush, Texas carried out the **death penalty** on 152 people, making him the deadliest governor of any state, ever.

He was a "compassionate" governor in other ways, too. When the national minimum wage was raised to $5.15 an hour, Bush kept Texas' at $3.35. When Congress passed a law to help states provide health insurance for kids, Bush opposed its expansion to 220,000 children in Texas. A federal judge had to step in, ruling that Texas failed to provide adequate health care for children. (Texas under Bush ranked near the bottom among states on almost every measure of social well-being.)

CORPORATE INFLUENCE:
ONE GIANT CONFLICT OF INTEREST

"Put simply, the [Bush] administration is subservient to economic pressure groups to an extent that surpasses any administration in modern history," wrote *The New Republic*'s Jonathan Chait. "It is simply unnecessary for the White House to generate its own policies because that role has been filled by business lobbyists."[82] But even that assessment fell short. As Veterans for Justice put it, "Every presidential cabinet appointment in the Bush administration has been someone with strong corporate connections. What this means is that lobbyists are not necessary in Washington to buy our government anymore. Bush *gave* our country to big business lock, stock, and barrel."[83]

Radicals in business suits:
Corporate agents in the Bush administration.
This very partial list closely resembles the list of multimillionaires that filled most high-ranking administration positions. (Also see **Energy policy: *Industry insiders.***)

John Ashcroft, Attorney General. While never a corporate officer, his service to corporate interests while Missouri attorney general, governor, and U.S. senator—for example, his opposition to a tobacco control bill in the Senate and his softness on antitrust issues—deserves dishonorable mention, as do the hundreds of thousands of dollars his Senate campaign received from the oil and gas, auto, and pharmaceutical industries. Some of the contributions he received were from corporations with important cases pending in the Justice Department.[84]

Francis Blake, Deputy Energy Secretary. Former senior vice president of GENERAL ELECTRIC, whose pollution created more Superfund toxic waste sites (47) than any other U.S. corporation, and which was one of the largest GOP contributors.

George W. Bush. See **Bush's business career; Energy; Enron.**

Andrew Card, White House Chief of Staff. Former head of the AMERICAN AUTOMOBILE MANUFACTURERS ASSOCIATION and chief lobbyist for GENERAL MOTORS. Prime exemplar of the administration's close ties to the auto industry, which in the wild imaginations of environmentalists was linked to the Bushies' opposition to raising vehicle fuel efficiency standards.

Elaine Chao, Secretary of Labor. Sat on the boards of DOLE FOODS and CLOROX.

Dick Cheney, Former CEO of Dallas oil services and construction firm HALLIBURTON INC. See **Cheney and Halliburton; Energy.**

Mitch Daniels, Director, White House Office of Management and Budget. (Resigned May 2003.) Former vice president of pharmaceutical firm ELI LILLY. Listed the value of his Lilly stock at between $5 million and $25 million.

Gordon England, Secretary of the Navy. Former executive vice president of defense contractor GENERAL DYNAMICS. Bush's picks for secretaries of the Army (THOMAS WHITE), Air Force (JAMES ROCHE) and Navy were all top executives of major defense contractors. The military-industrial complex was never so alive and well.

Linda Fischer, Deputy Administrator, Environmental Protection Agency. Former VP of government affairs (i.e., lobbying) at agricultural chemical and biotech company MONSANTO, where she was in charge of lobbying against regulation of genetically engineered crops.

John Graham, Director of OMB's Office of Information and Regulatory Affairs—Bush's chief regulation-killer. Former director of the Harvard Center for Risk Analysis, an anti-regulation think tank funded by DOW CHEMICAL, the CHEMICAL MANUFACTURER'S ASSOCIATION, the CHLORINE CHEMICAL COUNCIL, and other industry groups. See **Deregulation.**

J. Steven Griles, Deputy Interior Secretary. Former energy industry lobbyist; "the poster child of the corporate influence on this administration."[85] See **Energy.**

Norman Mineta, Secretary of Transportation. Former vice president of defense contractor LOCKHEED MARTIN.

William Geary Myers III, Interior Department Solicitor. Former lobbyist for the NATIONAL CATTLEMAN'S BEEF ASSOCIATION and its arm, the PUBLIC LANDS COUNCIL. Myers energetically fought Clinton's "Roadless Policy," designed to protect public lands from road-building and development, and opposed fees for grazing cattle on public land.

Gale Norton, Interior Secretary. Former lobbyist for NL Industries, a lead-paint manufacturer that was a defendant in at least fourteen federal environmental and personal injury lawsuits. Former national chairperson for the industry-backed COALITION OF ENVIRONMENTAL ADVOCATES—a "greenscam" group (right-wing anti-environmentalists, like Bush, who pose as environmentalists) funded by, among others, FORD, BP AMOCO, the AMERICAN FOREST & PAPER ASSOCIATION and the CHEMICAL MANUFACTURER'S ASSOCIATION. Supported abolishing Interior's Bureau of Land Management and "the transfer to private ownership of federally held, so-called public lands." As Colorado attorney general (1990–98), she fought vigorously against enforcement of environmental laws. NRDC called her "an ideological extremist who has worked for more than two decades to systematically dismantle our nation's environmental protections. The direct beneficiaries of her views on enforcement are mining, grazing, timber, oil and other multinational corporations."[86]

Paul O'Neil, Secretary of the Treasury until axed in late 2002. Former chairman of ALCOA, the world's largest aluminum manufacturer. Former president of INTERNATIONAL PAPER. Served on the boards of EASTMAN KODAK and LUCENT TECHNOLOGIES. In May 2001, he called for the elimination of all taxes on corporations, suggesting they be replaced by higher taxes on individuals, and said he hoped to eliminate the public "subsidizing" of Social Security and Medicare.

Richard Perle, Pentagon Defense Policy Board (DPB) member and former chairman. Managing partner of TRIREME PARTNERS and board member of AUTONOMY, firms whose clients included the defense and homeland security departments. Was hired by bankrupt telecom company GLOBAL CROSSING to win Pentagon approval for its sale to a Hong Kong firm with close ties to the Chinese government. Global's fiber optic network was extensively used by the U.S. government. Perle's $725,000 fee was contingent on the deal being approved by the man he advised at the Pentagon, his friend Donald Rumsfeld. Publicity about the deal led to Perle's resignation as Defense Policy Board chair. Of DPB's thirty members, nine were executives or lobbyists for defense contractors with combined DOD contracts of $75 billion.

Colin Powell, Secretary of State. Former board member of AMERICA ONLINE. On joining the administration, his stock portfolio was worth between $18 million and $65 million.

Anthony Principi, Secretary of Veteran's Affairs. Former executive at military contractor LOCKHEED MARTIN.

Condoleezza Rice, National Security Adviser. Former board member of energy giant CHEVRON, financial services firm CHARLES SCHWAB, and insurance company TRANSAMERICA.

James G. Roche, Secretary of the Air Force. Former corporate vice president of defense contractor and aircraft manufacturer NORTHROP GRUMMAN.

Karl Rove, Bush senior political adviser. Lobbyist and consultant for PHILIP MORRIS, 1991–96. Didn't unload his $100,000–250,000 worth of Boeing, General Electric, and Enron stock—which all benefited from Bush policies— until five months after taking office.

Donald Rumsfeld, Secretary of Defense. Former CEO of pharmaceutical company G.D. SEARLE and of GENERAL SIGNAL CORP. Sat on the boards of KELLOGG, biotech company GILEAD SCIENCES, and the TRIBUNE COMPANY, which owned the *Chicago Tribune* and the *Los Angeles Times*. On joining the administration, he had stocks and other investments worth $50–210 million.

Ann Veneman, Secretary of Agriculture. Former lobbyist for DOLE FOODS. Former board member of CALGENE INC., a pioneer in genetically engineered food. Served on the International Policy Council on Agriculture, Food and Trade, a group funded by CARGILL, NESTLE, KRAFT, and ARCHER DANIELS MIDLAND.

Thomas White, Secretary of the Army. Resigned April 2003. Former vice chairman of ENRON ENERGY SERVICES, one of the shadiest of Enron's businesses, which lost upward of $500 million. See **Enron** for details on some of the other fifty-two former Enronians who ended up in the Bush administration.

CORPORATE SCANDALS (AND "REFORM")

In January 2002, the media were treating the collapse of energy giant **Enron** Corp., Bush's biggest corporate backer, as virtually the story of the century. In the months that followed, scandals involving phony accounting, fraudulent stock recommendations, insider trading, tax evasion, and looting of their own companies by CEOs brought down one high-flying company and executive after another. Tens of thousands of employees lost their jobs and retirement savings. Investors lost hundreds of billions. A lineup of other energy companies—El Paso, Williams, Duke, Dynergy, Mirant, Reliant—at least half of them Texas-based and with close ties to Bush—were implicated along with Enron in manipulating power prices in **California**. "Boiler-room" ethics, it was discovered, prevailed at the nation's biggest investment firms. Crime rates were in decline across the country, but were evidently surging in corporate America.

After a decade or two of rampant **deregulation**, the crucial role of government in protecting the public from the excesses and abuses of the market system, and indeed, protecting capitalism from itself, had seemingly been rediscovered. It was unthinkable that before the year's end, Bush & Co. would be (a) trying to block, then to undermine, a major new corporate reform law; (b) cutting funding for the Securities and Exchange Commission (SEC); (c) refusing to sack an SEC chairman who was an accounting industry lobbyist and arch-antiregulator; and (d) blocking the appointment of a tough new commissioner to oversee the accounting industry because the industry wanted a friendlier one.

From the start, the Bushies' posture was to minimize the extent of the rot (it was a few bad apples; "most of the people that run the businesses in America are aboveboard [and] honest," Bush assured us)—and to insist that it was merely a corporate, not a political, scandal. Never mind all the adminstration figures with "Enron" on their résumés. Never mind the millions Enron had contributed to Bush and other pols—and the deregulation it had received—or that the White House had essentially let Enron and its peers write national **energy policy** and pick key regulatory officials. Never mind that fifty-one of fifty-six members of the House Energy and Commerce Committee, which led the Enron investigation, had taken money from Enron or Arthur Andersen, as had forty-nine of the seventy members of the House Financial Services Committee. Never mind how much it all resembled the "crony capitalism" that four years earlier had led to financial collapses across Asia, where business leaders' political connections had given them such a sense of immunity, they felt no need to tell investors the truth about their companies' finances.

In the summer of 2002, while a bill to toughen accounting standards and oversight, written by Paul Sarbanes (D-MD), took shape in the senate, the White House insisted no new laws were needed—only tougher enforcement of existing ones. (Under Bush, tough enforcement of laws protecting public interests was nowhere to be found.) Bush gave a speech outlining his own ten-point plan, in which, as in all Bush "regulation," the emphasis was on self-policing by business. Meanwhile, as Robert Kuttner observed, the fact that **Bush's** own **business career** "epitomized the kind of corruption that Enron and Global Crossing raised to new heights" did not stop Karl Rove from positioning Bush "as the champion of corporate reform."[87]

Chief accounting industry ~~lobbyist~~ regulator. While Enron's management was ruining its investors and employees, the accounting firm that was supposed to be checking the books, Arthur Andersen, was separately being paid $27 million to serve Enron as a consultant. (Andersen, caught shredding Enron documents, became the first of the corporate wrongdoers to be convicted, in June 2002.) In 2001, before Enron unraveled, the Clinton-appointed SEC chairman, Arthur Levitt, proposed a ban on such conflict-of-interest dual relationships. That ban was blocked by furious lobbying led by the accounting industry's leading lawyer/lobbyist, HARVEY PITT, whose clients included Andersen and the other Big Five firms. So who, in the midst of the epidemic of corporate and accounting scandals, did Bush name that August as the new SEC chairman? None other than this arch-SEC and accounting-regulation foe, this walking conflict of interest, Pitt. It was "a little like naming Osama bin Laden to run the Office of Homeland Security," Arianna Huffington remarked.[88]

The Sarbanes-Oxley Act was passed by Congress in July 2002 with overwhelming bipartisan support. Bush had no choice but to sign it. (Enforcing it would be another matter.) The act created a new accounting industry oversight board; hiked the SEC's budget by 77 percent; barred firms from providing accounting and consulting services to the same client; toughened penalties for fraud; and prohibited excessive loans to executives from company funds (such as the one CEO Bernie Ebbers received from WorldCom, or

George W. Bush received from Harken Energy, or the $24.5 million "sweetheart loan" Bush Treasury Secretary John Snow received as CEO of railroad company CSX—whose stock undperformed its peers by two-thirds during his twelve-year tenure).

Refusing to end the stock-options scam. Not addressed by Sarbanes-Oxley was business's favorite loophole—indeed, the black hole at the center of the corporate scandals: Salaries and bonuses paid in stock options, unlike regular salaries, did not have to be declared as business expenses. This had allowed, for example, Cisco Systems, a poster child for the 1990s "new economy," to consistently show giant profits instead of giant losses, wich kept the stock price inflated as a "currency" with which to pay more salaries and buy up other companies. Cisco was likened to a pyramid scheme—and ended much the same way: From 2000—when CEO John Chambers was paid $157 million—to 2002, the stock lost 84 percent of its value, or $400 billion—five times more than Enron investors lost. Yet Chambers was invited as a star speaker to Bush's farcical "economic forum" in Waco, Texas, in August 2002. "They really don't get it, do they?" The *New York Times*'s Paul Krugman remarked. The Bushies and their congressional allies consistently opposed changing the rules to require "expensing" of options. During Senate debate on Sarbanes-Oxley, no debate on the issue was permitted. Sen. John McCain (R-AZ) blamed business lobbyists: "The fix is in."[89]

Undermining Sarbanes-Oxley. As soon as the reform bill was passed, the administration began issuing "guidance" to prosecutors that undermined enforcement of key provisions, and letting the SEC interpret others to death (much as they did, for example, with **Campaign finance reform**). Among the first to go was the crucial ban on "dual relationships"; the SEC adopted language permitting the big accounting firms to continue providing audit clients with some of their most lucrative "non-audit" services, such as tax consulting. As Andersen/Enron had shown, providing these services easily tempted an auditor to "see things management's way"; the SEC had delivered "a huge concession to the Big 4 accounting firms."[90]

Slight oversight. Among the next things to go was Pitt, who was finally forced to resign after he backed former FBI and CIA head WILLIAM WEBSTER to head the new oversight board, but failed to disclose to his colleagues or the White House that Webster chaired the auditing board of a company whose own accounting practices were under investigation. (A previous candidate for the post, JOHN BIGGS, had been nixed because the White House didn't like his labor union backing and the accounting industry regarded him as too independent.)

To replace Pitt, Bush named WILLIAM DONALDSON, a former investment banker, New York Stock Exchange (NYSE) chairman, and Nixon official whose track record *Fortune* magazine described as "unimpressive" ("Is Donaldson the Best We Can Do at the SEC?" the headline asked)—but who, on the other hand, was Bush's fellow Yale *and* Skull and Bones society alum, and who had repeatedly fought with the SEC to permit *less* corporate financial disclosure.[91]

Underfunding the SEC. Meanwhile, though there was clearly enough corporate malfeasance around to keep ten SECs busy, Bush refused to give the commission the $776 million budget for 2003 provided for under Sarbanes-Oxley, insisting on no more than $568 million. Bush was "not fully committed to corporate reform," Sen. Jon Corzine (D-NJ) noticed; efforts to beef up SEC enforcement, he said, were being undermined by the White House "with a wink and a nod." The SEC, with 2,900 employees and a budget that is "puny by federal standards," had to police 17,000 corporations, 34,000 investment company portfolios, 8,000 brokerage firms and 7,500 financial advisers.[92]

Refusing to close the Bermuda Loophole: See **Tax evasion.**

DEATH PENALTY:
"THAT HANGMAN'S GRIN . . . "

It was another one of those headlines that told you it wasn't just a bad dream—George W. Bush *was* president: "Ashcroft Orders Prosecutors to Seek Death in More Cases" (*The New York Times*, February 6, 2003).

This came just a month after the convictions of five teenagers who had served from six to eleven and a half years in prison for the 1989 Central Park jogger attack in New York were overturned because DNA evidence proved someone else had committed the rape, and came a few weeks after departing Illinois Governor George Ryan commuted all 167 of the state's death sentences because, since 1976, twenty-five prisoners on Illinois's death row had been found to be innocent; thirteen of them were released—twelve had already been executed. In ten Illinois death-row cases, convictions had been based on confessions obtained by the police through torture.

In 2003, the U.S. remained among only a handful of countries that still executed people. We were in the company of such bastions of democracy and human rights as China and Saudi Arabia. More than 3,500 people—the highest number ever—were on death row in the U.S., more than 75 percent of them nonwhite. A death sentence was far more likely when the victim was white than black. More than 75 percent of all executions since 1976 took place in Southern states.

Chief executive officer. As governor of Texas, Bush signed death warrants for 152 executions—an average of one every two weeks—making him (in just one and a half terms) the deadliest governor in U.S. history, and making Texas a more prolific executioner by far not just than any other state but than any *country* in the Western world outside the U.S. From 1982 until Bush became governor in 1995, Texas had carried out eighteen executions. Bush achieved 152 in just six years.

"I do not believe we've put a guilty—I mean, innocent— person to death in the state of Texas." So said then-governor Bush. Well, nationwide, from 1976 to 2002, more than eighty-two people who were sentenced to death, or one in seven of those on death row, were released from prison after being fully exonerated. From 1900 to 1992, there were 416 documented cases of innocent people convicted and sentenced to death; twenty-three of these were executed.[93] There is every reason to believe Texas's record—especially under Bush—is much worse.

Governor Bush the Compassionate vetoed legislation to provide funding for legal defense for the poor.[94] He called the bill, which had bipartisan support, "a threat to public safety." Bush opposed legislation instituting life without parole and banning the execution of people with IQs below sixty-five. The governor also steadfastly opposed legislation to reform Texas' shocking clemency procedures. From 1982 through 1999, the state executed 170 people. The Texas Board of Pardons and Paroles recommended commuting the death sentence only once. Its eight members received more than seventy clemency petitions but did not consider even one worthy of a hearing. A judge called this "incredible" and "very troubling."

In fact, Bush apparently found clemency requests amusing. In a 1999 *Talk* magazine interview, the governor was asked about a woman recently executed in Texas to whom he had refused clemency. In response, Bush mockingly impersonated a woman begging for her life—distorting his face and whimpering, "Please, don't kill me!" Bush's good humor about executions was evident again during an October 11, 2000, debate with Gore, where he explained why Texas didn't need tougher anti-hate-crime laws by smiling and boasting that the three white killers of a black man in Texas were going to be executed. Columnist Lars Erik Nelson wrote that he supported the death penalty, "but that hangman's grin gives me the willies."[95]

Forcing the death penalty on Puerto Rico. In July 2003, **Ashcroft**'s Justice Department sought the death penalty in the trial of two men accused of kidnapping and murder in Puerto Rico, which had outlawed the death penalty in 1929. "This island, it is safe to say, hates capital punishment," *The New York Times* reported. Puerto Ricans in all walks of life "have denounced the trial [as] a betrayal of the island's autonomy, culture and law, in particular its Constitution."[96]

DEFENSE SPENDING

While freezing, slashing, or nickel-and-diming just about all domestic spending that might benefit ordinary Americans, Bush pushed through defense budgets that, for profligacy and waste, made the days of those famous $1,000 toilet seats look like an era of Puritan frugality. Journalist Robert Scheer called Bush's military buildup "the most preposterous in human history."[97]

Bush's 2003 budget called for $396 billion in military spending, representing a one-year increase of $48 billion—more than the increase Bush had promised over *nine* years during his election campaign; more than the *total* increase he promised for health, education, *and* defense; and more than any other nation's *entire* military budget. The $396 billion was more than the twenty-five next-largest military budgets in the world combined; more than six times Russia's, the world's second largest; and more than three times the combined spending of Russia, China, and the seven "rogue" states then identified by the Pentagon as our most likely adversaries (Cuba, Iran, Iraq, Libya, North Korea, Sudan, and Syria).

The Bushies' rationale for this buildup was, of course, the **war on terrorism**. Strange, then, that while we were fighting what Bush repeatedly called "a new kind of war"—against underground, urban terrorist cells and Afghan tribesmen holed up in caves—Bush & Co. were lavishing billions on weapons conceived for a land war against the Soviets on the plains of Europe; billions more on weapons that had been in development since the first Bush administration and had since proven deadly (killing U.S. personnel) failures; and new weapons systems that would do nothing that existing ones didn't already do far more cheaply. "These proposals are a refutation of [Bush's] own campaign pledges, the promise to transform the Pentagon into the 21st century," wrote Al Hunt.[98]

As Robert Scheer noted, "There is not an item in the Bush budget that will make us more secure from the next terrorist attack." So what *was* in it?

The ill-conceived (and ill-named) Crusader. One of the more notorious items was a forty-two-ton self-propelled howitzer that could not be carried by the military's biggest cargo planes. Before being canceled in late 2002, the Crusader—which was manufactured by the Bush-connected CARLYLE GROUP—got $475 million for the 2003 fiscal year on top of billions already spent. One year's funding, Al Hunt noted, could have restored the Bush cuts to the Low-Income Home Energy Assistance Program or provided Head Start for another 65,330 kids.

Three fighter programs for the price of . . . three. A National Defense Panel report on which candidate Bush based some of his main defense positions questioned the desirability of funding three separate new jet-fighter programs—but that is what Bush went on to do. For 2003 he threw $12 billion at the new Joint Strike Fighter, the F/A-18E/F, *and* the F-22 Raptor. The F-22 was already $9 billion over budget, making it the costliest fighter aircraft ever built; and, according to many experts, it did nothing the Joint Strike Fighter didn't do, nor was it a great improvement on the existing F-15 and F-16. Restricting production of the F-22 in favor of the other planes would have saved $10 billion over the next decade.

Osprey—or turkey? In March 2000, the Congressional Budget Office (CBO) recommended ending the V-22 Osprey tilt-rotor aircraft program, which, wrote Jason Vest in *The American Prospect*, "has killed more Marines than the Taliban"[99]—thirty, to be exact, in four crashes of prototypes—and which even Cheney, as defense secretary under Bush I, tried to quash. This, the CBO estimated, would save $6.6 billion. Bush proposed *adding* $2 billion to the program.

Chop this chopper. Initiated in 1983, the Army's hopeless Comanche helicopter program had yet to fly $48 billion later. The CBO recommended cutting the losses and saving $6.3 billion by buying new choppers that *work*. Bush wanted to pour another $900 million down this drain—maybe that would unclog it. A senior Pentagon analyst quoted by Vest wondered if "this money can be followed and frozen by law enforcement as part of the war on terrorism, as the program is clearly as much of a threat to the U.S. military as any marauding armed force in the world."

Misguided missile defense. Bush budgeted $8–9 billion a year to ramp up this quixotic program, which had an estimated cost of at least $230 billion. (See **Missile defense**.)

"Mr. Bush insists that the assumption that more government spending gets more results is not generally true," Hunt observed. "That is, unless it's the defense budget." Vest called it "curious" that Bush, who professed outrage at **Enron** and Arthur Andersen, shoveled these billions into the Pentagon, whose accounting practices "make Enron and Andersen look like sticklers for detail." In recent years, he noted, the General

Accounting Office (GAO) and the Defense Department's inspector general found trillions of dollars the Pentagon couldn't account for. "The books are in such disarray that the Defense Department can't even be effectively audited."

The Bushies' solution? *Less* oversight of and accountability by the Pentagon:

The "Defense Transformation for the 21st Century Act." That legislation, proposed in early 2003 by Secretary of Defense Rumsfeld, would have been better named the Colossal Pentagon Waste Protection Act. It would:

- Allow the Department of Defense (DOD) to award major contracts without Congressional review or public accountability.
- Exempt the DOD from numerous Congressional oversight rules, such as the need to notify Congress of significant cost increases in weapons programs, or when it leases major equipment. At the time, the Pentagon was arranging a notorious sweetheart deal with BOEING whereby the Air Force would lease 100 FUEL-TANKER AIRCRAFT at a cost to taxpayers of billions more than buying the planes outright. (In a May 2002 report, the GAO concluded that with relatively cheap upgrades, the Air Force's current fleet of 545 tankers could serve for another forty years.)[100]
- Reduce Congressional oversight of the missile defense program, granting the DOD's Missile Defense Agency spending authority "reaching far beyond that of any other federal agency."[101]
- Strip DOD employees of union rights, annual pay

raises, whistle-blower protections and the right to appeal disciplinary actions.

- Exempt the DOD from environmental protection rules on 23 million acres of public land.[102]

(See **Budget; Foreign policy; Nuclear weapons.**)

DEREGULATION: *"SOMETHING ROTTEN IN WASHINGTON"*

Under the "pro-business" fanaticism of the Bush administration, the twenty-year process of deregulation reached new heights of absurdity and new depths of betrayal of the public interest.

The Bushies insisted we must replace outdated, "heavy handed," centralized, "command-and-control" regulation with modern, streamlined, more efficient, and economical "self-regulation" by industry. We were asked to believe that if we just removed regulations that industry fought tooth and nail against, industry would comply voluntarily. As governor of Texas, Bush introduced "self-regulation" of air pollution emissions by the power industry (even for plants near schools). By the end of his governorship, not one company had complied, Houston had passed L.A. as America's smog capital, and "self-regulation" in Texas was scrapped. But the concept remained alive and well: It simply followed Bush to Washington and became the basis of all his regulatory policy.

In just their first year and a half, the Bushies abandoned a campaign promise to regulate carbon dioxide emissions by power plants, repealed a rule requiring plants to upgrade their antipollution equipment, raised the permitted level of arsenic in drinking water, repealed workplace safety rules, attacked regulations protecting 60 million acres of national forest from logging and road building, killed measures to raise automobile fuel efficiency standards, and rolled back dozens of other health, safety, and environmental regulations.

Enron's implications were simply denied. It "doesn't seem to be tied too much to deregulated energy markets," said Pat Wood, head of the Federal Energy Regulatory Commission (appointed by Bush but anointed by Enron CEO Kenneth Lay). As Arianna Huffington remarked, "You know that something is rotten in Washington when the top energy industry regulator is so unabashedly anti-regulation."[103]

The same month that Enron declared bankruptcy, December 2001, the Bushies *lowered* standards of corporate behavior by repealing a Clinton-era rule that barred the federal government from awarding contracts to businesses that had broken environmental, civil rights, labor, tax, or other laws. With the repeal, the government *could no longer consider* corporations' lawbreaking records when granting contracts. Hundreds of corporations remained eligible for federal contracts despite having been convicted of or sued for defrauding the government. But, as columnist Molly Ivins noted, "Lawbreakers have to make a living, too, so why not reward them with millions of taxpayer dollars?"[104]

Pity the "sovereign consumer." As Robert Kuttner wrote, the "conceit" that capitalism functions best if simply left alone "came back into intellectual fashion around the time that the last economists who personally remembered 1929 died or retired."[105] But to the true believers, regulation was best left to consumers looking out for their own well-being and exercising consumer choice. Were "consumers," then, to determine the safety of medicines by trial and error? Soon enough, perhaps; in its first year under Bush, the Food and Drug Administration's enforcement actions against false and misleading drug advertising fell by 70 percent. A Department of Health and Human Services report on nursing homes in February 2002 showed that more than 90 percent were chronically understaffed and patient care suffered as a result. Bush's response? Consumers should try to be better informed.

The "purity" canard. Deregulators also long argued that government regulation only created opportunities for corruption and influence-peddling. But as Kuttner pointed out, the age of deregulation had been "an age of intensified corporate lobbying and heightened conflicts of interest, not market purity." Enron, he noted, did not favor deregulation "that would help sovereign consumers to shop around for the best deal. It favored rigging the rules so it could make a killing—and spent a fortune politically to get the rules it wanted." As for the supposed economic benefits of deregulation, average economic growth in the last quarter-century lagged behind that of the previous one, when capitalism was more regulated.

The "science-based" ploy. While slashing staff at the Environmental Protection Agency (EPA), the White House was hiring scientists at its regulatory review office, the Office of Information and Regulatory Affairs, whose mission it became to promote "science-based regulation"—**BushSpeak** for using "scientific" arguments to eliminate health, safety, and environmental regulations that business wanted to be rid of. Heading this enterprise was Bush's (de)regulatory czar JOHN D. GRAHAM, former head of the Harvard Center for Risk Analysis, where he led industry-funded studies that tended to conclude the costs of regulations outweighed the benefits. His center solicited tobacco industry money while disparaging the risks of secondhand smoke, and published a study, funded by AT&T Wireless, downplaying the danger of using cell phones while driving.[106]

In a report to Congress in March 2002, Graham boasted that his office had already rejected twenty significant rules on grounds of "inadequate analysis." Industry was overjoyed. (*The Washington Post* broke the news: Industry "believes the administration is sympathetic to its plaints."[107]) Graham was "creating a wholesale shift away from environmental protection," a law professor told the *Post*.

The "senior death discount." The heart (-lessness) of Graham's report was the introduction of two creative new methods of cost-benefit analysis. The really interesting one was to stop analyzing benefits on the basis of lives saved and instead use "life-years"—the number of *years* of life saved, taking into account people's ages. Based on surveys showing that younger people were willing to pay more than older people for life-saving measures such as car air bags, Graham's office calculated that the life of a person under seventy was worth $3.7 million, while one over seventy was worth $2.3 million—$1.4 million less. (A previous method used by the feds reckoned the value of a life at $6.1 million.) Graham's brave new method was, at his own insistence, immediately pressed into service by the EPA to lower the supposed benefits of clean air regulations. News of what was dubbed the "senior death discount" triggered protests, and in May 2003, EPA administrator Christie Whitman disavowed it, saying that henceforth, all lives were equal again.

In September 2003, in its annual review of the costs and benefits of regulations, the White House Office of Management and Budget reported that the benefits of 107 major environmental regulations enacted over the previous decade outweighed the costs by three to eight times. Given the well-known fact that the Bush administration could not do the right thing except by accident of for some nefarious political purpose, it must be assumed that this surprising admission was intended to blur the Bushies' anti-environmentalist image as part of their fake-to-the-center reelection strategy, or else that they figured they'd been caught cooking the books too many times to risk it again.

(See **Environment; Health and safety; Science policy.**)

DRUGS, "WAR ON"

While even many Republicans and right-wing libertarians were softening on the use of mandatory minimum sentences for low-level drug crimes, Bush's two top drug enforcement officials—his appointed drug czar, John Walters (who held the same job under Bush Sr., and who likened medical marijuana to "medicinal crack") and AG John Ashcroft—clung to a policy of harsh punishments and a view of the drug problem as an issue of individual moral responsibility, or rather, failure. As Diana Gordon wrote in *The Nation*, "These must be the last two guys in America who don't believe in treatment [for drug users]."[108]

In the immediate aftermath of 9/11, Ashcroft found time to order the Drug Enforcement Agency (DEA) to take action against doctors in California and Oregon who, under state laws, prescribed marijuana to dying patients.

The week of the first anniversary of 9/11—with the country eagerly awaiting some good news about the war on terrorism—the Feds struck again: In an early-morning raid, the DEA stormed a dangerous medical-marijuana hospice in Santa Cruz, California that catered to terminally ill patients and that was praised by local law enforcement officials for its good works. The agents burst in with guns drawn, cut down the pot garden, and took ailing patients, including a paraplegic, away in handcuffs. "Compassionate conservatism" in action.

ECONOMY: *THE BUSH RECESSION*

According to the Census Bureau's annual report on income and poverty—but contrary to Republican claims—the recession of 2001–2003 began in March 2001, and not under Clinton. Some of its effects:

- **Job losses.** In Bush's first twenty-seven months, the economy lost 3 million jobs, after having *created* 1.7 million in 2000 alone. It was the longest sustained period without job growth since the 1930s, and Bush

was, to date, the first president since Hoover to give
the country a net job loss. Unemployment went from
4.5 to 6.1 percent. More than 8.6 million Americans
were out of work at the end of 2002—a twenty-year
high. (The real figures were far higher; the official figures did not include those who had given up looking
for work.) The slump "dwarfs the jobless recovery following the '90–'91 recession," an economist told *The
New York Times*.[109] The administration touted an
August 2003 report by the National Bureau of Economic Research that declared the recession had ended
in November 2001. The economy had since lost
another million jobs.

- **Growing poverty.** After decreasing for eight straight
years, the number of Americans officially living in poverty
rose in 2001 and 2002 by 3 million, to 34.6 million, *or 12.3
percent of the population*. The number of "severely
poor"—those whose incomes are less than half of the official poverty level—rose from 12.6 million to 13.4 million.
(The official poverty levels were defined as income less
than $18,104 for a family of four, $9,039 for an individual.)
From 1993 to 2000, the poverty rate had fallen from 15.1
percent to 11.3 percent, and the number of officially poor
people had dropped by 7.7 million.

- **Middle-class decline.** The income of middle-class
households fell in 2001 for the first time since the previous recession ended in 1991. Median household
income fell to $42,228, a 2.2 percent decline from the
prior year. All regions except the Northeast experienced a decline in income. Figures for 2002 were
expected to show another decline. This was also the

group that would assume an increasing share of the federal tax burden under Bush's tax cuts.

- **Increasing inequality.** The gap between rich and poor grew, continuing a fifteen-year trend. The wealthiest fifth of the population now received half of all household income; the poorest fifth received 3.5 percent.

- **Health insurance crisis.** The number of Americans without **health insurance** increased by 1.4 million to more than 40 million in 2001, after declining by 600,000 from 1999 to 2000. Health insurance costs rose by 12.7 percent in 2002, the largest one-year increase since 1990.

- **The grizzly bear.** In Bush's first year and a half, the stock market (S&P 500) fell by 37 percent, almost twice the percentage decline under Hoover.

- **Bankruptcies.** There were 1.6 million new personal bankruptcy filings—a new record—in the twelve months between March 2002 and March 2003.

EDUCATION

"There's something surreal about the fact that the United States of America, the richest, most powerful nation in history, can't provide a basic public education for all its children ... Strike the word 'can't.' The correct word is 'won't.'"
—Bob Herbert, *The New York Times*, March 6, 2003

Candidate Bush said education would be one of his two top priorities as president; the other was tax cuts. It soon became apparent which was the higher priority. On education, Bush failed to put money where his mouth was. It is unlikely he ever intended to: The Bush/Republican ideology of "public bad, private good" pointed not toward *saving* public schools but replacing them with private and religious schools. Under the counterfeit promise of NO CHILD LEFT BEHIND, the title of Bush's education initiative and the act passed by Congress in January 2002, Bush's education policy consisted of requiring schools to increase students' test scores without giving them sufficient funding to do so, then cutting off federal funding if they failed. The policy also encouraged students to transfer to private (and religious) schools, using vouchers paid for with taxpayer dollars.

School funding under siege. By 2002–03, amid their worst fiscal crisis in decades, states across the country were cutting millions, even billions, from public school budgets, forcing districts to lay off teachers, increase class sizes, shorten the school week and year, and eliminate teacher training, remedial classes, after-school programs, and more. In Oregon, parents took to selling their blood to help pay for teachers' salaries. Nationally, elementary and middle-school teachers spent an average of $521 of their own money on classroom supplies in 2001, and some spent thousands.[110]

Moreover, schools' budgets were being slashed just as they faced the increased student achievement standards imposed, under the banner of "accountability," by Bush's No Child Left Behind (NCLB) initiative. NCLB was supposed to increase federal education funding by more than 40 percent; but even if that promise had been kept, it would not have been enough to offset the cuts at the state level because federal funding accounted for only around 8 percent of K–12 education spending nationally. As New Jersey Education Association president Edithe Fulton noted, "The Bush administration—which would deregulate everything from business to health care to toxic emissions—has imposed the most onerous federal regulations imaginable on the public schools," despite contributing only 8 percent of their funding.[111]

"Set up for failure." The new law required every state to make "adequate yearly progress" (AYP), measured solely by improvements in mandatory tests for all students in grades three through eight.[112] Any school receiving federal funding for disadvantaged students that failed to make "AYP" for two consecutive years would be labeled "failing" and lose those funds, and their students could transfer out immediately. In its first year, the law had already labeled 8,000 schools in poor areas as "failing." The law required that every class have a "highly qualified teacher" by 2005, and that all students test as proficient in reading by 2012. These goals required the very kinds of programs that states had created in the 1990s to help raise school standards, and that were now falling victim to states' budget crunches and federal cutbacks.

In February 2003—just as Bush was proposing $700 billion in new tax cuts—his 2004 budget proposal reduced spending for NCLB programs and entirely eliminated some, including rural education, dropout prevention, gifted and talented education, and after-school programs for 500,000 children. It cut $50 million from the Even Start Family Literacy Project, which Bush previously lauded. Overall, Bush's budget contained $6 billion less for NCLB than the $18.5 billion called for by the act. "As soon as the Klieg lights were off and the bunting came down, the Bush administration turned its back on school reform and America's children," said Sen. Ted Kennedy (D-MA), who had worked closely with Bush to help pass NCLB based on assurances of adequate funding.[113]

Vouchers and charter schools. It was hard not to conclude, as did Edithe Fulton, that public schools were "being set up" to fail, and that "'No Child Left Behind' is the ultimate Trojan Horse, labeling schools as failures in order to pave the way for vouchers."[114]

Vouchers for tuition at private and religious schools—the right's ticket to undermining public education—were included in Bush's first draft of NCLB but were so controversial that Congress removed them. The administration, however, found $75 million for voucher "demonstration projects." After they recaptured the Senate in November 2002, Republicans said they would try to expand the program.

In June 2002, the U.S. Supreme Court ruled 5–4 that a Cleveland, Ohio, voucher program was constitutional—a ruling the right hailed as the first step toward dismantling public education in America. In a speech, Bush shamelessly compared it to *Brown v. Board of Education*, the Court's landmark 1954 desegregation ruling.

The Cleveland program *was* instructive as a model. It provided vouchers worth a maximum of $2,250 to children from the poorest families to, in theory, transfer from public to private schools or to better public schools in the suburbs. "Things, however, did not work out that way," Brent Staples reported in *The New York Times*. Suburban schools were not interested in Cleveland's students, whose vouchers covered less than a third of the cost of educating them. Nonreligious schools had few vacancies and were swamped with more affluent applicants. More than 96 percent of the voucher students ended up in religious schools—a result that the program was *structured* to produce, as dissenting Supreme Court Justice David Souter noted.

Bush also backed CHARTER SCHOOLS—experimental, privately owned, publicly funded schools that operated with minimal regulation. Some, like Edison Schools, were large, for-profit chains. The "experimental" aspect of some charter schools seemed to consist of finding new ways to misuse public funds and to fail to educate. Investigators in Texas, for example, found that funds intended for charters were being used to buy Victoria's Secret lingerie. (Sex education class?) One school proved to have twenty felons on its staff. "Barely half of charter students passed basic Texas performance tests, compared with an 82 percent pass rate for the rest of the state's public school students. . . . The dropout rate among students at Texas charters is more than three times the rate for other public school children."[115] Bush's 2003 budget gave charter schools $200 million.

Turning Head Start into "Slow Start or No Start." The Bushies obviously couldn't leave a Great Society program that had been working well for nearly four decades unmolested. In July 2003, Bush announced a plan to let Head Start, which provided medical care and meals to a million poor preschool children, be taken over by state governments and given an "academic focus." Critics feared that states already staggering under deficits would divert federal Head Start funds to other uses, and that an "academic focus"—for three- and four-year-olds in need of health care and decent food!— would diminish the program's nurturing role. "We think [the Bush plan] would absolutely destroy Head Start," Sarah Greene, president of the National Head Start Association, told *The New York Times*.[116]

Cutting college tuition aid. In May 2003, without congressional approval or public comment of any kind, the Department of Education altered the formula governing financial aid to college students to cut the federal government's contribution by hundreds of millions of dollars. As a result, it was estimated, students would pay anywhere from $100 to over $1,000 extra in tuition, and many fewer students would qualify for federal financial aid. The altered formula also governed—and would therefore shrink—state and private tuition aid. Another example of how ordinary Americans benefited from Bush's tax cuts . . .

ELECTION 2000, THEFT OF

"The fundamental maxim of republican government requires that the sense of the majority should prevail."
—Alexander Hamilton

The prophesied Y2K apocalypse never materialized, but 2000 did bring a catastrophe—not on January 1, but on November 7.

Some Americans may remember—despite all the

Bushies' and the media's enjoinders to forget—that Gore got 500,000 more votes than Bush. But few ever even heard that while Gore lost the recount battle, based on Florida's statutory standard of "clear voter intent," he won Florida, and therefore the election, according to a meticulous study of all 175,000 disputed Florida ballots sponsored by a consortium of newspapers and media organizations, conducted by the National Opinion Research Center (NORC) of the University of Chicago, and published in November 2001.

The NORC Florida Ballots Project did find that the hand recount in four counties, which Gore sought and was denied by the U.S. Supreme Court in *Bush v. Gore*, would still have given Bush a victory, by a hair. And that was the way the media—against the backdrop of the war on terrorism, Bush's sky-high approval ratings, and low public interest in such ancient history[117]—played the story: Bush did win after all. But what if there had been a statewide recount, *as Florida law required* and Gore said he would welcome—and the Supreme Court endorsed in principle (i.e., *if* the state could devise an acceptable method and complete it in the two hours remaining before the deadline to submit voting results)? The NORC study showed that, overall:

- Tens of thousands more Florida voters went to the polls intending to vote for Gore than Bush.
- Thousands of Gore voters were prevented from voting by numerous problems ranging from the infamous and technically illegal ballot designs in Palm Beach and Duval Counties to the purge of thousands of legally registered African-American Democratic voters at the behest of Republican state election officials.

- Despite all that, Gore still received the majority of legal ballots in Florida; and had a recount of all disputed state ballots been conducted in the strict manner that Bush wanted—indeed by *all* recount standards—Gore would have been declared the winner in Florida by 105 votes. As the *Washington Post* reported—on page 10— statewide, "Full Review Favors Gore."

THE THEFT OF ELECTION 2000 began well before election day. The real blame, and shame, lies in the legal, or not so legal, shenanigans of Bush campaign officials and—what were often the same people—Republican state officials, most notably Secretary of State KATHERINE HARRIS, who also happened to serve as Bush's Florida campaign co-chair (while, just as notably, Florida's governor, Jeb Bush, also happened to serve as W.'s brother).

Among other services to Bush, Harris sent local election officials a list of more than 57,000 mostly black Florida citizens to be removed from the voter rolls because they were "possible" convicted felons—prohibited from voting by a Confederate-era Florida law—even though most of the convictions were for nonviolent drug offenses. The names came from a list compiled by a private, Republican-connected firm her office hired. Thousands of people on it were completely innocent but had the same names as convicted felons, or somewhat similar names. Some differed from the supposed felons in race, gender, age, address, and social security number. Around 8,000 of those on the list had (like George W. Bush following his 1976 DUI arrest) only been convicted of misdemeanors. In an election officially decided by 537 votes, this purge may have made all the difference. But so might any of these other apparent efforts to disenfranchise likely Gore voters:

- Local election supervisors said Harris had ignored their pleas for help in providing voter education—which might have prevented fiascos such as the more than 20,000 would-be Gore voters in Palm Beach County who accidentally voted for Pat Buchanan because of confusing and probably illegal ballot forms.
- In Republican-controlled Duval County, 26,000 ballots were disqualified, an estimated 60 percent of them cast by blacks; this was four times the number of votes disqualified there in 1996. At least 9,000 were disqualified because, due to confusing ballot design, a vote for Gore was marked *twice.*
- Minority voters were reportedly harassed by police and poll workers. Some were prevented from reaching the polling place by mysterious new roadblocks. And large numbers of black voters found themselves standing in line and unable to vote when polls closed prematurely.

Other improprieties:

- While thousands of technically invalid Gore ballots were disqualified, a *New York Times* investigation found that Florida election officials, under intense GOP pressure, counted 680 absentee ballots, largely military, that failed to comply with state election laws. The number exceeded Bush's 537-vote margin of victory.
- Most critically, while carrying out the Florida felon law and purging voters a tad *over*zealously, Harris

failed to do what another law required of her as Secretary of State—to order a full, automatic recount of every ballot in every county because the margin separating the candidates was less than one-half of 1 percent. Around 1.58 million votes in eighteen counties were never recounted as the law prescribed—"an extraordinary violation that Ms. Harris and her aides knew but never mentioned, let alone remedied," Joe Conason reported. "Sworn to uphold the law and conduct a fair election despite her allegiance to Mr. Bush and his brother Jeb . . . Ms. Harris did the opposite."[118]

John W. Dean, former counsel to President Nixon, concluded, "In truth, [Gore] won the Florida vote but lost the recount." Jeb's "presence was felt everywhere during the recount, assuring his brother's team a win."[119]

DeLay and Lott's thugs. Credit also goes to Rep. Tom DeLay (R-TX) and Sen. Trent Lott (R-MS), who rounded up goon squads of Republican Congressional staffers and flew them from Washington to Florida—many on company planes provided by **Enron** and Halliburton (see **Cheney**). They besieged the building where Miami-Dade County supervisors were conducting their recount and staged what was widely described as a riot, physically attacking and intimidating election officials until they stopped the recount. All DeLay and Lott's thugs were missing were the brown shirts. No wonder many observers concluded that Bush won because winning was all he and his team cared about.

The old College jeer. To historian Arthur Schlesinger Jr., the Florida results mattered less than the issue of the popular vote versus the electoral college, an undemocratic relic whose survival he deplored. "The true significance of the disputed 2000 election has thus far escaped public attention," he wrote. "A reasonable deduction from [Alexander] Hamilton's premise [quoted at the top of this section] is that the presidential candidate who wins the most votes in an election should also win the election." But the "astounding fact" that the 2000 election gave the presidency to the popular-vote *loser* was ignored by the National Commission on Federal Election Reform, the body appointed in the wake of the 2000 election; and this same astounding fact was then obscured "by the political astuteness of the court-appointed president in behaving as if he had won the White House by a landslide; and now by the effect of September 11 in presidentializing George W. Bush and giving him commanding popularity in the polls."[120] Schlesinger might have added the role of the media, which immediately dropped the story once the election was awarded to Bush, as though all questions were settled.

ENERGY POLICY

It would hardly be an exaggeration to describe Bush's election as a hostile takeover of the White House by the energy industry. To be more precise, a buyout. Energy companies were Bush's biggest contributors from the start, giving around $1.5 million to his 1994 and '98 Texas gubernatorial campaigns. In 2000, oil and gas companies and their executives gave nearly $2 million to the Bush campaign (and another $1 million to the Bush inaugural committee)—more than to any previous presidential candidate; indeed, more than any federal candidate got from the industry *in total* over the previous decade. Bush's single biggest contributor from 1994 through 2000 was **Enron.** Overall, the oil and gas industry gave more than $32 million in political contributions for the 2000 election—funding Republicans over Democrats by a 9–1 margin.

These investments yielded fabulous returns. Every Bush policy and action affecting the energy industry confirmed that this administration did not merely happen to be packed with people—from Bush and Cheney on down—who came *from* the industry; the administration *was* all but an energy lobbying group—the industry's Washington headquarters. It was aptly dubbed an "oil-igarchy."

Bush's first big favor to the energy lobby came in March 2001, when, caving to the coal mining and power utility industries, and against the urging of his own Environmental Protection Agency (EPA) administrator, he reneged on his campaign promise to require reductions in power plants' carbon dioxide (CO_2) emissions, the principal human cause of **global warming.** (Half of all U.S. electricity came from coal-fired power plants.) The same month, he took the U.S. out of the Kyoto accord, which called for modest U.S. reductions in CO_2 and other "greenhouse gas" emissions.

Cheney's energy task force. Cheney, the former CEO of Halliburton, one of the world's largest oil-service firms, took charge of energy policy, appointing and heading the National Energy Policy Development Group. Cheney's "energy task force" met behind closed doors (contrary to federal law, according to some Congress members) in early 2001 to vet the nominees for political posts within the

Energy Department and plot the course of U.S. energy policy. Of the task force's sixty-three members, fifty came from the energy industry: twenty-seven from oil and gas, seventeen from nuclear power and uranium mining, sixteen from electric power, and seven from coal. Only one was from the renewable-energy sector. Energy industry representatives said this reflected "a more balanced position" than that of the previous administration. While meeting in person with energy lobbyists again and again, Bush officials only gave environmental groups three days to provide input in writing.

The White House refused to release any records of task force meetings or names of those with whom Cheney and other Bush officials met—defying repeated requests from members of Congress (see **Secrecy**). The nonpartisan General Accounting Office, the investigative arm of Congress, finally sued Cheney to release the names. The lawsuit was dismissed in December 2002 by U.S. District Judge John Bates, a recent Bush appointee.

As a result of related lawsuits brought by public-interest groups, the Energy Department released 11,000 records in March 2002; however, according to the plaintiffs, the administration withheld more than 25,000 documents, and of those that were released, large portions had been deleted.

But they were damning enough. Documents showed that, from January to May 2001, ENERGY SECRETARY SPENCER ABRAHAM met with more than 100 energy industry representatives, many of whom were among the most generous Bush and GOP contributors. Eighteen of the companies and trade groups represented had given a total of more than $16 million to the GOP since 1999—three times what they gave Democrats. They included Enron, ChevronTexaco, Exxon-

Mobil, British Petroleum (BP), the Edison Electric Institute, the Nuclear Energy Institute, and the Independent Petroleum Association of America.

And they received quick and courteous service. A week after Abraham met secretly with the American Gas Association (AGA), Bush issued executive orders—bypassing Congress—that were almost identical to written recommendations from the AGA and the American Petroleum Institute to ease regulations and speed up federal approvals of oil and gas drilling on public lands.[121] Both groups were major Bush and GOP contributors.

Meanwhile, Abraham met with *no* representatives of environmental or consumer groups. Nearly thirty had asked for meetings, but the Energy Department declined, citing the secretary's busy schedule. (Abraham said the process was "open and appropriate" and "included all viewpoints," and called the resulting energy plan "balanced.")

Although all documents relating to meetings with **Enron** were missing, Cheney admitted he or his aides met with Enron executives at least six times. The day after a meeting with Enron CEO KENNETH LAY—the only executive who got to meet with him alone—Cheney announced he would not support price caps on wholesale electricity in California, which Enron was seeking to block (see **California energy crisis**). Rep. Henry Waxman (D-CA) subsequently identified seventeen different provisions of Bush's National Energy Plan that would benefit Enron.

The Bush energy plan. The released task force records showed how directly the energy cabal's "recommendations" were translated into the "National Energy Plan,"

Bush's proposed energy bill, released in May 2001. The plan consisted of 105 industry-friendly energy proposals, of which, the administration estimated, eighty-five could take effect without Congressional action. Highlights include:

- *No* significant support for ENERGY CONSERVATION or developing RENEWABLE ENERGY sources—indeed, Bush's first budget slashed funding for such initiatives by a third.
- *No* significant increases in the FUEL EFFICIENCY of cars, SUVs, or other light trucks. The Bushies, at the behest of the auto industry, consistently opposed any substantial increases.

Instead, the Bush plan called for:

- More and more oil, gas, and coal production.
- Opening up publicly owned land and wilderness preserves to oil and gas exploitation.
- $33 billion in taxpayer subsidies and tax cuts for the oil, coal, and nuclear power industries.
- Building 1,300 new coal-fired power plants.
- Rolling back regulations limiting power plant air pollution emissions, water pollution caused by coal mining, and other environmental harm caused by fossil fuel production and use. (See **Air pollution** and **Environment**.)

"It's patriotic to pollute": 9/11, ANWR, and the phony imperative to drill, drill, drill. The **war on terrorism** provided the Bushies with a new pretext for their energy policy (and for the rest of their pre-9/11 agenda). The lesson many Americans took from 9/11 was that the U.S. should *reduce* its dependence on fossil fuels and redouble its efforts to conserve energy and develop alternative sources. The U.S. consumed 25 percent of global oil production, but had only three percent of the world's known oil reserves. Domestic reserves made up an ever-shrinking portion (less than 50 percent) of U.S. consumption. As long as we depended on oil, we would remain dependent on, and embroiled with, unstable Mideast suppliers—some of whom were also global suppliers of Islamic-extremist ideologies and of financing for terrorist groups (see **Oil, appeasement and the war on terrorism**).

Nonetheless, the Bushies would have us believe we could drill our way to energy independence by drilling in federally owned lands and wilderness areas. Thus, after 9/11, the Republicans' age-old[122] obsession with opening the ARCTIC NATIONAL WILDLIFE REFUGE (ANWR)—one of America's last pristine wildernesses—to drilling was repackaged as a vital "matter of national security," a bold bid for "energy independence," and "a jobs bill." The *Philadelphia Inquirer* called it the "It's patriotic to pollute" ploy. Indeed, with the Bushies, anything became an excuse to drill in ANWR, from the California energy crisis to the great Northeast power blackout of August 2003—both of which had nothing whatsoever to do with oil and gas supplies.

The Bush Energy Department itself estimated that ANWR could produce no more than 600,000 to 900,000 barrels a day—barely a dent in the 20 million barrels the U.S. consumed. The amount of economically recoverable oil in ANWR was estimated at 3.2 billion barrels—less than a six-month supply. Increasing new vehicles' fuel efficiency by just three miles per gallon, the EPA calculated, would save five times as much oil per day as ANWR was likely to provide.

But in March 2002, the Bushies were blocking a bipartisan Senate bill to increase fuel efficiency (see below), and at the same time playing up the fact that the U.S. imported at least 700,000 barrels a day from Saddam Hussein's **Iraq**—even though they were quietly planning to do something about *that* much sooner than any oil could be made to flow from ANWR, which would take at least eight to ten years of exploration and development. Meanwhile, however, Democratic opponents of drilling in ANWR could be, and were, tarred as allies of Saddam. (Never mind that those actually buying Saddam's oil—ChevronTexaco, Exxon-Mobil, ConocoPhillips, BP—were the ones lobbying for drilling in ANWR.)

Here's your conclusion—now bring us the study. The Bushies were even more deceptive about the environmental impact of drilling in ANWR. In claiming that drilling and support facilities would be limited to 2,000 of the refuge's 1.9 million acres, they omitted all the new roads that would link the widely scattered facilities. In counting the area affected by pipelines resting on posts, they counted only the ground on which the posts rest, not the ground under the pipelines![124]

In April 2002, the U.S. Geological Survey (USGS), a branch of the Interior Department, released a seventy-eight-page report that concluded after twelve years of study that drilling in ANWR posed a serious hazard to wildlife. INTERIOR SECRETARY GALE NORTON ordered the scientists to reevaluate their conclusions and report back within ten days—just in time for a Senate debate on Bush's energy bill. In just two pages, the politically "corrected" report concluded that drilling in ANWR would have little or no impact on wildlife. And Norton got the headlines she needed—e.g., "Limited Arctic Drilling Won't Harm Caribou, Scientists Say."[124] Norton—the official responsible for administering and protecting federally owned lands in the public interest—recommended the president veto any final energy bill that failed to include drilling in ANWR.

The great Interior land rush. The Interior Department's Bureau of Land Management (BLM) managed some 260 million acres of public land, of which more than 90 percent was already open for energy leasing and development. Under Norton and Deputy Interior Secretary STEVEN GRILES, (formerly) a leading energy lobbyist, in 2001 alone the BLM opened 4 million new acres for oil and gas exploration and coal mining, up from 2.6 million acres in 2000. BLM managers sent field personnel a memo describing oil and gas leases and drilling permits as "their No. 1 priority," and directing them to speed up environmental reviews of energy projects. In January 2002, the department gave the green light to the drilling of more than 50,000 environmentally destructive COALBED METHANE natural gas wells in vast areas of Wyoming, Colorado, and Montana (see **Environment**). The drilling companies were to be subsidized for this, while paying next to nothing for the drilling rights and reaping windfalls on the gas.[125]

Ask not what you can do for your country—just gas-guzzle away. In 2002, passenger vehicles averaged twenty-four miles per gallon—the lowest level since 1980, largely because of increased sales of SUVs, pickups, and minivans. Raising the standard for these vehicles to 40 miles per gallon, which was already feasible, would save more oil per day than the U.S. imported from the Persian Gulf or could extract from ANWR combined; cut carbon dioxide pollution, the chief man-made cause of global warming, by 600 million metric tons; and save vehicle owners over $2,000 in fuel over the life of their vehicles, even allowing for their slightly higher cost. Instead:

- Bush's energy plan called for no significant increases in auto and light truck fuel efficiency.
- In March 2002, the White House, siding with the auto industry, helped kill a Senate proposal by John Kerry (D-MA) and John McCain (R-AZ) to increase fuel efficiency standards on cars and trucks by up to 50 percent by 2015. This would have saved about 2.5 million barrels of oil a day—about the amount the U.S. currently imported from the Middle East.
- In October 2002, the Bush administration actually sued the state of California for imposing a higher fuel efficiency standard than required under federal law. The suit was in accordance with the letter of the Clean Air Act, but against its clear intent. "For those keeping score," Arianna Huffington noted, "the Bush administration is in favor of states' rights when the states want to weaken federal safety standards of any kind, and against states' rights when the states want stronger measures."[126]
- Bush's 2004 budget included an increase of at least 50 percent, or up to $100,000, in tax deductions for business purchasers of the biggest SUVs and pickups—the "HUMMER DEDUCTION"—an incentive to buy the least fuel-efficient and most polluting vehicles.

- In his 2003 State of the Union address, Bush dramatically announced an initiative to develop HYDROGEN POWERED FUEL-CELL VEHICLES—which would likely take twenty years to become commercially viable. This "initiative" was widely viewed as a ploy to avoid the fuel-efficiency improvements in conventional vehicles that could be made far sooner. Tellingly, a House version of the Bush energy bill approved in April 2003 contained $1.8 billion for the hydrogen inititiative but $18 billion in subsidies and tax breaks for oil, gas, and coal producers. "This is an oil-company bill," remarked Rep. Jim McDermott (D-WA)."[127] Actually, it also put a cap on the nuclear industry's liability for accidents.

Disdain for renewables and conservation. The Bush energy plan included no significant support for energy conservation and developing renewable energy sources. In fact:

- Bush's first budget (fiscal 2002) cut $277 million, or 27 percent, from the Energy Department's (DOE) energy efficiency and renewable energy programs; some specific programs were cut by 50 percent. This slowed down development of more efficient lighting, appliances, heating and cooling systems, and building designs, and hampered efforts to cut waste in federal buildings. The DOE had recently documented that these programs had saved consumers and businesses $30 billion.[128] In a quintessential Bushie gesture, the White House even "dipped into [these programs'] already meager funds . . . to come up with over \$135,000 for the printing of 10,000 copies of its industry-friendly energy plan."[129]

- Bush opposed the so-called RENEWABLE PORTFOLIO STANDARD—a Democratic-supported measure requiring utilities to generate 10 percent of their electricity from renewable energy sources by 2010. Meanwhile, wind energy alone, with existing technology, could supply 20 percent of America's electricity, while the sunlight the Earth receives in thirty minutes was equivalent to all the power consumed globally in one year.

- While endlessly insisting on the urgent need for more energy supplies, Bush did not deliver a single speech calling on Americans to conserve.

King Coal. The coal industry made out like a bandit under Bush. In the 2000 election, the industry provided (in addition to \$100,000 in contributions) critical support for Bush in traditionally Democratic coal-mining states, especially West Virginia. A responsive Bush White House:

- Vastly increased mining access to public lands.
- Reneged on its promise to regulate carbon dioxide (CO_2) emissions and refused to label CO_2 a pollutant. More than 30 percent of U.S. CO_2 emissions came from coal-fired power plants.
- Effectively legalized the practice of "MOUNTAINTOP REMOVAL" coal mining, in which the entire mountaintops are blasted off, leaving a lunar landscape and generating huge volumes of waste, which is dumped into nearby streams and wetlands.

- Raised permitted levels of MERCURY POLLUTION, which is emitted by coal-fired power plants and causes brain, lung, and kidney damage and reproductive problems. (See **Air pollution**.)

The ultimate energy lobby.

At least thirty high-level Bush administration officials were former energy executives, lobbyists, or lawyers. Many others were eminently industry-friendly and -funded.Among them were:

Spencer Abraham, Energy Secretary. As a Michigan senator, Abraham led the Senate effort to defeat higher fuel-efficiency standards for SUVs; fought to cut research into renewable energy, wipe out the federal gasoline tax, and privatize federal-owned power generating operations. He also attempted three times to abolish the Energy Department, which he viewed as merely a regulatory thorn in the side of the industries he supported—and that supported him. For his failed 2000 Senate reelection campaign Abraham received $449,000 from the energy lobby, more than any other Senate candidate; $700,000 from the auto industry; and $178,674 from Coalition for Vehicle Choice, an industry lobby group that opposed raising fuel efficiency standards.

George W. Bush. Former oilman (see **Bush's business career**). In 2000, Bush became by far the biggest federal recipient of energy industry campaign contributions in history, receiving $2.8 million.

Andrew Card, White House of Staff. Former chief lobbyist for the auto industry and for GM.

Robert Card, Under Secretary of Energy. Former president and CEO of KAISER HILL, a nuclear waste cleanup contractor that was fined almost $1 million for nuclear safety violations at the abandoned Rocky Flats nuclear weapons factory in Colorado.

James E. Cason, Associate Deputy Secretary, Interior Department. As Principal Deputy Assistant Secretary of the Interior, 1985–1990, Cason played a key role in a decision to resume selling titles to federal oil and shale tracts for $2.50 an acre, far below their market value, and "approve[d] the granting of titles to some 82,000 acres, even though Congress had made clear its intent to revise the program. One set of claims, 17,000 acres, was purchased for $42,000 and sold months later for $37 million. . . . Two years later when Congress considered trying to change the law that made these transfers possible Mr. Cason rushed out to Colorado to urge more claimants to 'line up to the trough while they could.'"[130]

Dick Cheney. CEO of Houston oil-services giant HALLIBURTON, 1995–2000. Was also a member of the industry front-group COMPASS, the Committee to Preserve American Security and Sovereignty, which worked to oppose the Kyoto treaty on **global warming.** See **Cheney and Halliburton.**

James Connaughton, Chairman of the White House Council on Environmental Quality. Previously a lobbyist for GE (the top SUPERFUND polluter), oil giant ATLANTIC RICHFIELD and ARCO COAL, chiefly on environmental issues.

Donald Evans, Secretary of Commerce. Former CEO of Denver-based oil company TOM BROWN. Came to office holding 940,000 Tom Brown stock options worth between $5 million and $25 million. Described as Bush's best friend, he headed the Bush-Cheney 2000 campaign, for which he raised $100 million.

J. Steven Griles, Deputy Interior Secretary. Former lobbyist for UNITED COMPANY, a coal, oil, and gas development firm. Former vice president of NATIONAL ENVIRONMENTAL STRATEGIES, a DC-based lobbying firm representing oil, coal, and utility interests. Known as one of the energy industry's most powerful lobbyists, Griles focused his efforts on opening public lands to COALBED METHANE drilling. Appointed to Interior after promising "to avoid any actual or apparent conflicts of interest," Griles then met repeatedly with, and intervened with the EPA on behalf of, his former energy industry clients in order to, in his own words, "try to expedite [coalbed] drilling."

Gail A. Norton, Interior Secretary. Career-long advocate of opening public lands, including ANWR, to oil and gas drilling. Filled top positions at Interior with "former" energy lobbyists.

Condoleezza Rice, National Security Adviser. Board member of energy giant CHEVRON CORP. from 1991 to 2000. Chevron named an oil tanker after her in August 2000.

Thomas Sansonetti, Assistant Attorney General for Environment and Natural Resources. In private law practice, represented coal and mining companies seeking more access to federal lands.

Carl Michael Smith, Assistant Secretary of Energy for Fossil Energy. Oil driller, lawyer for oil companies, President of the OKLAHOMA INDEPENDENT PETROLEUM ASSOCIATION. In a speech to the Independent Oil and Gas Association of West Virginia in January 2002, Smith said his role was to figure out "how best to utilize taxpayer dollars to the benefit of the industry." Also, "Our tax code is not real favorable to the petroleum and pipeline sector of our industry." That was the *lowest*-taxed industry in America, paying 5.7 percent of its U.S. profits in federal income taxes in 1998. Half its companies paid no income tax at all, but got rebates.

ENRON: *AMERICA'S WORST CORPORATE CRIMINAL, BUSH'S BEST CORPORATE FRIEND*

"We are a loyal member of your team and are prepared to do whatever fits your strategic plan. . . . In public policy, it matters less who has the best arguments and more who gets heard—and by whom."
—Memo to Enron executives from Bush campaign adviser and former Christian Coalition leader Ralph Reed, seeking $380,000 from Enron to lobby for deregulation of electricity markets, October 2000.[131]

Before its collapse in 2001 in one of the biggest **corporate scandals** and bankruptcies in history, no company was more closely tied to the Bush administration, or stood to gain more from Bush-Cheney **energy** policies, or had more say in *shaping* those policies, than Enron, the Houston energy and commodities trading conglomerate. State and federal deregulation of energy distribution and trading delivered in the 1990s by Enron's Republican allies—including

Texas Governor Bush—had enabled Enron's fraud-ridden
growth into the seventh largest U.S. corporation. Enron and
its executives were Bush's biggest campaign contributors.
Former Enron executives, lobbyists, shareholders and
donees filled high positions throughout his administration.
Yet not even a scandal of this magnitude—which shook the
political ground under Bush, ravaged thousands of Enron
investors and employees, and set the stock market and the
economy reeling—could induce the Bushies to get tough on
corporate governance.

At the heart of Enron's collapse was the systematic inflation of company profits, hiding of debts through hundreds of
phony "special-purpose" partnerships, and avoiding taxes
through 881 subsidiaries in offshore tax havens (see **Tax
evasion**). When the company admitted in October 2001 to
inflating profits, the stock nosedived, vaporizing $70 billion
in shareholders' wealth. Top insiders had been selling quietly all along—CEO KENNETH LAY, for example, got out with
more than $100 million—even while encouraging employees
to invest more, indeed, *all* of their 401k retirement funds in
the stock and preventing them from selling as the shares
were dropping. Enron's bankruptcy in December 2001 cost
15,000 company employees their jobs and cost many their
life savings.

It was also revealed that the **California energy crisis**
had been propelled by Enron and other large traders' manip-
ulations, which created artificial shortages and drastically
drove up prices—and their own trading revenues.

Enron's support for Bush and its extraordinary White
House access threatened to become a full-fledged political
scandal, but for the **war on terrorism** diverting attention

and buoying Bush's popularity. As for his cronies at the head of Enron, despite eighteen criminal indictments of Enron executives, including the chief financial officer, and guilty pleas by four others, as of December 2003, no charges had yet been brought against the company's two top executives, Bush's old pal "Kenny boy" Lay and former CEO Jeffrey Skilling, although the court examiner concluded that the two shared responsibility for the collapse. (The Justice Department touted its conviction of Enron's accounting firm, Arthur Andersen, but as one lawyer commented, "It's like focusing on the guy who drove the getaway car.")

Covering his tracks: The fifteen-year Bush-Enron relationship. A month after Enron's bankruptcy, Bush raced to distance himself from "Kenny boy." He dissembled about the extent of his relationship with Lay, describing him as having been merely "a supporter" and denying knowing him before 1994. In fact, Enron and Lay were major financial supporters of President Bush Sr.—who considered Lay for a cabinet position—and W.'s oil company, Spectrum 7, did business with Enron as early as 1986, when Lay already headed Enron[132] (see **Bush's business career**). Bush even claimed that Lay had supported his opponent, Democrat Ann Richards, in the '94 Texas governor's race. Lay did contribute to Richards's campaign, but he gave three times as much to Bush.

Dozens of letters exchanged between Governor Bush and Lay showed a close personal and political relationship and made clear that Lay's single-minded goal in supporting Bush was to win more and more deregulation of the electricity business, from which Enron stood to make a killing— and which Bush pushed through the Texas legislature immediately after his reelection in 1998. "These documents suggest that Bush was acting as promoter in chief for Enron and its business interests at a time when he was getting ready to raise money for his run for president," Joan Claybrook of Public Citizen told CNN.[133]

Bush and Lay take the White House.[134] In 1999 and 2000, Enron and its executives gave more than $2 million to GOP causes (four times as much as to Democrats), including more than $1 million (mostly through the Republican National Committee) and use of the company jet for the Bush-Cheney campaign. Those petty outlays were repaid handsomely. Dozens of former Enron executives, lobbyists, lawyers, or substantial shareholders ended up working for the Bush administration. Lay served on the Bush transition team, and Bush even considered making him Treasury Secretary. No company had more pull than Enron in shaping national energy policy under the closed-door auspices of Cheney's energy task force. Cheney and/or aides met with Enron executives at least six times. Lay was the only CEO who got private meetings with Cheney.

Lay was allowed to vet, and veto, candidates for the Federal Energy Regulatory Commission (FERC), which oversees the gas pipelines and electricity grids that were key to Enron's business. After FERC chairman Curt Hebert, a Clinton appointee, refused to go along with Enron on electricity deregulation, Bush replaced him—reportedly at Lay's behest—with arch-deregulator Pat Wood III (whom Governor Bush had, with Lay's endorsement, named chairman of the Texas Public Utility Commission).

In the wake of Enron's collapse, the White House claimed it had never done the company any favors. To be sure, intervening to try to save Enron in its death throes was politically unthinkable. But by taking Enron's campaign donations and then opening their doors to Enron's policy and personnel recommendations—scandalous in itself—the Bushies could well have encouraged Enron executives' belief that their White House connections made them untouchable.

"Enron's Washington Branch."

A few of the fifty-two former Enron executives, lobbyists, lawyers or significant shareholders and Enron donees who ended up working for the Bush administration deserve special mention:

John Ashcroft received nearly $61,000 from Enron and its executives, including $25,000 from Kenneth Lay, for his unsuccessful 2000 Senate run.

Dick Cheney, the day after meeting personally with Lay, announced he would not support price caps on electricity in California, which Enron wanted blocked.

Lawrence Lindsey, Bush's chief economic adviser until his resignation in December 2002, was formerly a $50,000-a-year Enron consultant and board member.

Marc Racicot remained an Enron lobbyist even after Bush appointed him Chairman of the RNC in December 2001. As governor of Montana in the 1990s, Racicot enacted Enron-style deregulation of Montana's electricity market, which resulted in 40 percent rate increases, business shutdowns, and the ruin of Montana's leading utility.[135] In 2000, Racicot turned down Bush's offer to become Attorney General and instead went to work with the law/lobbying firm Bracewell & Patterson, using his connections to Bush to lobby states and Congress on behalf of Enron and other energy companies.

Karl Rove held $100,000–$250,000 in Enron shares when appointed Bush's chief political advisor. His refusal to sell those shares, as required, upon taking office meant that he held them, along with other energy stocks, while taking part in meetings that helped shape Bush energy policy. (He sold them well before they collapsed.)

Thomas White, Secretary of the Army until he abruptly resigned in April 2003, was previously chairman and CEO of Enron Operations Corp. and vice-chairman of Enron Energy Services, whose dubious accounting practices concealed around $500 million in losses on White's watch. When White heard of the losses, his emailed response summed up Enron strategy: "Close a bigger deal. Hide the loss before the 1Q [first quarter]." He sold $12 million in Enron shares just before they became worthless. In appointing him Army secretary, Bush entrusted White with overseeing the biggest military budget expansion since Vietnam.

Robert Zoellick, U.S. Trade Representative, was a paid consultant on the Enron advisory board before joining the Bush administration.

ENVIRONMENT

Almost from day one, the Bush administration waged all-out war on environmental protection regulations, attacking and rolling back one hard-won measure after another. Virtually every rule opposed by Bush and Cheney's most special interests—including the energy, electric power, mining, logging, and auto industries—came under assault.

Bush kicked off this war in March 2001 by breaking his campaign promise to regulate power plants' emissions of carbon dioxide (CO_2), the main "greenhouse gas" implicated in causing **global warming.** The decision came after furious lobbying from the coal industry, which fueled half the country's power plants. In backing out of his pledge, Bush said he had not been aware that CO_2 was not designated a "pollutant" under the Clean Air Act. Which was exactly why it *needed* to be regulated!

Within two years, Bush & Co. had racked up many other proud achievements:

- **Clean Air Act crippled.** Bush suspended enforcement of a critical provision—"NEW SOURCE REVIEW"— which required power plants to install anti-pollution equipment if and when they expand. The Bushies also replaced CLEAN AIR ACT limits on the main air pollutants with the laxer limits of Bush's cynically titled "CLEAR SKIES INITIATIVE." (See **Air pollution.**)
- **Global warming accord ditched.** Bush pulled the U.S. out of the 1997 Kyoto treaty, which aimed to reduce greenhouse gas emissions (principally CO_2) produced by the burning of fossil fuels, and which 165 other nations signed in October 2001. (With just 4 percent of the world's population, the U.S. produced nearly a quarter of the world's CO_2.)
- **Global warming, uh, eradicated.** The Bushies ended the threat of global warming—by simply

deleting the subject from the Environmental Protection Agency's (EPA) annual federal report on air pollution trends—"much as [Enron's] accountants [Arthur] Andersen might have cleaned up a balance sheet by hiding an unprofitable division," *The New York Times's* Frank Rich remarked.

- **EPA funding, staff, and enforcement slashed.** In their first two years, the Bushies cut the EPA's enforcement program by at least 100 staff positions. After 9/11, about 40 percent of the EPA's criminal enforcement division was diverted to anti-terrorist activities. "This may well be advisable," wrote Molly Ivins, "but it also would be smart to remember that more people were killed by the 1984 chemical plant accident in Bhopal [India] than died on Sept. 11."[136] EPA enforcement actions cut pollution by 60 percent less in 2002 than in 2001. Bush's fiscal 2004 budget cut environmental funding by another $1.6 billion.

- **Arsenic limits raised.** In April 2001—during National Poison Prevention Week—Bush, caving to the mining industry, rescinded Clinton's rule lowering permitted arsenic levels in drinking water from fifty to ten parts per billion. Even Clinton's reduced levels were subsequently proven to significantly increase the risk of cancer. The move generated toxic levels of publicity, and the Bushies later backed down.

- **Arctic National Wildlife Refuge (ANWR) under assault.** Bush & Co. joined other oil-industry lobbyists in pressing relentlessly for oil drilling in Alaska's ANWR, one of America's last pristine wilderness areas, and misled the public about the benefits and environmental impact. (See **Energy**.)

- **Interior Department taken over by industry lobbyists.** Bush picked GALE A. NORTON for Interior Secretary, in charge of federal decisions on the use of 436 million acres of public land and much of the country's water management. A former industry lobbyist and a leading advocate of "voluntary compliance" by corporations with environmental rules, Norton had been devoted to *fighting* the Interior Department on behalf of industries that wanted to mine, drill and log freely on public lands. She picked a lobbyist for Arctic oil drilling, Camden Toohey, as her top official for Alaska and another energy lobbyist, Kit Kimball, to be her "ambassador" to the West. Deputy Interior SECRETARY J. STEVEN GRILES, formerly a powerful energy industry lobbyist, worked hard at Interior to expedite the following:

- **Coalbed methane drilling.** The Bushies gave the green light to—and budgeted millions in new subsidies for—the drilling of more than 50,000 coalbed methane natural gas wells on vast areas of public land in Wyoming, Colorado, and Montana. This process involved pumping out and wasting huge amounts of groundwater and allowing salt-contaminated water to flow into surrounding streams, and would cut up the land with tens of thousands of miles of new roads and transmission lines.

- **Padre Island National Seashore opened up for gas drilling.** The eighty-mile-long barrier island in Texas was the longest stretch of undeveloped beach in the U.S., home to eleven endangered wildlife species and destination for 800,000 visitors per year. The National Park Service, part of the Interior Department, decided to allow heavy trucks to drive along the island about twenty times a day, all year round, for the construction of gas wells by BNP Petroleum of Corpus Christi, Texas.

- **Mining operations let loose on public land.** Reversing a Clinton rule, the Bushies reinstated the 1872 Mining Law, which prevented the federal government from blocking mining on public land even if it caused "substantial and irreparable" environmental harm. That law, Molly Ivins noted, had been "meant to help small-time pick-and-shovel miners back in the day, is now the protector of giant corporations mining for gold, silver, copper and uranium."[137] According to the EPA, 40 percent of Western watersheds were already polluted by mining. The public did not even receive royalties for this "use" of its land.

- **Repeal of the "roadless rule."** Gutted a key regulation protecting 60 million acres of national forest from road building and logging. (See **Forests**.)

- **Snowmobiles over nature.** Pushed back the planned phase-out of snowmobiles in Yellowstone and Grand Teton national parks.

- **Automobile fuel (in)efficiency.** Successfully opposed Congressional efforts to raise vehicle fuel efficiency (CAFE) standards; canceled an impending deadline (set by Clinton) for automakers to develop prototype high-mileage cars; and increased tax deductions for business purchasers of gas-guzzling and polluting SUVs and pickups.

- **Wetlands protections gutted.** Relaxed the rules on developing wetlands. Meanwhile, the total wetlands area which the federal government claimed the right to regulate shrank by at least 40 percent in Bush's first two years. (See **Water.**)
- **Clean water funding dried up.** Opposed a bipartisan House bill to help states clean up water supplies, saying defense spending must take priority.
- **Endangered species get more so.** Abandoned legal protections for dozens of endangered species and millions of acres of habitat across the country. In lawsuits brought by real-estate developers, the administration did not *lose* but rather *asked the judges to rule in favor of the developers* and to rescind legal protections for some two dozen endangered species.[138] The Fish and Wildlife Service also said it would "temporarily" stop designating "critical habitats" because it was running out of money. In fact, the agency hadn't bothered *requesting* the funding it needed. "They've engineered a budget crisis," said the director of the Center for Biological Diversity.
- **Military exemption.** In April 2003, the Bushies proposed exempting 25 million acres of military bases, ports, and airfields from key environmental laws. At stake were endangered species protections, air and groundwater pollution, and cleanups of toxic rocket fuel and other hazardous wastes. The Pentagon was America's biggest polluter, producing more hazardous waste than the top three chemical companies combined.
- **Land and Water Conservation Fund looted.** The

148 *Environment*

Bushies cut the Fund's spending on land acquisitions in 2004 by 56 percent, or $242 million, from the 2002 level, by diverting its funds to pay for other programs. The fund used revenues derived from offshore oil and gas drilling to acquire and preserve land and water resources.

- **Toxic pesticide un-banned.** Effectively removed the ban on METHYL BROMIDE (MB), a toxic pesticide used by golf courses to kill unwanted grasses and weeds on greens. MB can cause failure of the central nervous or respiratory system, along with permanent disabilities and fetal defects. It also contributes significantly to the destruction of the ozone layer. In 2000, the U.S. agreed to a complete ban by 2005. In 2003, the Bush administration said it would grant "critical-use exemptions" to as many as 56 industry groups, including golf courses, allowing them to use 734,000 pounds of MB from 2005 to 2007—the "critical use" being to make their greens pretty. The industry gave upwards of $220,000 to federal candidates in 2001–2002—more than two-thirds of it to Republicans—and many times more to local candidates

- **Ships to go on polluting.** The EPA ruled in January 2003 that large seagoing vessels—oil tankers, cruise ships, cargo ships—would not have to cut emissions until at least 2007. These are among the fastest-growing and least regulated sources of air pollution, accounting for 14 percent of global nitrogen oxide and 16 percent of sulphur oxide emissions. In the large U.S. ports they frequent, several of these ships can emit as much air pollution as 1 million cars. The EPA sought a more stringent regulation but was overruled by the White House.

- **"Bush to shift toxic cleanups to taxpayers."** Could the essence of Bushism be conveyed more starkly than in that *New York Times* headline (February 24, 2002)? The story referred to funding of the SUPER-FUND, which was founded in 1980 to pay for the cleanup of toxic waste sites, under the slogan "the polluter pays." It was funded mostly by a special tax on industry, which had to be renewed every five years or so. In 1995, at the behest of the chemical and oil industries, the Republican-controlled House of Representatives refused to renew. As a result, by 2002, the fund had dwindled by more than 99 percent. Bush refused to reauthorize the tax in his 2002 and 2003 budgets—ensuring that by 2004 all the money would come from individual taxpayers, none from the corporate tax. Meanwhile, fewer sites were being cleaned up: Around forty in 2002 and 2003, compared to eighty in each of Clinton's last four years.

- **New York lied to about World Trade Center pollution.** One week after 9/11, EPA Administrator Christie Whitman assured New Yorkers the air was safe to breathe, even though the towers' collapse threw more than a million tons of pulverized cement, glass and insulation dust into the air, and the site spewed toxic gases "like a chemical factory" for at least the next six weeks, a University of California study reported in September 2003. That same month, the EPA's inspector general reported that the White House Council on Environmental Quality had "convinced EPA to add reassuring statements and delete cautionary ones," such as information on the potential health hazards of breathing asbestos, lead, concrete and pulverized glass, and that the White House had the National Security Council control EPA communications in the days after 9/11.

- **The "communications battle."** Republicans may be evil, but they're not, on the whole, stupid. By the lead-up to the 2002 mid-term elections, they realized they were losing what GOP strategist Frank Luntz called the "environmental communications battle," and proceeded to change their "message" to counter what Luntz called "the single biggest vulnerability for the Republicans and especially for George Bush." On Luntz's advice, the words "global warming" and "environmentalist" disappeared from Bush's speeches—replaced by "climate change" and "conservationist." Republican candidates began speaking out for clean water and forest preservation. The new strategy was credited with helping win some important races in November. "We are going to talk about these issues a lot over the next [2004] election cycle," said GOP chairman Marc Racicot.

ESTATE TAX: *RELIEF FOR MILLIONAIRES AND THE FALSE ADVERTISING BUSH SOLD IT WITH*

Abolishing a tax that affected only the richest 2 percent of Americans was an urgent priority for Bush. He campaigned hard for repeal of the "death tax" and got it passed (a one-year repeal plus ten-year phase out) through Congress in early 2001 as part of his $1.35 trillion tax-cut package.

Supporters of estate tax repeal portrayed it a populist measure benefiting Americans of all classes. They especially emphasized small business owners and farmers—claiming time and again that farm families were often forced to sell the land after a parent died in order to pay the tax. In fact, not a single example of the loss of a family farm because of estate-tax liability had ever been identified.

The benefits of repeal were quite obvious, on the other hand, for the corporate elite—as personified, for example, by Bush's own cabinet. According to one estimate, Bush's cabinet members stood to save $5 million to $120 million apiece if the estate tax was abolished.[139] When fully in effect, the Center on Budget and Policy Priorities calculated, the repeal would save America's 4,500 largest estates as much in taxes as Bush's tax cuts gave to the 142 million lowest-income Americans combined.

The "double-taxation" myth strikes again. Bush & Co. kept claiming—as a newspaper ad placed by a group of wealthy businessmen put it—"The estate tax is unfair double taxation since taxpayers are taxed twice—once when the money is earned and again when you die." *Slate* editor Michael Kinsley described this "most tediously repeated sound bite of the estate tax debate" as "out-and-out false." Most of the accumulated wealth that was subject to the estate tax represented unrealized capital gains, and was never subject to the income tax. "Anyone with the slightest business or financial experience surely knows it," Kinsley wrote. "Even George W. Bush. Yet he keeps on repeating the lie."[141] (The right propagated a similar myth with regard to taxes on stock dividends; see **Budget and taxes**.)

Opponents of repeal, strange as it seemed, included Microsoft chairman Bill Gates and gazillionaire investor Warren Buffet—perhaps the two richest people in America— who started an organization of millionaires against estate-tax repeal. They argued that those who merely inherit rather than earn fortunes should be expected to pay tax on them. A hundred years earlier, Andrew Carnegie went much further and proposed that estates be taxed 100 percent. Let the sons of the rich earn their own fortunes, he thought. They have already enjoyed plenty of advantages, such as fancy educations, social and business connections, and the family name, just by *being* sons of the rich and powerful. What better example of that than George W. Bush. (See **Bush's business career; Budget and taxes; State and local governments**.)

FEDERALIST SOCIETY: *RISING POWER OF THE LEGAL PROFESSION'S RIGHT WING.*

Under Bush, a right-wing lawyers' group seeking to bring about a radical transformation of the American legal system quietly gained powerful influence through appointments of its members to high positions throughout the administration. The Federalist Society for Law and Public Policy Studies was co-founded in the late 1970s by Bush energy secretary SPENCER ABRAHAM—then a Harvard law student. By 2000, the Washington-based group had about 40,000 members, including lawyers, policy experts, and business leaders. Backed by millions of dollars from right-wing foundations for its advocacy, litigation, publications, websites, and conferences, the Society waged war on a wide range of issues—civil rights, minority and women's rights, **environmental, health and safety regulations,** and **church-state** separation—by targeting the courts, the American Bar Association, and federal judicial and political appointments. The Society also recruited tomorrow's shock troops through its Student Division, which had more than 5,000 members at 145 law schools. It was, if not the heart, then the brain, or at least the gall bladder, of the vast right-wing conspiracy.

Federalist Society members were instrumental in winning the Florida recount battle for Bush and securing him the presidency (see **Election 2000**). Washington, D.C. chapter president THEODORE OLSON argued Bush's case before the U.S. Supreme Court in *Bush v. Gore.* (Olson allegedly took part in the ARKANSAS PROJECT—a $2.4 million, five-year effort to dig up dirt on President Clinton—and was a close associate of arch-Clinton-hunter and fellow Federalist KEN STARR.) Bush subsequently appointed Olson Solicitor General—the country's chief trial lawyer, who represents the administration before the Supreme Court. Olson had also represented plaintiffs in a successful challenge to the University of Texas affirmative action program.

Society members were instrumental in securing the nomination of member JOHN ASHCROFT as Attorney General. According to the liberal Institute for Democratic Studies (IDS) in early 2001, "It is impossible to grasp the potential significance of [Ashcroft's appointment] without understanding the key role that the Federalist Society . . . is playing in the challenge to democratic legal values. The leadership of the Federalist Society is, quite simply, poised to transform the landscape of American law and society [and has] changed the course of American politics."

Society members appointed to the Bush administration included, among many others, Interior Secretary GALE NORTON (whom the Society had honored as their Young Lawyer of the Year); Solicitor of Labor EUGENE SCALIA (son of Supreme Court Justice ANTONIN SCALIA, also a member), Deputy Attorney General LARRY THOMPSON; Assistant Attorney General for Legal Policy VIET DINH; Assistant Attorney General for Environment THOMAS L. SANSONETTI; and Director of the National Institute of Justice SARAH V. HART. Society cofounder LEE LIBERMAN OTIS played a key role in setting up the administration's judicial selection process. She played a similar role as assistant White House counsel under Bush I, examining "all candidates for federal judgeships for ideological purity . . . It is well known that no federal judicial appointment is made without her imprimatur," a U.S. Court of Appeals judge wrote in 1992. Otis herself boasted openly that no one who was not a Federalist Society member had received a judicial appointment from President Bush Sr.

Society members' core belief was that the Constitution should be interpreted according to their own dubious claims about the original intentions of the Framers. In practice, this gave conservative judges a rationale for enforcing the oppressive and undemocratic social and moral values of a happily bygone era of gross economic, social, and racial inequality and radical, unfettered capitalism. Judicial actions that did not accord with the Society's philosophy, the group attacked as "judicial activism" and as unconstitutional.

The group advocated severely limiting the regulatory power of the Environmental Protection Agency (EPA) and Occupational Safety and Health Administration (OSHA), and *abolishing* outright the Securities and Exchange Commission (SEC)—which would mean no regulatory oversight whatsoever of the financial dealings of companies like Enron or their accounting firms. Society publications and speakers also frequently targeted federal civil and labor rights laws, including desegregation orders and voting rights, gender equity, age discrimination and sexual harassment laws, even the Americans with Disabilities Act. Theirs was the Bush (de)regulatory agenda: Give free rein to the Enrons and Arthur Andersens and polluters of the world while attacking the legal protections of workers, women, minorities, the aged, and the handicapped.

Reflecting the presence of the religious right in its leadership and membership, the Society also targeted the **church-state** separation and advocated for "school choice," "charitable choice," teaching creationism and distributing religious materials in public schools. Among fifteen broad areas for which the Society organized special "practice groups" were "religious liberty," national security, cyberspace, corporate law, and environmental law. The goal was right-wing legal control over every area of economic, social, and political life.

Despite all this, the Society assiduously portrayed itself as nonpartisan! In his keynote address at a 1999 Federalist convention, for example, Justice CLARENCE THOMAS denounced the American Bar Association as an "interest group" and commended the Federalist Society "for maintaining the wall of separation between law and politics."[141]

FOREIGN POLICY AND NATIONAL SECURITY DOCTRINE: *US VS. THE WORLD*

"World domination . . . same old dream."
—James Bond, "Dr. No."

Polls consistently showed far higher public approval for Bush's handling of the war on terrorism, defense, and security matters than for his domestic policies. But were they so different? In both, the Bushies displayed a disdain for consensus (bipartisanship at home, multilateralism abroad); an arrogation of a right to rule without interference; similar ideological radicalism and aggressiveness in the exercise of power; the same privileging of business interests over all others, except perhaps their own political gain; the same disregard for truth-telling.

It seemed forgotten that Bush had come into office with little interest in and even less knowledge of international affairs. As he admitted during his election campaign, "I'm not going to play like I've been a person who's spent hours involved with foreign policy." (Not even *hours!*) And he had a foreign policy to match—namely, as little foreign policy as possible; he said he thought the U.S. had been over-involved abroad, and promised to scale back on international economic aid and "nation-building" projects—even as he advocated huge military spending increases.

But **September 11** brought to the fore the most aggressive, right-wing elements in the defense and foreign-policy apparatus—those who believed the U.S. should freely exercise its power, particularly in the Middle East, to "redraw the map" in its own perceived interests. Within a year, Bush—who as a candidate had said the U.S. should be "humble"—had made clear his intention to invade **Iraq** and depose Saddam Hussein, with or without the cooperation or approval of the U.N. or of our closest allies, and he announced a radical national security doctrine that reserved the right to attack "preemptively" any country the U.S. labeled a threat. At home, total control by one party—abroad, total domination by one country.

"A disdain for allies, treaties, and international organizations," wrote journalist Fareed Zakaria, was what the Bush administration had shown from the start. "In its first two years it has reneged on more international treaties than any previous Administration."[143] The Bushies tore up, rejected, or undermined the ABM Treaty (see **Missile defense**), the **Biological Weapons** Convention, the **nuclear weapons** Comprehensive Test Ban Treaty, the INTERNATIONAL CRIMINAL COURT; the convention on banning **landmines**, the U.N. conference on small arms (see **Gun control**), and the Kyoto accord on **global warming**. (Also see **Trade and tariffs.**) "There is something almost comical about the prospect of George Bush waging war on another nation [Iraq] because that nation has defied international law," noted *The Guardian*'s George Monbiot. The Bush administration "has torn up more international treaties and disregarded more U.N. conventions than the rest of the world has in 20 years. . . . Even its preparedness to go to war with Iraq without a mandate from the U.N. security council is a defiance of international law far graver than Saddam Hussein's non-compliance with U.N. weapons inspectors."[143] In rejecting multilateralism, according to former U.N. ambassador Richard Holbrooke, the U.S. made "a radical break with 55 years of a bipartisan tradition that sought international agreements and regimes of benefit to us." It was time, some said, for a "Declaration of Interdependence."

Bush foreign policy hastened the evaporation of the international goodwill and sympathy the U.S. enjoyed briefly after 9/11. Within a year, resentment and hostility toward the U.S., even among our closest allies—especially over Iraq— was at its highest pitch in decades, perhaps ever.

An unrivaled U.S. imperium: The Bush doctrine. In 2002, the U.S. military budget was larger than the world's next fifteen largest combined. Its one-year defense spending *increase* alone was larger that the entire military budget of Britain or Russia. Clearly—to the Bushies—U.S. military dominance wasn't overwhelming enough. And to go with their out-of-control military buildup, they adopted a national security doctrine that was breathtakingly radical in its assertions of U.S. prerogatives.

Belying Bush's claim that it was a necessary response to 9/11, the new doctrine had in fact been laid out two years earlier in a report issued by the PROJECT FOR THE NEW AMERICAN CENTURY, a group of right-wingers whose great fear was that the U.S. might forfeit its chance at a global empire. Among the report's authors were such future Bush foreign policy makers as Deputy Defense Secretary PAUL WOLFOWITZ, Pentagon Comptroller DOV ZAKHEIM, Under Secretary of State JOHN BOLTON, head of the Pentagon's Office of Program, Analysis and Evaluation STEPHEN CAMBONE, Defense Policy Board members ELIOT COHEN and DEVON CROSS, and Cheney chief of staff "SCOOTER" LIBBY. Their report became a virtual blueprint for Bush defense policy:

It advocated the repudiation of the Anti-Ballistic Missile Treaty (done in 2001) and the building of a **missile defense** system (under way); huge military-spending increases (done and done); and the development of a new generation of small **nuclear weapons** for actual battlefield use (okayed by Congress in 2002).

"A formula for international anarchy." Bush first outlined the new doctrine publicly in a commencement speech at West Point in June 2002. "America," he read, "has, and intends to keep, military strengths beyond challenge, thereby making the destabilizing arms races of other eras pointless." (A policy of keeping far ahead of likely challengers like China would seem rather to ensure a permanent arms race.) The "Bush doctrine" was formalized in the "National Security Strategy" report Bush submitted to Congress in September 2002. Along with the reliance on overwhelming military power, its crux was the replacement of deterrence by "preemptive" military action whenever the U.S. sees fit—a policy that "overturns 500 years of international practice and law," said Clyde Prestowitz, author of a book about U.S. foreign policy titled *Rogue Nation*. Critics warned of a Pandora's box. Rep. Lloyd Doggett (D-Tex.) wrote that "America will now attack first with pre-emptive strikes in what could spiral into wars without end, because other countries will likely copy this model. . . . This is a formula for international anarchy, not domestic security."

Learning from Ghenghis Khan. Parts of the paper sounded "like a pronouncement that the Roman Empire or Napoleon might have produced," according to a *New York Times* editorial. Indeed, in the summer of 2001, Donald Rumsfeld's office had sponsored a study of ancient empires—Alexander the Great's, the Romans, the Mongols—to determine how they had maintained their dominance. "The vision laid out in the Bush document is a vision of what used to be called, when we believed it to be the Soviet ambition, world domination," wrote Hendrik Hertzberg in *The New Yorker*. "There's a name for the kind of regime in which the cops rule, answering only to themselves. It's called a police state."

"Better to be feared than loved." The Bushies' position, Hertzberg noted, was "essentially this: Hey, we're the good guys. . . . [Whereas] Osama is evil; the axis of evil is evil. Nothing more need be said, nothing more need be understood. And if the other side is absolutely evil then we must be absolutely good, so it's fine for us to be absolutely powerful." Lacking any vision of a world governed democratically by law, "[t]he Bush vision is in the end a profoundly pessimistic one, and, as such, more than a little un-American. It is, among other things, a vision of perpetual war. . . . It's a dismal dream, and an ignoble guide for American foreign policy." [144]

Indeed, Fareed Zakaria noted, in a world of suicide bombers and suitcase bombs, "America's overwhelming military power cannot keep it safe." That would take close international cooperation—on intelligence, customs and immigration controls, and so on. "'It is better to be feared than loved,' Machiavelli wrote. But he was wrong. The Soviet Union was feared by its allies; the United States was loved, or at least, liked. Look who's still around."

Foreign views of the U.S.: Measuring the Bush Effect.
In March 2003, the Pew Research Center for the People and the Press released the results of a poll comparing foreign attitudes toward the U.S. and the Bush administration in July 2002 and March 2003. During that time, the "unfavorable" opinion of the U.S. went, in Britain, from 16 to 40%; France, from 34 to 67%; Germany, from 35 to 71%; Italy, from 23 to 59%; Spain, 79% (no 2002 survey taken); Poland, from 11 to 44%; Russia, from 33 to 68%; and Turkey, from 55 to 84%. Disapproval of Bush's foreign policy, March 2003: Britain, 60%; France, 87% Germany, 85%; Italy, 76%; Spain, 79%; Poland, 54%; Russia, 83%; Turkey, 85%.

A Bush foreign policy rogues gallery:

Elliott Abrams, National Security Council (NSC): Assistant Secretary of State under Reagan. Convicted of lying to Congress about his role in the IRAN-CONTRA scandal; later pardoned by President Bush I. In 2001 Bush II, perhaps trying to be funny, appointed him NSC Senior Director for Democracy, Human Rights, and International Operations, and in 2002 he got the NSC's top Middle East policy spot.

Richard Armitage, Deputy Secretary of State, was Assistant Secretary of Defense under Reagan. Investigated by Reagan's Commission on Organized Crime in 1984 for alleged links to gambling and prostitution. Denied appointment as Assistant Secretary of State by Bush I because of links to IRAN-CONTRA and other scandals.

John Bolton, Under Secretary of State for Arms Control and

International Security Affairs, was assistant attorney general under Reagan and Assistant Secretary of State under Bush I. In 1999, Bolton complained bitterly that the U.N. wished to limit America's freedom to use force at "its discretion . . . to advance its national interests," and said "nothing more should be paid to the U.N. system." Bolton signed the letter renouncing any U.S. role in the International Criminal Court, supported U.S. renunciation of the ABM Treaty, and opposed ratification of the Comprehensive Test Ban Treaty on **nuclear weapons**. In a speech in May 2002 titled "Beyond the Axis of Evil," Bolton hinted that after **Iraq**, Cuba might be the administration's next target. On North Korea, he said the U.S. should "make it clear . . . that we are indifferent to whether we ever have 'normal' diplomatic relations with it."

Otto Reich, Assistant Secretary of State for Latin American Affairs. Supported by the powerful Cuban-American lobby, the Cuban-born Reich was so controversial, Bush had to sneak him in through a recess appointment. As a corporate lobbyist, Reich helped draft the Helms-Burton Act tightening the Cuba embargo. Under Reagan, he was the first director of the State Department's Office of Public Diplomacy (OPD) for Latin America and the Caribbean, whose main mission was to put out frightening and usually false stories about Nicaragua's left-wing Sandinista government—such as the story fed to the press on the night of Reagan's reelection that Soviet MiG fighters were arriving in Nicaragua, or that the country had acquired chemical weapons. A senior U.S. official described the OPD as "a vast psychological warfare operation" (it involved CIA and military intelligence covert- and psy-ops specialists, including OLIVER NORTH)—except that its targets were the U.S. public and Congress. The OPD was finally shut down after a U.S. comptroller general's report concluded it had used federal funds to engage in "prohibited, covert propaganda activities."

Paul Wolfowitz, Deputy Secretary of Defense. Formerly Reagan State Department official; Under Secretary of Defense for policy under Bush I; member of the PROJECT FOR THE NEW AMERICAN CENTURY, a group of proponents of a new American empire forged through military might. Leading proponent of war in Iraq.

Dov Zakheim, Under Secretary of Defense and Chief Financial Officer for the Pentagon. Defense policy adviser under Reagan; private defense consultant during the 1990s; policy adviser to the 2000 Bush campaign; PROJECT FOR THE NEW AMERICAN CENTURY member; leading Iraq hawk.

Read his lips: No nation-building. "During the campaign, the president did not express, as you put it, disdain for nation-building."

—White House Press Secretary Ari Fleischer,
February 28, 2003

"I think what we need to do is convince people who live in the lands they live in to build the nations. Maybe I'm missing something here. I mean, we're going to have kind of a nation-building corps from America? Absolutely not."

—George W. Bush, October 11, 2000

FORESTS AND LOGGING:
THEY CAME, THEY SAWED . . .

When it came to protecting national forests, you could say the Bushies couldn't see the forest for the valuable trees the logging companies (valuable Republican contributors) wanted to cut down. In their eagerness to hand over public lands for private exploitation by timber, mining, and oil and gas companies, the Bushies showed their intention to literally undermine, drill, and attack with chain saws the very concept of *public* property.

Under Bush, the U.S. Forest Service became an instrument for turning national forests into private logging operations. That Bush's appointee for the nation's top forest management position, MARK REY, was a former logging-industry lobbyist went without saying.

Attacking—after pledging to uphold—the crucial "Roadless Rule" and promoting logging on public land in the name of fire prevention were but two of the Bushies' efforts on behalf of the timber industry (which in the 2000 election cycle gave 82 percent of its contributions to Republicans). Most of these efforts not only opened more national forests to road-building and logging operations but subsidized them with hundreds of millions of taxpayer dollars annually.

The Roadless Area Conservation Rule, passed in the Clinton administration's final days, was designed to protect the remaining one-third of national forest lands not already open to logging, mining, and drilling. These forests—some 58 million acres' worth in thirty-nine states—were used for recreation; provided critical habitat for some 1600 species of fish and wildlife, including many threatened and endangered species; and contained the sources of drinking water for millions of people.

The "roadless rule" *allowed* logging and road-building on these lands as necessary to reduce the risk of fire, and permitted expansion of oil and gas operations within existing lease areas. Not good enough for the Bushies; the rule became an immediate target for the new administration. The Bushies tried to portray it as flawed last-minute regulation; in fact, it was the fruit of a three-year process that included a record 1.6 million public comments, 95 percent of which supported strong protection for national forests. When industry groups challenged the rule in court, the administration, in March 2001, offered to suspend it indefinitely and began to draft a permanent rollback. Under pressure from Congress and the public, the administration then pledged to uphold the rule—but meanwhile began to allow local forest officials to opt out of it. But the whole purpose of the rule had been to prevent the case-by-case handover of wildlands to loggers, miners, and oil drillers that had gone on for decades.

Forest fires and how to profit from them. In the summer of 2002, fires destroyed thousands of acres of forest across the country and many adjacent homes. Bush quickly blamed anti-logging environmentalists for the accumulation of flammable small trees and underbrush that fueled forest fires, and proposed as the solution a policy he'd favored all along, emergency or no emergency: Rev up the chain saws and turn the loggers loose. He neglected to mention that loggers were not after the small stuff that posed the fire hazard but the big, old, profitable trees—which were not the cause of forest fires and often, in fact, survive them and even help prevent them by shading the forest floor and keeping it cool. Bush also ignored the Forest Service's own research showing that the best way to protect homes was to clear brush in their immediate surroundings. Instead, the Bush plan—bearing the classic **BushSpeak** title, "HEALTHY FORESTS INITIATIVE"— allowed timber companies to log hundreds of thousands of acres far away from homes, as well as old-growth trees in remote forest areas. The plan, in short, was just more Bush corporate welfare in the guise of forest fire prevention.

FREE SPEECH AND CENSORSHIP: SUPPRESSING CRITICISM, DISSENT, AND DEBATE

> *"All Americans . . . need to watch what they say, watch what they do."*
> —White House spokesman Ari Fleischer, September 26, 2001

The Bush administration's assaults on **civil liberties** following 9/11 were accompanied by stepped-up pressures on the public, the media, and Congress to curb any criticism of the administration's policies. These pressures intensified in the lead-up to Bush's war on **Iraq**.

Silencing dissent in the media. Fleischer's ominous warning (quoted above) was in response to a remark by Bill Maher, host of ABC's *Politically Incorrect*, who said shortly after 9/11, "Staying in the airplane when it hits the building, say what you want about it, it's not cowardly," whereas "lobbing

cruise missiles from 2,000 miles away—that's cowardly."
Compounding censorship with censorship—and with lies—
the White House removed Fleischer's comment from the
transcript available on the White House website—then, in
response to criticism of *that*, said it had been a transcription
error. But the remark remained a virtual motto for the right's
thuggish efforts to stifle criticism.

Granted, the media and their sponsors did most of the
administration's job of policing and censoring dissent for it.
But blame the Bushies for setting the tone. Right-wing media
pundits joined Bushies like **Ashcroft** and Fleischer in
painting criticism of the administration as treason and terrorism. Maher, for instance, was immediately targeted as
unpatriotic by right-wing talk show hosts; sponsors pulled
out of his show; an ABC affiliate in Washington, D.C.
dropped it; Michael Eisner, the chairman of ABC's corporate
parent, Walt Disney Corporation, publicly criticized Maher;
and the show was eventually taken off the air. Elsewhere in
the media:

- In the weeks following 9/11, *Washington Post* columnist Michael Kelly wrote that pacifists opposed to war
  in Afghanistan were "on the side of the [terrorist] mur-
  derers"; Ann Coulter accused liberals of "20 years of
  treason"; Fox News host Bill O'Reilly accused antiwar
  protesters of being "un-American"; and Rush Limbaugh
  referred to three prominent Democrats as "Abdullah
  Begala," "Mustafa Stephanopoulos," and "Sahib
  Carville." The slur was as much against Arabs and Muslims: To Ayatollah Limbaugh, those Arabic names
  simply signified "enemies" and "terrorists."

- The country music group the Dixie Chicks were targeted for boycotts and protests—including some organized by the Clear Channel Communications radio chain, a major GOP and Bush supporter—and received death threats after Texas-born lead singer Natalie Maines told a London audience, on the eve of the Iraq war, "Just so you know, we're ashamed the president of the United States is from Texas."

Meanwhile, back in Washington:

- After Ashcroft testified in support of the USA PATRIOT ACT at a House Judiciary Committee hearing in September 2001, committee Democrats called on civil liberties advocates to testify, whereupon the committee's Republican staff, in violation of House rules, ordered all TV camera crews, including C-SPAN's, to leave.
- At a Bush press conference on the eve of the Iraq war, the White House introduced a new format, summoning the press corps in pairs "as if we were in grammar school," a reporter said; not calling any reporters known to ask hard or critical questions, and refusing to answer any; and for the first time, taking no follow-up questions. "Veterans say they hadn't seen such a stifling atmosphere since the 1980s," *USA Today* reported.[145] Before long, regular presidential press conferences were ended entirely. (See **Media, manipulation of.**)

Silencing dissent in Congress. A palpable fear of expressing any criticism of Bush or his foreign and national security policies prevailed in Congress after 9/11, maintained by Republican intimidation and smear tactics. In February 2002, when then–Senate Majority Leader Tom Daschle (D-SD) dared question Bush's vast military spending increases and military goals—what about getting bin Laden, he wondered, the man Bush had declared "Wanted, dead or alive"?—Republicans all but took him out and shot him for treason. "How dare Senator Daschle criticize President Bush while we are fighting our war on terrorism," bellowed then–Senate Minority Leader Trent Lott, who accused Daschle of trying to "divide the country" (this from an old crypto-Confederate and segregationist). Rep. Tom Davis (R-VA) said Daschle was "giving aid and comfort to our enemies." Senate Majority Whip Don Nickles said two House Democrats who accused Bush of misleading the people "both sound somewhat like spokespersons for the Iraqi government." Daschle's opposition to oil drilling in the Arctic National Wildlife Refuge prompted a Republican ad with the caption "Why is America buying 725,000 barrels of oil a day from this man [picture of Saddam Hussein]? Because this man [picture of Daschle] won't let America drill for oil at home."

Silencing dissent by the public. An American Civil Liberties Union (ACLU) report in May 2003 described how, after 9/11, government officials, including local police, went "to extraordinary lengths to squelch dissent wherever it has sprung up, drawing on a breathtaking array of tactics—from censorship and surveillance to detention, denial of due process and excessive force," including police violence against antiwar demonstrators in every part of the country. Examples cited in the report illustrated "how dangerous it has become . . . to criticize the President of the United States or his policies."[146]

- A favorite Bush administration tactic cited in the
  ACLU report was to herd protesters at presidential
  appearances into 'designated protest zones,' out of
  sight of his motorcade (and of most TV cameras) and
  to arrest those who refused to be moved. In city after
  city—St. Louis, Pittsburgh, Phoenix, Tampa—police
  only removed (or arrested) people carrying signs critical of the president, allowing those with pro-Bush
  signs to remain. The purpose was not to protect
  Bush's safety: Those removed or arrested were often
  grandmothers, and some were told, "Lose the sign and
  you can stay." At a Cheney appearance in Indiana, an
  environmentalist was arrested for carrying a sign
  reading "Cheney—19th c Energy Man."
- Before and during the Iraq war, in cities across the
  country, antiwar protesters were denied the right to
  protest or march in traditional locations, such as past
  U.N. headquarters in New York. Hundreds of protesters were injured by police; thousands more alleged
  wrongful arrest and excessive force. Protesters in St.
  Louis said they were maced after being handcuffed
  and that police had hurled epithets like "traitor," "anti-
  American," and "unpatriotic" at them. In New York,
  hundreds arrested for minor offenses like blocking the
  sidewalk were taken to police headquarters and inter-
  rogated about their political affiliations and prior political activities. Police entered the information into a
  database. Requests to see counsel were ignored or met
  with threats of prolonged detention. Protesters in
  Albuquerque, New Mexico, were teargassed and beaten
  with batons before being taken into custody.

- A sixty-one-year-old lawyer was arrested at a mall in Guilderland, New York for refusing to leave or to remove a "Give Peace a Chance" T-shirt he'd bought there. Similar incidents occurred in other cities. As the ACLU noted, at the height of the Vietnam War, the Supreme Court had upheld the right of a protester to wear a jacket emblazoned "Fuck the Draft," even inside a county courthouse. The times they *are* a changin'.

- Ashcroft's Justice Department asserted the right to seize protesters' assets.

- Under Ashcroft's USA PATRIOT ACT (see **Civil liberties**), federal agents could secretly search records of citizens' book purchases, library loans, and website visits without having to show a judge probable cause.

- Ashcroft said those who raised concerns about curtailments of civil liberties—or, as he put it, who "scare peace-loving people with phantoms of lost liberty"—"aid terrorists" and "give ammunition to America's enemies"—which, by the provisions of the USA PATRIOT ACT, meant such critics could be subject to detention, deportation, and even the death penalty.

Silencing dissent in the schools. At schools and universities across the country, students and teachers were harassed, suspended, questioned by authorities and/or threatened with arrest for displaying antiwar or anti-Bush symbols, artwork, and other expressions. In Albuquerque, New Mexico, teachers were suspended for displaying students' poster designs that a principal termed "not sufficiently pro-war." (Pro-war and recruitment posters were allowed to be prominently displayed.) A student in Dearborn, Michigan was sent home after refusing to turn his anti-Bush T-shirt inside out. Police in Iowa threatened to arrest two college students for hanging a U.S. flag upside-down from their dorm window. An Alabama high school senior was spanked three times for remaining silent during the class recitation of the Pledge of Allegiance. A freshman at a Durham, North Carolina college was visited by U.S. Secret Service agents and local police, responding to an anonymous report that she had an "anti-American" wall poster. It was in fact an anti–death penalty poster that noted that Texas under Bush executed 152 people. The agents asked the student if she had any information about Afghanistan or the Taliban. An FBI agent and a campus police officer visited an Iraqi-American economics professor at his office at the University of Massachusetts and questioned him on his loyalty to the U.S. and his opposition the war, telling him they were acting on a tip that he held "anti–American views." The professor, a U.S. citizen, had fled Iraq in 1982 because of similar political witch hunts (he was not a Baath party member).

(See **Media, manipulation of; September 11; War on terrorism.**)

GAY RIGHTS

When asked at a news conference in July 2003 about his view of homosexuality, Bush replied, "We're all sinners." Evidently "sinner" was the first word that came to his mind in connection with gays, and he considered being gay in itself a sin. He went on to reiterate that he opposed gay marriage and said White House lawyers were looking into ways of banning it. (He had signed a bill banning it in Texas.) He did not address the question of same-sex civil unions, but had said in 2000 he would oppose them.

Actually, Bush was trying both to placate the right, which was still enraged over the Supreme Court's June 2003 decision striking down a Texas sodomy law (which Governor Bush had supported), and to soothe moderates with expressions of tolerance (we must "respect each individual"—just not give equal rights to all). The right referred to this as "courting the homosexual lobby," which they warned could put Bush's reelection in jeopardy.

Over Rove's dead body. Republican strategists assured the media that Bush understood where his core support lay. Bush had, it was true, left in place Clinton's executive orders barring discrimination against gays in federal employment and boosted federal spending on global AIDS. But he:

- Opposed giving gay couples legal recognition and the health, tax, and other benefits that afforded.
- As governor, supported a Texas law not only banning gays and lesbians from adopting children or providing foster care, but allowing the state to remove children from the homes of gay and lesbian couples.
- As a candidate, assured a conservative lobbying group he would not appoint people who espoused a "homosexual lifestyle" and refused to meet with representatives of the gay and lesbian Log Cabin Republicans.
- Opposed the federal Employment Non-Discrimination Act, which would ban discrimination on the basis of sexual orientation.
- Continued the military's "Don't Ask, Don't Tell" policy, under which service members who acknowledged

being or were discovered to be homosexual were discharged.

- His Faith-Based Initiative provided federal funding to religious organizations while leaving them exempt from anti-discrimination laws. (See **Church and state**.) Many of these organizations were virulently anti-gay. The Bush White House promised the Salvation Army a regulation protecting it and other religious charities from local laws banning discrimination in hiring gays and lesbians in return for the organization's lobbying support for the Faith-Based Initiative.[147]

- Bush's judicial nominees were largely anti-gay religious ultra-conservatives. And he appointed John **Ashcroft** Attorney General. Ashcroft, to cite but one example, opposed the Mychal Judge Act, which permitted police and firefighters to designate a $250,000 death benefit to the survivor of their choice, even (gasp) a same-sex partner.

Hate crimes laws. Both as governor and as president, Bush opposed expanding hate crimes laws to cover crimes based on sexual orientation—the third highest category of hate crimes after race and religion. Reported incidents more than tripled in the 1990s (while crime rates in general were falling); 1,317 such crimes were reported in 1999. Bush's stated position was, "All crime is hate crime," and no new laws were needed.

The Texas bill Bush opposed as governor, which would have toughened penalties and covered sexual orientation, was introduced after the hate-murders of Matthew Shepard, a gay man, in Wyoming, and James Byrd Jr., a black man who was dragged to death behind a pickup truck in Texas. Bush was denounced by the families of both victims. Without his support for the James Byrd Jr. Hate Crimes Bill, state Senate Republicans were able to kill it—saving Bush from having to sign it and jeopardize right-wing support or veto it and anger moderates.

Bush also refused to endorse a strengthened federal hate crimes law to cover crimes based on sexual orientation and authorize federal prosecution of hate crimes when local officials fail to do so. He bragged about what a great job Texas did in prosecuting the James Byrd Jr. case but omitted to mention that Texas got nearly $300,000 from the federal government to assist with the case only because race was specifically covered under the federal hate crime law. Because sexual orientation was not, Wyoming received no federal help in prosecuting the Matthew Shepard murder, the cost of which resulted in state police layoffs.

As Richard Goldstein remarked in *The Village Voice*, far-right criticism of Bush as too gay-friendly created "the illusion that Bush is standing up to his right flank on gay rights," when in fact, "He will do the right thing only when he risks the least capital to get the greatest return."[148]

GLOBAL WARMING AND CLIMATE-CHANGE POLICY: *IGNORE, DENY, CENSOR*

It was another of those "welcome to the Bush era" headlines. This one pretty much summed up the Bushies' attitude toward global warming: "With White House Approval, EPA Pollution Report Omits Global Warming Section" (*The New*

York Times, September 15, 2002). "For the first time in six years," the article explained, "the annual federal report on air pollution trends has no section on global warming, though President Bush has said that slowing the growth of emissions linked to warming is a priority for his administration."

The report covered a range of air-polluting emissions—most of which had been reduced in the past decade—but not carbon dioxide (CO_2), which is emitted into the atmosphere in increasing quantities by the burning of fossil fuels and is the main contributor to global warming. The decision was yet another Bush administration gift to the oil, coal, and auto industries, which had pushed for CO_2 not to be labeled a pollutant.

The newspapers that year were full of stories of freakish and frightening weather-related phenomena. Chunks of the Antarctic ice cap the size of U.S. states were breaking off into the ocean. The northern tundra was thawing. From the Alps to the Himalayas, the glaciers were melting, threatening to dry up within a few decades the great rivers they fed . Floods ravaged cities in Central Europe. Drought devastated the U.S. agricultural heartland. The oceans were warming. Violent weather was becoming more frequent. Habitats were shifting; infectious diseases were migrating. Most if not all of this was the result of just one degree of global warming. According to the Intergovernmental Panel on Climate Change (IPCC), a group of 2,000 of the world's leading climate scientists, the earth would warm from four to eleven degrees more in the twenty-first century.

But in Washington, denial and deception remained the basis of Bush climate-change policy. The Bushies were just about the last people on Earth even to acknowledge the reality of global warming—much less its connection to the burning of oil and coal. The IPCC concluded in 1995 that, as had long been suspected, the burning of fossil fuels had caused most of the global warming over the past fifty years. The panel reaffirmed that conclusion in 2000, saying the evidence was growing; it was now "very unlikely" that global warming is due only to natural climate variability; and predictions of potentially disastrous climate change due to human activity were becoming more and more reliable.

Bush—determined to hear the *right* answer—asked the National Academy of Sciences (NAS) to review the IPCC's findings. Only after the NAS came back with overwhelming support for the IPCC conclusions did Bush finally concede a link between carbon dioxide and rising temperatures. But by February 2002, he had backslid into casting doubt on its validity. Moreover, the Bushies, at the urging of Exxon-Mobil, orchestrated the replacement of the IPCC chair, an eminent and outspoken climate scientist, with, fittingly enough, an economist.[149]

Kyoto: An environmental *and* foreign relations fiasco. One of the administration's earliest and most infamous anti-environmental acts was its withdrawal from the Kyoto Protocol on global climate change, which aimed at modest decreases in global emissions of greenhouse gases. As a result, the U.S., which had 4 percent of the world's population but produced 25 percent of its greenhouse gases, was not among the 165 nations that signed the Kyoto agreement in October 2001.

Kyoto's goals, reached after six years of study and negotiation, had been so reduced—partly in hopes that the U.S. would sign on—that critics called it "Kyoto Lite." The treaty required thirty-eight leading industrial nations to reduce CO_2 emissions an average of 5.2 percent below 1990 levels by 2012. The U.S.

Oceans of evidence. Even as the Bushies were trying to censor global warming out of existence, evidence was literally flooding in. In March 2002, two pieces of Antarctic ice shelf, each roughly the size of Delaware, broke off and shattered, dumping more ice into the ocean than the previous fifty years' worth of icebergs combined. It was predicted that if temperatures in Antarctica—which were now believed to be the warmest in more than 1,800 years—continued to rise, the whole West Antarctic Ice Sheet could eventually collapse, leading to a rise in sea levels of *fifteen to twenty feet*. The disappearance of large quantities of ice would further accelerate climate warming because 80 percent of the heat and light of the sun is reflected back into space from ice or snow.

- Over the past century, global average temperature increased faster than at any time in 10,000 years, probably as a result of human activity. According to the IPCC, global temperature may rise as much by 2100 as it has since the last Ice Age.
- The 20th century was the warmest, and the 1990s were the warmest decade, of the last 1,000 years. Globally, 1998 was the warmest year on record.
- Atmospheric CO_2, which accounts for about two-thirds of the human-induced greenhouse effect, has increased by about 30

percent in the last 200 years, mostly due to the burning of fossil fuels, and is now higher than at any time in the past 400,000 years and probably the last 20 million. If we continue to burn fossil fuels at the current rate, atmospheric CO_2 will be twice pre-industrial levels by 2030 and three times that figure by 2100.

- Global average sea level has risen between 4 and 8 inches in the past century. A much greater rise in sea level is expected by 2100, threatening low-lying coastal areas around the globe that are home to hundreds of millions of people.

- A warmer globe means more energy in the climate system, fuelling more frequent phenomena such as hurricanes and El Niño, and more extreme weather events. In 1998 (an El Niño year), natural disasters produced more refugees than did armed conflicts and cost around $65 billion.

- Rainfall will decrease in drier areas and increase in wetter ones, increasing the likelihood of floods and droughts worldwide and of conflicts as nations compete for limited water supplies.

- Ecosystems and agricultural zones will shift towards the poles by as much as 200 miles per degree Celsius of average temperature increase, causing lower crop yields and food shortages in some regions. By 2100 up to one-third of natural habitats may be destroyed by climate change. Animal and plant species that cannot adapt or migrate will become extinct.

had committed to a 7 percent reduction. Because of various loopholes, the real reductions would be more like 3 percent.

Whatever the environmental implications of Bush's move, its effect on the geopolitical climate was immediate. It provoked angry demonstrations in European capitals and protests from EU leaders. It confirmed the image of Bush's America as a go-it-aloner, indifferent to the global good, and strained relations with allies the U.S. looked to for support against terrorism. As noted in *Foreign Policy*, the prediction was widespread that Bush's decision "could become a turning point in trans-Atlantic relations."[150]

Bush's alternative "plan": Let the polluters regulate pollution. Bush promised to come up with an alternative to Kyoto—and kept his word, announcing the new plan in a February 2002 report: It was, in effect, to do nothing.

The plan rejected setting any targets for reducing CO_2 emissions, saying that imposing timetables and targets would hamper industry. Instead, the U.S. would rely on industry to come up with solutions and would "adopt a flexible agenda to avoid [God forbid] imposing any regulations." It also backed away from the Bushies' earlier, reluctant acknowledgment that global warming was real, citing "scientific uncertainty" and "competing concerns about energy security," and saying the evidence was not yet clear enough to require CO_2 reductions. (Compare and contrast the Bushies' standards of proof on **Iraq**'s WMDs.)

Then-chairman of the Senate Environment and Public Works Committee, Jim Jeffords (I-VT), called Bush's plan "A love letter to the status quo and the polluting past" and "divorced from the reality of global warming," and said real reductions of CO_2

emissions "have completely fallen off the table." "We've found that these voluntary programs just don't work," said Sen. Joseph Lieberman (D-CT), pointing out that U.S. emissions were now 13.6 percent above the target set in the 1992 "Rio" treaty.

Indeed, by linking CO_2 goals to gross domestic product, Bush's plan *guaranteed* that CO_2 emissions would continue to grow as long as the economy did. By 2010, these emissions were now expected to increase by 31 percent over 1990 levels, versus the 7 percent drop the U.S. had agreed to under Kyoto and the 8 percent cut Europe committed to. Meanwhile, even if emissions remained constant, the earth's climate would continue heating up because of the greenhouse gases already in the atmosphere.

(See **Energy policy; Environmental policy; Science policy.**)

GOD AND BUSH, GOOD AND EVIL

Oh-oh: "I've heard the call. I believe God wants me to run for president."

—George W. Bush[151]

Few things could induce more Bushophobia than Bush's routine, facile references to "good" and "evil," his apparent simple moral certainty, and apparent belief that God was on his and America's side. This was frightening (if not blasphemous) to anyone who, unlike Bush, knew a little history—who could indeed draw what seemed an obvious lesson from **September 11**—and to whom it seemed that moral and religious absolutes like Bush's had been the cause of a lot of trouble for a very long time.

"The lure of this kind of reductionist thinking is not a new one," remarked Arianna Huffington. "Alexander Solzhenitsyn, himself a victim of some of the most horrific evil of the twentieth century, warned against it in *The Gulag Archipelago*: 'If only there were evil people somewhere insidiously committing evil deeds and it were necessary only to separate them from the rest of us and destroy them. But the line dividing good and evil cuts through the heart of every human being.'"[152] Which is what made Bush's tidy moral bisection of humanity so dangerous: Who could tell who would end up cast into the "evil" category—and for what political or ideological sins?

Bush's "good-evil" dualism grew from his deep Christian faith—that prerequisite to Southern political success. Not, God forbid, to question its sincerity. If only. As a *Newsweek* essay on "The Sin of Pride" put it, "Few doubt that Mr. Bush is sincere in his faith. The problem is with the president's evident conviction that he's doing God's will."

"We have had other 'religious' presidents," wrote Catholic theologian Jeffrey S. Siker. "But no other President has so clearly perceived his calling in such epic biblical terms." Siker recounted how Bush got religion following a weekend with Billy Graham in 1986, and how, in 1998, he was inspired by a sermon about Moses as a model of political leadership. (According to Bush's autobiography, his mother later said to him, "He [the minister] was talking to you.") "And so it was," Siker wrote, "that Bush took up Moses' mantle, as he saw it, and entered the Presidential race."

According to Siker, Bush "sees America as a kind of new Israel called by God to be God's people on the international stage. . . . Bush appears to believe that through his redemption in Christ he . . . now has a clear vision of what is morally right and wrong, both personally and as the leader of the free world"—a vision of a "righteous nation vs. evil **axis**," one in which "some people simply deserve the wrathful judgment of God, and if God chooses to use him as the vehicle of punishment . . . so be it, whether for death row inmates in Texas or for governments such as Iraq . . . white hats on one side, wanted posters on the other, with little doubt as to who's on which side of divine truth and justice."[153]

(See **Church and state.**)

GUN CONTROL

As Al Gore put it in 2000, Bush "wants to take the gun lobbyists out of the lobby and put them right into the Oval Office." Gun violence, Gore noted, was straining the health care system to the tune of $2.3 billion annually, but Bush was too deeply in the pocket of the gun lobby to recognize the problem.

So it had been in Texas, where Bush:

- **Ended the state's 125-year-old ban on the carrying of concealed handguns by civilians.** Bush signed this NRA-backed legislation in his first year as governor. In fourteen "may issue" states, local police *could* issue or deny such licenses; Bush's bill made Texas a "shall issue" state, meaning every "qualified" applicant *must* be given a permit. Who is "qualified"? The Violence Policy Center reported in 1998 that 2,000 of Bush's "concealed-carry" permit-holders had been charged with crimes in the previous three years, including five cases of murder and attempted murder.

- **Let guns into churches.** No joke. In 1997 Bush signed an amendment to his "concealed-carry" statute removing houses of worship from the list of places where permit-holders were forbidden to bring their weapons—reportedly because gun-owning clergy members felt deprived of their rights!

- **Shielded gun manufacturers from lawsuits.** Signed a bill that prevented local governments from suing firearm and ammo manufacturers for the public costs associated with gun violence. Said the reason was to curb "frivolous" lawsuits. (Over "frivolous" gun violence?)

- **Opposed mandatory child safety locks on guns.** Handgun Control, Inc. gave Bush's Texas the sixth worst grade in the nation on protecting kids from guns, citing Texas's failure to prohibit juveniles from owning handguns and its prohibition of municipal gun laws that were stricter than state law.

- **Failed to enforce existing gun laws.** The *Houston Chronicle* reported that on Bush's watch, Texas authorities knew of more than 600 convicted felons who may have illegally possessed firearms but did nothing to prosecute them.

- **Refused to close the "gun show loophole" that let**

criminals buy guns without background checks.
Texas hosted nearly 500 gun shows a year—around
twice as many as second-place Pennsylvania. The federal Brady Gun Control bill—which required licensed
dealers to check buyers' backgrounds with a
national data center to prevent sales to felons or
illegal immigrants—exempted non-licensed dealers
selling from "personal collections." As a result, gun
shows and even flea markets had become havens for
gun sales to criminals (or, just as easily, terrorists, as a
couple of cases in 2001 proved). A bill to close this loophole in Texas would have passed "if [Governor] Bush
had lifted a finger to help," the bill's sponsor said.

The day after the bill died, in April 1999, a dozen students
and a teacher were shot to death at Columbine High School
in Colorado by two students using guns bought at gun
shows. Bush then said he supported expanding background
checks, but soon retreated to the position that *federal* legislation should close the loophole—a position he then
retreated *from* as president. He called for "character education" (code for religious indoctrination?) in public schools
to reduce school violence. As the *Economist* observed,
Bush "places the blame for America's frequent gun mas-
sacres on negligent parents, a 'wave of evil' and the culture of violence"[154]—i.e., on anything but guns.

What's good enough for Texas . . . To be sure, as the
Washington Post noted, Bush "has reflected not only the
NRA's line, but the enduring pro-gun passion of the state that
twice elected him."[155] But Bush brought the same views to

Washington. As president, he promised the gun lobby he would only support background checks on buyers at gun shows if the results could be returned instantly. In March 2001, Congress's General Accounting Office reported that investigators had consistently been able to get through "instant checks" and purchase firearms with fake IDs. Effective background checks could take up to a few days. Bush also promised to introduce no new gun controls, except possibly harsher penalties for criminals using guns; support concealed-weapon laws (as he did in Texas); restrict lawsuits against gun manufacturers (ditto); and to oppose mandatory safety locks, photo licensing for handgun purchases, limiting gun purchases to one per month, and requiring manufacturers and federally licensed sellers to report sales to a state authority. "If the NRA could pick a candidate," *The Economist* concluded during the 2000 campaign, it would "undoubtedly" be Bush.

And if the NRA could pick an Attorney General, it would undoubtedly be John **Ashcroft**, who:

- Moved in July 2001 to further protect gun buyers' anonymity by reducing the amount of time that background-check records must be held, from ninety days to one.
- Drafted an "anti-terrorism" bill after September 11 that intruded on Americans' rights in myriad ways, but not the right—even of foreign visitors—to buy guns at gun shows without effective background checks. On September 10, as it happened, a federal court in Detroit convicted a Lebanese man who was a convicted felon of conspiring to ship weapons he purchased at Michigan gun shows to Hezbollah in Lebanon.

- Blocked efforts by law-enforcement agencies to check the Justice Department database to determine if any of his 1,200 or so detained terrorism suspects had bought or attempted to buy guns—which as a federal agent told PBS, "could have really opened up a lot of doors" in tracking down terrorists.[156]

Protecting international gun runners. In July 2001, the Bush administration rejected an international treaty on SMALL-ARMS PROLIFERATION aimed at cutting off the flow of weapons that fed civil wars, terrorists and drug-traffickers and caused half a million deaths a year.[157] The U.S. was, incidentally, the world's leading small-arms exporter. Reading as though from the NRA script, Under Secretary of State for Arms Control John Bolton told a U.N. conference the U.S. would not sign any document that infringed on U.S. citizens' constitutional right to bear arms. Bush "ordered the U.S. delegation . . . to block the main proposals because he fears inflaming the U.S. gun lobby," Britain's *The Guardian* reported.

HEALTH INSURANCE

Before Bush, the U.S. already lagged far behind every other industrialized country in providing medical coverage for all. Under Bush it fell even farther behind, as the numbers of Americans lacking health insurance grew. Bush's "solutions" would enrich the powerful private insurance and HMO industries while leaving individuals and families to fend more and more for themselves.

While the right loved to spread horror stories about Canada's single-payer, state-sponsored health-care system—which, despite problems and rising costs, remained overwhelmingly popular in Canada—it was the U.S. "system" that was truly broken:

- After declining in 1999 and 2000, in Bush's first year as president the number of Americans without health insurance increased by 1.4 million to 41.2 million, largely because they lost job-based coverage as unemployment increased[158] (see **Economy**). In May 2003 the Congressional Budget Office found that nearly 60 million Americans lacked health insurance for at least part of the year.
- In 2001, about 12 percent of U.S. children (roughly 9 million), 21.3 percent of poor children, and 30.7 percent of all poor people lacked any health insurance.
- Lack of coverage was not limited to low-income Americans. In 2001 the number of uninsured people with household incomes of $75,000 or more jumped to 6.6 million, a 14 percent increase from 2000.
- Because of rising costs, more and more small businesses were unwilling or unable to provide health insurance for their employees. In September 2003, it was reported that the share that employees paid for "employer-sponsored" health care jumped by 48 percent since 2000.
- Doctors and hospitals began to turn away **Medicare**

patients as the government cut Medicare reimbursements. And across the country, state governments
drowning in deficits were slashing **Medicaid**
spending and coverage.

Faced with this crisis, the Bushies responded first by blaming
the exploding costs of medical care and insurance indirectly on
patients themselves by blaming lawyers who represent patients
bringing "excessive" malpractice suits (see **Tort reform**). Every
one of the Bushies' other "solutions," oddly enough, aimed to
divert more and more of the nation's health care spending into
the coffers of insurance companies and HMOs.

But there was already plenty of evidence that serving
patients and pursuing profits were fundamentally con-
flicting goals. For corporate health-care providers, every
dollar of revenue actually spent on health care was a dollar
of profit lost. HMOs had become justly notorious and hated
for questioning, delaying, and/or refusing treatments sought
by doctors and their patients (see **Patients' rights**). And
the big, for-profit hospital chains—led by Columbia/HCA,
the hospital giant founded and part-owned by the family of
Dr. Bill Frist, Bush's hand-picked Senate majority leader and
point-man on health-care "reform"—had discovered the
profit value of cutting back staff essential to patients' well-
being, such as nurses and social workers.

Bush's 2003 budget proposal included two "solutions":

- **Tax credits,** ostensibly to help low- and middle-
  income individuals and families obtain health insurance coverage. But the credits were too small ($3000
  for families, $1000 for individuals) for most to buy

insurance on the open market. As these credits would cover only the lowest-cost, lowest-coverage plans, they would likely siphon off the healthiest segment of the market and thus drive up rates for everyone else. Moreover, employers might be encouraged to drop coverage for workers. The net result, therefore, would be no net gain for individuals—but another taxpayer subsidy to businesses.

- **Expanded Medical Savings Accounts (MSA).** These would appeal only to the relatively healthy and wealthy because they required signing up for high-deductible catastrophic coverage that is neither comprehensive enough for the less healthy nor affordable enough for lower-income people. MSAs, too, would cause the healthy and wealthy to opt out of the group market, causing premiums to increase for the remaining, older and sicker members, many of whom would likely end up priced out of insurance entirely. See **Medicaid** and **Medicare**.

HEALTH AND SAFETY REGULATIONS: INDUSTRY WRITING THE RULES

Throughout the Bush administration—from the Department of Health and Human Services (HHS) and its Centers for Disease Control (CDC) to the Environmental Protection Agency and the Food and Drug Administration—noted academic experts were systematically replaced by industry-friendly appointees who were typically former (and future) industry employees or lobbyists. And research findings unfavorable to Bush's big-business clientele were routinely suppressed. As Frank Rich commented in *The New York Times*, "This administration no longer cooks the books merely on fiscal matters. Disinformation has become ubiquitous, even in the government's allegedly empirical scientific data on public health." [159]

For example, the CDC's Advisory Committee on Childhood Lead Poisoning Prevention was charged with assessing whether the government's blood lead level limits are adequate. (According to CDC estimates, in 2002, 890,000 U.S. children ages one to five had elevated levels of lead in their blood, as did more than one-fifth of African-American children living in pre-1946 housing.) Nominations made by the committee and CDC staff members were, for the first time ever, nixed by the HHS secretary (Tommy Thompson). Instead, the Bushies packed the committee with new members affiliated or openly sympathetic with the views of the lead industry—such as Dr. William Banner, expert witness for the industry, who maintained that lead is harmful only at levels seven to ten times as high as those currently deemed safe by the CDC; and Dr. Kimberly Thompson of the Harvard Center for Risk Analysis (HCRA).[160] "Risk analysis" was conservative code for "scientifically" demonstrating that the costs of environmental, health, and safety regulations outweigh the benefits. The HCRA was heavily industry-funded—and twenty-two of its corporate funders had financial interests that would benefit from an easing of regulations on lead. (Bush appointed the HCRA's director, JOHN GRAHAM, to head the White House regulatory "review" office; see **Deregulation**.) Commenting on the new appointees, Rep. Edward

Markey (D-MA) said, "It makes you wonder, if the Bush Administration was seeking advice on whether the sun revolved around the earth or vice versa, would it take Galileo off the committee and replace him with the Inquisition?"

Siding with the junk-food industry. In November 2002, HHS Secretary Thompson, addressing the Grocery Manufacturers Association (GMA), whose members include such companies as Coca Cola, Mars, PepsiCo, and Philip Morris, urged the junk food lobby to "go on the offensive" against critics blaming the food industry for obesity. This was the country's top *health* official siding with pushers of sugar, empty calories, and fat in the midst of a national obesity epidemic. Thompson chose not to ask them why they manufacture the garbage they do and barrage kids with advertising for it, but rather, to tell them the problem was their critics. "To deny that the junk food industry, and its artillery of marketing, has any role in the epidemic of childhood obesity is as absurd as the size of the soft money contributions that some GMA members made to the Republican Party during the 2002 election cycle," the consumer group Commercial Alert wrote Thompson.

Food safety: The Bushies' deadly refusal to beef up inspections. In October 2002, the discovery by Agriculture Department inspectors of a deadly bacterial infection called listeria at a Pilgrim's Pride meat-packing plant in Pennsylvania led to the largest recall of meat in U.S. history. It came in the wake of a listeria outbreak that had caused at least seven deaths and 120 illnesses in the Northeast. A few months earlier, 19 million pounds of meat sold by another packing giant, ConAgra, had had to be recalled.

New regulations mandating tougher inspections for listeria, which consumer groups said would have prevented the outbreak, were initiated by the Clinton administration in its final months, but two years later, Bush's Agriculture Department had still failed to adopt them, insisting that existing regulations and inspections were adequate. (Agriculture's inspector general concluded that department inspectors' failure even to enforce existing regulations had led to the ConAgra recall.)

As it happened, Texas-based Pilgrim's Pride, the fourth largest U.S. poultry producer, was Bush's 10th largest campaign contributor in the 2000 election. In 1989, the company's chairman, Lonnie "Bo" Pilgrim, gave out $10,000 checks on the floor of the Texas Senate while lobbying lawmakers to gut workers compensation legislation. (As they say in Texas, "*Plus ça change . . .* ") From 1992 to 2002, the company was fined more than $500,000 for pollution violations (or should we say, *only* $500,000?)

(See **Pharmaceutical industry; Science; Tobacco.**)

HOMELAND SECURITY: ONE OF BUSH'S TOP TEN PRIORITIES

At least according to Republican polls, a majority of Americans consistently trusted Republicans more than Democrats to protect national security. To be sure, the Bushies forged an image of themselves as implacable defenders of America's security—and I mean *forged*. Time and again, both before and after **September 11,** they let pre-9/11 priorities—tax cuts for the rich, **Iraq** (a counterfeit and counterproductive part of the **war on terrorism**), attacking **labor unions**—take precedence over, and direct resources from, homeland security. When Congress tried to shift $600 million from **missile defense** to counterterrorism, Defense Secretary Rumsfeld *demanded that Bush veto the measure*. That was on September 9, 2001.

During their eight months in office prior to 9/11, among many other warnings ignored and measures not taken (see **September 11**), the Bushies:

- Ignored the HART-RUDMAN COMMISSION (see below).
- Ignored repeated urgings from Sen. Diane Feinstein (D-CA), a member of the Intelligence Committee and chair of the Technology and Terrorism Subcommittee, to restructure U.S. counterterrorism and homeland defense programs, saying the system was "seriously broken and needs to be fixed." On September 10, Cheney's chief of staff "Scooter" Libby told Feinstein he might review her proposals within six months. She replied she did not believe we had six months.
- Despite warnings of Al Qaeda plans to hijack airliners, ignored the recommendation of the Gore Commission on Aviation Safety and Security to improve cockpit security.
- Sound and fury: Announced a new Office of National Preparedness for terrorism within the Federal Emergency Management Agency, but cut FEMA's budget by $200 million.
- Promised, but never delivered, reviews of preparedness for the consequences of a terrorist attack on the U.S.

Hart-Rudman Commission brushed aside by the White House. (Too bipartisan.) Among the Bushies' most notable failures was their politically motivated disregard for the U.S. Commission on National Security, set up by President Clinton in rare partnership with then-House Speaker Newt Gingrich (R-GA), and headed by former senators Gary Hart (D-CO) and Warren Rudman (R-NH). Its final report, issued in January 2001, warned of large-scale terrorist attacks on American soil, and specifically of "a weapon of mass destruction in a high-rise building"; said the country and the government were woefully unprepared; and recommended the creation of a cabinet-level department of homeland security (a measure the Bushies delayed until a year after 9/11). The report also warned of "a terrific sense of the resentment building against the U.S. as a bully . . . exercising its power with arrogance and self-absorption." Congress scheduled hearings on the report for the week of May 7, 2001, but the White House stymied the move: "It did not want Congress out in front on the issues, not least with a report originated by a Democratic president," publisher Harold Evans wrote. The administration announced that instead it was forming its own committee, headed by Cheney—who was expected to report in October. "The administration actually slowed down response to Hart-Rudman when momentum was building in the spring," Gingrich said.[161] In an effort to get the administration moving faster, Hart met with National Security Adviser Condoleezza Rice, who told him she would "pass on" his concerns. That was on September 6.

After 9/11: Tax cuts, corporate interests, and union-bashing *still* come first. Even *after* 9/11, the White House:

- Repeatedly rejected increased funding requests for homeland security, even while doling out tax cuts to the wealthy in amounts that dwarfed those requests.
- Sided with corporations lobbying to oppose tougher safety rules at industrial and commercial facilities.
- Categorically opposed the creation of a new DEPARTMENT OF HOMELAND SECURITY (it was a Democrat's idea, would cost money the Bushies preferred to spend on tax cuts, and, God forbid, expanded federal government)—then, after agreeing to it, held up the legislation for months over Bush's insistence on stripping the department's nearly 200,000 workers of union rights, both to undermine the unions (see **Labor**) and accuse the Democrats heading into the 2002 elections of putting union interests ahead of national security.
- Named as homeland security chief former Pennsylvania Governor Tom Ridge, "a decent politician with no expertise in intelligence or counterterrorism . . . a frivolous choice," wrote Frank Rich.
- Continued to oppose for more than a year any independent investigation of the intelligence failures that preceded 9/11.

A Kmart war on terrorism. In July 2003, amid new government warnings of possible Al Qaeda suicide hijackings, the Transportation Security Administration (TSA) announced it wanted to cut $104 million from the air marshal program to help offset a budget shortfall. (Think $2.5 *trillion* in Bush tax cuts.) Around the same time, an air marshall service memo was leaked, which, citing budget problems, urged that the service drop flights requiring overnight stays. "We're pursuing the war on terrorism with a management style that's pure Kmart," Frank Rich wrote.

The pattern had begun immediately after 9/11, when ranking Democrats and Republicans on the House Appropriations Committee wanted to add $8 billion to the $20 billion Bush had requested for homeland security. They compiled a list of only those areas of vulnerability that both parties agreed were most critical and that had not been funded—including improved security at airports, seaports, power plants, chemical plants and nuclear weapons facilities; hiring more INS and customs agents; upgrades for the FBI's antiquated computers; personnel and equipment for local police and fire departments; and bioterrorism-related vaccine research. *Republicans* came up with estimated funding needs of $1.5 *trillion* over five years.

The Congress members met with Bush, who, according to Rep. David Obey (D-WI), told them: "My good friend [budget director] Mitch Daniels here assures me that our request is adequate. . . . I want to make it clear that if Congress appropriates one dollar more than we have requested, I will veto the bill."[163] He added that he had time to hear four comments before he had to leave. The congressmen told Bush the additional funding requests had come from his own agency appointees. But "there was no give," said Obey, adding that it was "the first time in thirty years that I've been coming down here that any president has told me his mind was closed before the subject was even opened."

The plain fact was that for Bush, tax cuts came first. As Jonathan Chait noted in *The New Republic*, growing deficits were "undermining political support for Bush's signature tax cuts, and a spending outburst, however necessary, would increase the pressure even more."[163] So, in November 2001, Cheney was dispatched to Congress to lobby against further spending on homeland security. Republicans got into line, and the House voted along party lines not to even permit debate on the matter.

Phony "fiscal discipline" versus security. In August 2002, Congress overwhelmingly approved a $5.1 billion spending bill, half of which consisted of desperately needed homeland funding. Bush declared he would veto it. As a result, the Customs Service, Energy Department, and other critical anti-terrorism agencies had to freeze planned improvements. As *The Washington Post* put it, the nonmilitary side of government was still operating, a year later, "as if Sept. 11 never happened."

After the Republicans took control of Congress in November, Bush demanded and got another $10 billion in spending cuts, which further delayed and reduced homeland spending. The Bushies—fresh from turning a projected $5.6 trillion budget surplus into a $4 trillion deficit—touted this as a victory for "fiscal discipline." According to Chait, the White House believed Bush's standing on national security was "so unassailable that he does not need to shore it up. Instead, the administration seems to view his wartime popularity as a massive bank of political capital from which they can withdraw and spend on other, unrelated issues."

Bush's fiscal 2004 budget proposal included $41 billion for homeland security and $100 billion in further tax cuts for the rich. He had also by this point "vetoed several specific (and relatively cost-effective) measures proposed by Congress that would have addressed critical national vulnerabilities," the Brookings Institution noted. The Council on Foreign Relations reported in December 2002 that "America remains dangerously unprepared to prevent and respond to a catastrophic terrorist attack on U.S. soil." Let us count the ways:

- **Laissez-faire security.** Bush did nothing to require owners of power plants, chemical plants (see next item), office buildings, shopping malls, etc., to institute safety measures or obtain terrorism insurance. The administration said, "sufficient incentives exist in the private market to supply protection," and even suggested that owners could be counted on to take the necessary precautions out of their sense of civic duty.
- **Chemical plants left wide open.** In the summer of 2002, the Senate Committee on the Environment and Public Works approved by nineteen to zero a bill toughening security standards at chemical plants, which Al Qaeda was known to have studied. The chemical industry lobbied Republicans to reject it, and the White House stood by while they killed it. In 2002, the *Pittsburgh Tribune-Review* investigated sixty chemical plants and found a pattern of lax security. At a plant in New Jersey where an incident could endanger more than 7 million people, gates were left open and unguarded and there was almost no security at all.
- **Nukes left unprotected, for God's sake.** In March 2002, Energy Secretary SPENCER ABRAHAM wrote to Bush budget director Mitch Daniels pleading for $380 million to protect various Energy Department nuclear

weapons facilities where, he warned, "vast amounts of materials" were stored "that remain highly volatile and subject to unthinkable consequences if placed in the wrong hands. . . . The Department now is unable to meet the next round of critical security mission requirements." The White House approved $26 million, or 7 percent of Abraham's request.[164]

- **Soviet nukes left lying around.** The $1 billion per year the U.S. spent to help secure and/or dismantle the decaying and poorly guarded nuclear weapons facilities scattered across the former Soviet Union— and notoriously accessible to terrorists—was widely regarded as one of the most cost-effective parts of the entire budget. Even before 9/11, a bipartisan Energy Department study had recommended tripling it. In 2002, Bush proposed cutting it, and the following year proposed a bare increase. (See U.S. forces' failure to secure nuclear materials in **Iraq**.)

- **Airports unsecured.** Nine months after 9/11, only 190 of 1,300 bomb-detecting machines mandated by Congress had been installed in U.S. airports; the airport security staffing company Argenbright, which had been found to employ convicts and illegal aliens, was still providing the security at five major airports; the TSA had failed to fix known security flaws that could easily allow bombs to be planted aboard aircraft, and had cut back on marksmanship training for federal air marshals. Fortunately, however, little old ladies were now being thoroughly searched as they checked in, and passengers were being relieved of their nail clippers.

- **Seaports unsecured.** Ninety-five percent of U.S. imports arrived by sea; only one in fifty cargo containers was ever searched. The author of a Council on Foreign Relations report on port security said, "We have virtually no security there." The Coast Guard estimated it would cost $1 billion immediately and $4.5 billion over the next nine years to secure U.S. ports. In the year and a half following 9/11, they received just $318 million. Bush, typically, touted a new program that would screen U.S.-bound cargo at the ports of origin, but provided not one new penny for it in his budget.

- **INS understaffed, overwhelmed, incompetent.** A year and a half after 9/11, the Immigration and Naturalization Service had 14 agents to track down 1,200 illegal immigrants from countries where Al Qaeda was active. Bush turned down an INS request for $52 million (a few billionaires' one-year tax cuts) to hire more agents. INS failure to coordinate with the Social Security Administration still allowed tens of thousands of foreigners to secure illegal Social Security numbers to help create fake identities. (Six months after 9/11, the INS mailed student visa approvals for Mohammad Atta and another of the 9/11 hijackers to their Florida flying school. No one at INS was fired as a result.)

- **First responders double-crossed.** After 9/11, Bush repeatedly posed with firefighters, praised their heroism, and promised first responders (police, fire and emergency medical personnel) the funding they needed for adequate equipment and staffing. In August 2002, he vetoed $5.1 billion approved by

Congress for homeland security, including $340 million for equipping fire departments across the country. That same month Bush promised $3.5 billion to help states equip and train first responders; $2.7 billion of these "new" funds, it turned out, were merely being shifted from existing programs with the same purposes. According to *Congressional Quarterly*, "the Bush plan for funding new responders amounts to double-entry bookkeeping: changes in the ledger that would result in no net increase in the amount of federal funding flowing to cities, counties, and states."

According to Jonathan Chait, Bush's homeland security record barely became a story because "it's simply hard to believe that something as essential . . . would be resisted by any serious person in Washington. . . . It's even harder to believe that the resistance would come from Bush. The president has asserted over and over that he has made homeland security his 'highest priority'. . . . The disturbing truth is that Bush's domestic agenda has not only made the nation less prosperous and less fair, it has also made it less safe."

Divvying up the dollars: Pork and homeland security.
The Bush administration's formula for apportioning the $600 million in federal homeland security assistance for fiscal 2003 clearly reflected terrorists' prime targets—Cheyenne, Wyoming; Anchorage, Alaska; and major cities and landmarks in Iowa, North Dakota, and Idaho. Or so it would seem. In per capita federal anti-terror assistance to the fifty states and Washington, D.C., four of the top five recipients

were Wyoming, Vermont, Alaska, and North Dakota. (The fifth was D.C.) New York was fiftieth. Only Democratic-dominated California, out on the left coast, got less. Well, who would want to blow up Golden Gate Bridge when there's the World Pork Expo in Des Moines?

Iowa, in fact, got $8 million, to train cattlemen and veterinarians to spot signs of biological attacks and to protect livestock. That came to twice as much per capita (or was it per head?) as New York got to protect its people, which was $1.40, compared to the national state average of $3.29, or the $9.78 that went to first-place Wyoming—Cheney's home state.

Even after Homeland Security Secretary Ridge admitted the formula used didn't take into account that certain states' anti-terror needs "are substantially greater than others," the White House reused the same formula for dividing up $1.5 billion for 2004.[165]

HYPOCRISY AND DECEPTION

Yes, yes, *every* section of this book is in a sense about this. But Bush BS was so all-pervasive, so systemic and systematic, and so marvelously brazen, it demanded some special homage.

In a piece titled "For Bush, Facts Are Malleable," *The Washington Post*'s Dana Milbank cited fibs, large and small, from Eisenhower through Clinton, but quoted Brookings Institution scholar Stephen Hess, who said, "What worries me about some of these [from the Bushies] is they appear to be with foresight. This is about public policy in its grandest sense, about potential wars and who is our enemy." [166] The **war on terror** and the threat supposedly posed by **Iraq** were indeed vast fields of Bush BS. But was Bush domestic policy, especially **budget and tax** policy, any less? As Al Hunt noted, "What the president says—the **compassionate conservatism** rhetoric—resonates with many swing voters, usually political moderates or centrists. What he does— slashing taxes and cutting back government's role and responsibilities—is red meat for the base, mostly conservatives."[167] Let us consider just one special category of Bush bait-and-switch:

"The kiss of death." Paul Begala of CNN's *Crossfire* noted a pattern of W. posing at the sites of various social programs, praising their good work—then quietly cutting their funding; "case by case by case of Bush kissing the program and then killing it. It's the kiss of death. You know," he added, "all across America now, charitable groups are saying to the president, 'please don't come here.'"[168] (Columnist Molly Ivins noted another variation on this theme: "When George W. Bush was governor of Texas, many political observers had a theory that whenever he started holding photo-ops with adorable little children, it was time to grab your wallet because it meant some unconscionable giveaway to the corporations was in the wind."[169]) Examples:

- **Job training betrayed.** Days before declaring in his January 2002 State of the Union address that his number one economic priority was "jobs," Bush visited a "youth opportunity" job-training/search center in Portland and lauded the program that funded it. A month later, his 2003 budget proposal cut that program's budget by 80 percent and took the axe to most other job training as well. The White House then lied and said they had *increased* job-training funding for 2004; they counted federal money that had already been sent to the states and spent in 2003.

- **Hopes Six housing deep-sixed.** In June 2002, Bush held a photo-op at an Atlanta housing project founded by the Department of Housing and Urban Development's (HUD) Hopes Six program, on which he lavished praise. His next budget proposal eliminated its funding.

- **Boys and Girls let down.** In February 2003 Bush visited a branch of the Boys and Girls Clubs of America and praised the organization—whose funding his new budget proposal had just cut by $10 million.

- **Don't take him too literally.** Bush cut $50 million from the Even Start Family Literacy Project, another program he had previously lauded.

- **Not much of a reader himself.** In April 2001, Laura Bush, a former school librarian, visited Northeast Neighborhood Library in Washington to kick off "The Campaign for America's Libraries." A week later George announced a $39 million cutback in federal spending on libraries.

- **Children "left behind."** Bush even undermined funding for his own, much-ballyhooed "No Child Left Behind" program (see **Education**).

- **At least Scrooge didn't pretend.** A pediatric training program to help children with cancer moved Bush to tears during a 2001 visit to Egleston Hospital in Atlanta. After the photo-op, he went home and cut funding for it.

- **Winter in America.** In his 2000 campaign, Bush pledged "first and foremost" to "fully fund LIHEAP," the LOW INCOME HOME ENERGY ASSISTANCE PROGRAM, which helps the poor pay home energy bills. His first budget proposal cut its funding by $300 million, or 20 percent. He also repeatedly denied requests for emergency funding for the program during weather extremes.

- **Medical research cut.** After styling himself a champion of health research and calling the NATIONAL INSTITUTES OF HEALTH (NIH) "one of the most successful undertakings in our history," Bush's 2004 budget proposal gave the NIH a 1.8 percent increase (which, inflation-adjusted, was a decrease), most of which was for bioterrorism research, meaning a significant cut in funding for research on major diseases.

- **Under-mining safety.** In August 2002, even as Bush met with Pennsylvania coal miners rescued from a flooded mine and praised their and their rescuers' bravery, he was seeking for a second time to cut the budget of the Mine Safety and Health Administration, which ensured that mines meet safety standards.

- **Rx BS.** Bush praised a bare-bones $350 billion **Medicare** prescription drug plan proposed in Congress, then set aside little more than half that amount in his 2002 budget.

- **Welching on wetlands.** A few months after Bush pledged—on Earth Day, 2001—to protect wetlands, his administration revoked the tougher permit requirements enacted under Clinton to control wetlands-destroying development. A prime example of:

- **Greenscam**. A term for right-wing anti-environmentalists posing as environmentalists—as in Bush posing with trees on Earth Day, 2002, before turning timber companies loose on national forest lands (see **Forests and logging**), and making other solemn pledges to protect the environment while waging the most ferocious war on environmental protections in U.S. history.

- **Americorps abandoned.** As *The New York Times* put it, "Betraying his oft-repeated promise to expand opportunities for meaningful national service, President Bush has not lifted a finger to secure the extra money needed to avoid devastating cuts [20,000 positions] to . . . the federal government's flagship domestic volunteer program."

IRAQ: *W.'S FRAUDULENT WAR*

"Foreigners should stay out of Iraq"
—Deputy Secretary of Defense Paul Wolfowitz, July 2003,
following his return from an inspection tour of the U.S.
occupation forces in Iraq.

In May 2003, the International Institute for Strategic Studies (IISS), a respected British think tank, said al Qaeda was "now reconstituted and . . . more insidious and just as dangerous" as before 9/11. Senate Intelligence Committee member Bob Graham (D-FL) charged that Al Qaeda had been "on the ropes" a year earlier but was able to recover because U.S. military and intelligence resources were diverted to Iraq.

But, now we were safe from Saddam.

Did the Bushies ever tell the public a word of truth about why we were in Iraq, or about the seriousness of the threat Iraq posed? Depending when you asked—the rationale kept shifting as this or that claim fell apart—Saddam had to go because he was (a) defying UN resolutions to dismantle his weapons of mass destruction (WMDs) and continuing to develop chemical, biological, and nuclear weapons, long-range missiles, etc., while threatening the U.S., its interests and allies; (b) conspiring with Al Qaeda and other terrorists; (c) tyrannizing his people.

The basic lie was that war in Iraq was part of the **war on terrorism.** What had suddenly made Iraq—a regional power much diminished by the Gulf War, and which had been kept contained for eleven years—a threat the U.S. could not live with? September 11, supposedly, which Bush said brought home America's vulnerability and made the policy of containment obsolete. *The New York Times*'s Nicholas Kristof observed, "What changed? Not Iraq, but rather our own sensibilities after 9/11." Indeed, surveys showed that a majority of Americans thought some or all of the 9/11 hijackers were Iraqi, and up to 70 percent as of August '03 believed Saddam was involved—beliefs the Bushies were happy to encourage.

An Iraq that served as a WMD factory for terrorists *would* be intolerable. But the Bushies, it turned out, had grossly exaggerated the WMD story *and* invented the linkage with Al Qaeda—who detested Saddam's regime. Meanwhile, Al Qaeda, which had actually attacked us, was still out there—yet a year after declaring Osama bin Laden

"Wanted, dead or alive," Bush never even mentioned him anymore; it was all Iraq all the time.

Indeed, all the Bushies' arguments for war with Iraq applied as well to other countries with which the U.S. was quite cozy or was willing to deal peacefully. Nuclear weapons plus support for terrorists? Try Pakistan—the most likely current home of bin Laden and world headquarters of Al Qaeda. Brutally repressive regimes that export Islamic extremism? Try our good friends the Saudis (see **Oil**). Violations of UN resolutions? Other countries were in violation of ninety-one of those. In February 2003, the very eve of the invasion of Iraq, IRAN—long atop the U.S. list of states sponsoring terrorism—announced it had begun mining uranium and was preparing to start a nuclear power plant, which Iran, sitting on an ocean of oil, had no peaceful use for.

Most perplexing (or revealing) were the Bushies' contrasting approaches to Iraq and its fellow **axis of evil** member (along with Iran), NORTH KOREA. A month before invading Iraq, the administration acknowledged that the North Koreans already had nuclear weapons and that their recent moves could enable them to build four to six new nukes within months—a fact the White House had kept hidden from Congress until after the vote to authorize war with Iraq. The North Koreans also had sufficient bomb-grade plutonium to sell to terrorists or other rogue states, and missiles that might be able to reach the continental U.S. Iraq had none of these things. North Korea had "one of the best, most robust bioweapons programs on earth," according to Under Secretary of State John Bolton. It also had 1.1 million tough, disciplined troops and had just put its 1.8 million reservists on alert *and* threatened a preemptive attack against the U.S. or U.S. forces.

Yet North Korea, the Bush administration kept insisting, was "not a crisis." North Korea was assured the U.S. sought a peaceful solution through talks. *Iraq* was the crisis that necessitated immediate U.S. invasion.

No wonder, in a February 2003 Gallup poll, only 24 percent of Americans polled said they trusted Bush when it came to U.S. policy toward Iraq. Abroad, almost everywhere, huge majorities were intensely opposed to the war, whose real purposes, they suspected, were to (a) take control of Iraq's oil reserves, the world's second largest, and dominate the entire oil-rich Gulf region, (b) show they were acting vigorously against "terrorism," (c) extend Bush's war-leader popularity; (d) distract from Bush's lousy economic record and unpopular domestic policies; and/or (e) erase the Republican/Bush stain of having left Saddam in power at the end of Gulf War I, and avenge Saddam's assassination attempt on Bush Sr.

Anger at the U.S. reached multi-year highs. A poll in Britain, our staunchest ally, ranked the U.S. the world's most dangerous nation—ahead of North Korea and Iraq! The U.S. "has never been so isolated globally, literally never, since 1945," said former National Security Adviser Zbigniew Brzezinski. Little over a year after 9/11, international sympathy and solidarity with the U.S. had, thanks to the Bushies, been replaced by the perception of the U.S. as an arrogant, reckless, imperialistic global bully.

As for the UN inspections process, the Bushies refused to share information about weapons sites with the inspectors while belittling their abilities to find them. Indeed, their biggest fear seemed to be that Iraq would fully comply. The war, it seemed clear, had long been scheduled. The UN was to rubber-stamp it, or be "irrelevant."

Thanks to the Bushies' attempts to bully or bribe nations into backing their war plan—telling them to "line up" as if they were part of some "Warsaw Pact," as Brzezinski put it—America's foreign relations were in tatters and the futures of NATO and the UN were in doubt. The Bushies seemed well on their way to wrecking the international order they so detested.

Iraq and the "Bush doctrine." The hawks around Bush had in fact been determined to force regime change in Iraq ever since Gulf War I. For this group—which included DICK CHENEY, his chief of staff, I. LEWIS "SCOOTER" LIBBY, Defense Secretary DONALD RUMSFELD, Deputy Defense Secretary PAUL WOLFOWITZ, Under Secretary of State JOHN BOLTON, Defense Policy Board chairman RICHARD PERLE, and other Bushies connected with the PROJECT FOR THE NEW AMERICAN CENTURY (see **Foreign policy**)—it was not *just* about oil but about an America that would bestride the world with unrivaled military strength, and feel free to exercise it—even to strike first—when and wherever its interests or ambitions dictated. Iraq would be a pilot project, as it were, for this "Bush doctrine"—and would demonstrate what awaited other unruly regimes.

Disarming the Democrats. War in Iraq also promised Bush & Co. victories at home—starting in the run-up to the 2002 congressional elections. Cunningly forcing a vote in Congress on a resolution authorizing Bush to use force against Iraq meant Democrats would either fall in line behind the commander-in-chief, elevating his colossal stature even more, or be tarred by Republicans as appeasers, Saddam-lovers, traitors. (They "sound somewhat like spokespersons for the Iraqi government," said Sen. Don Nickles [R-OK] of

House Democrats who accused Bush of misleading America into war.)

Meanwhile, the more the country talked about Iraq, the less it talked about the lousy **economy**, a wave of **corporate scandals**, and the Bushies' regressive and unpopular social, environmental, and fiscal policies. (On the very day the war began, Republicans in Congress were working to pass Bush's latest, $700 million tax cut for the rich.) In a talk on White House strategy for the midterm elections, "General" Karl Rove said the focus on Iraq was key to maintaining "a positive issue environment." (As for timing, when asked why the administration waited until after Labor Day to sell the American people on the war, White House Chief of Staff Andrew Card answered, "From a marketing point of view, you don't introduce new products in August.") And indeed, the GOP increased its majority in the House and recaptured the Senate. The victory in the opening battle of the Iraq war was decisive.

Deceiving America into war. "Don't confuse us with facts," might have been the Bushies' motto with respect to Iraq.

- **Iraq–Al Qaeda links.** A steady Bush refrain. Defense Secretary Rumsfeld claimed there was "bullet-proof" evidence of close ties. None was ever put forward, other than the following: a report of a meeting in Prague between an Iraqi diplomat and Mohammed Atta, which was refuted by U.S. intelligence; the fact that an Al Qaeda operative received medical treatment in Baghdad; and the presence of a few hundred Al Qaeda–like extremists (actually backed by Iran) in a region of Iraq out of Saddam's control. The two top Al Qaeda planners in custody told U.S. interrogators Osama bin Laden had rejected the idea of working with Saddam. The Bushies kept this from the public. A tape of bin Laden calling on all Muslims to oppose U.S. aggression against Iraq, while reviling the "godless" Iraqi leaders, was cited by Secretary of State Colin Powell as proof of an Iraq–Al Qaeda "partnership." Would Saddam "pass nuclear technology" to such "partners"?

- **September 11.** The Bushies hinted Iraq was behind 9/11; as National Security Adviser Condoleezza Rice said deviously, "This is a story that is unfolding and is getting clearer, and we're learning more." We, the public, never did.

- **CIA pressured to produce "evidence."** CIA intelligence analysts said they were pressured by senior Bush officials to play up Iraqi links with Al Qaeda and attempts to procure nuclear weapons, whether they existed or not. "It was a foregone conclusion that every photo of a trailer truck would be a 'mobile bioweapons lab' and every tanker truck would be 'filled with weaponized anthrax,'" a former military intelligence officer told *The New York Times*. Powell reportedly told confidants he himself did not believe the arguments he made before the UN in February 2003 regarding Iraq's nuclear program and Al Qaeda connections. "At one point during the rehearsal [for the UN speech]," *U.S. News and World Report* commented, "Powell tossed several pages in the air. 'I'm not reading this,' he declared. 'This is bulls——.'"[170]

- **We were enforcing UN Security Council resolutions.** So the Bushies claimed—even while violating the articles of the UN Charter prohibiting the use of military force except when the UN Security Council had (a) determined there was a material breach of a resolution and all non-military means of enforcement had been exhausted, and (b) had specifically authorized the use of force.

- **Iraq "kicked out" UN weapons inspectors in 1998**. They were withdrawn by the UN after chief weapons inspector Richard Butler accused Iraq of not fully cooperating, and at the behest of the U.S. in preparation for the Desert Fox bombing campaign of December 1998.

- **UN weapons inspections couldn't do the job, Bush said.** But as proof of Saddam's intentions to acquire nukes, Bush in an October 2002 speech cited the weapons inspectors' success in the early 1990s in discovering and dismantling extensive nuclear weapons-related facilities in Iraq.

- **Iraq's nuclear threat.** In the same speech, Bush cited satellite photos (which the Bushies refused to show) as "evidence . . . that Iraq is reconstituting its nuclear weapons program." International Atomic Energy Agency (IAEA) inspectors visited and tested all of the sites in question, and concluded in January 2003 there was no evidence Iraq had revived its nuclear weapon program.

- **The aluminum tubes.** Bush repeatedly claimed Baghdad had made several attempts to buy aluminum tubes "used to enrich uranium for nuclear weapons," even after the IAEA—supported by U.S. Department of Energy scientists—concluded the tubes were not suitable for enriching uranium and were in fact meant for conventional artillery rockets.

- **Uranium from Niger.** In his January 2003 State of the Union address, Bush cited documents detailing alleged

Iraqi efforts to procure uranium from Niger. The CIA and IAEA had established the documents as crude forgeries nearly a year earlier; the CIA had warned the White House not to use the claim in Bush's speech.

"Leakgate": Bush critics beware. Former U.S. Ambassador Joseph Wilson revealed in a July 2003 *New York Times* op ed piece that the CIA had sent him to Niger a year earlier to investigate whether Iraq had tried to purchase uranium there for nuclear weapons, and that he had found nothing to substantiate the story. Wilson's piece broadly criticized Bush allegations and policies regarding Iraq. Several days later, Robert Novak revealed in his syndicated column that two administration officials, whom he would not name, had informed him that Wilson's wife was a CIA operative on WMDs. It is a crime for an official to leak the identity of an undercover intelligence operative; it not only ruins her career as an agent but potentially endangers her entire network of agents and operations. Bush officials reportedly "outed" Wilson's wife to several other reporters as well—according to Wilson, as retribution for his criticisms and to intimidate other critics of Bush Iraq policy. In September, at the CIA's request, the Justice Department began an investigation of the leak. The White House opposed the appointment of a special counsel to investigate, despite Attorney General Ashcroft's close ties to White House officials, particularly Karl Rove, who once worked for Ashcroft and who Wilson and others suggested might be behind the leak. The Bushies assured us they could be trusted to investigate themselves.

- **The "poison factory" in northern Iraq.** In his February 2003 presentation to the Security Council, Powell showed aerial photographs of an alleged poisons and explosives factory in a small area of northern Iraq occupied by Al Qaeda–like militants, Ansar al-Islam. Journalists who visited the site reported seeing only crude barracks and homes.

- **Iraqi drones could hit the U.S.** In October 2002, Bush claimed Iraq was "exploring ways" of using unmanned aerial vehicles (UAVs) "for missions targeting the United States." U.S. officials later admitted the UAVs had a maximum range of several hundred miles. As Peter Beinart wrote in *The New Republic*, "It's hard to believe such a whopping error made it into President Bush's speech by accident."

- **"Mobile labs": Hot air.** The White House, CIA, and Pentagon labeled two trailers found in Iraq after the war "mobile weapons labs," and "the strongest evidence to date that Iraq was hiding a biological warfare program." But State Department and British intelligence analysts had disputed that claim, and in August, it was learned that most of the Defense Intelligence Agency's engineering experts had concluded the trailers were used to produce hydrogen to fill weather balloons.[171]

- **Saddam had WMDs *and used them*.** Bush repeatedly told this lie of omission; he never mentioned that immediately after learning that Iraq had used chemical weapons against the Kurds in 1987–88, the Reagan administration blocked a Senate resolution imposing sanctions on Iraq, and the succeeding Bush I administration gave Saddam's government $1.2 billion in financial credits. Or that the U.S. helped cover up Saddam's poison gas attacks on the Kurds by claiming Iran was responsible. Or that while knowing Iraq was using chemical weapons against Iran, the U.S. gave Iraq satellite intelligence to help it target Iranians. Or that the U.S. supplied Iraq with anthrax. Or that Donald Rumsfeld was Reagan's envoy to cozy up to Saddam in 1983.

- **Saddam's threat to his neighbors.** So, how come the rulers of Turkey, Saudi Arabia, Jordan, Egypt, and just about every other country in the region, not to mention their populations, implored the U.S. not to go to war?

- **Saddam is a "danger to America and the world," and "grows stronger."** He was much more powerful and dangerous in the 1980s, when we supported him; he was dramatically weakened as a result of Gulf War I and UN sanctions through the '90s.

- **Our "coalition" of "many nations."** There was no UN Security Council resolution authorizing use of force. Three of the five permanent members—France, Russia, and China—remained opposed, and despite intense lobbying of the ten rotating members, the U.S. failed to muster the nine votes needed to pass such a resolution. Only three countries—the U.S., U.K., and Australia—sent combat forces to Iraq. Around thirty countries openly voiced support (according to the White House, another fifteen did so anonymously), a small minority of the 184 UN member nations. The thirty supporters did not include a single Arab country. (The list the White House proudly put out did, however, include such strategically important

allies as Bulgaria, Estonia, El Salvador, and the
Solomon Islands—whose prime minister, when asked
about this support, said he was "completely unaware"
of it.) Moreover, much of Bush's "coalition of the
willing" was more of a coalition of the bribed and brow-
beaten—and in most if not all of these countries, huge
majorities of the public remained vehemently opposed.

- **Iraqis would welcome us as liberators.** Many did.
  But within a week, those who *didn't* were turning out
  by the tens of thousands in almost daily demonstrations demanding that U.S. forces leave and featuring
  signs such as "Bush = Saddam." Soon, attacks on U.S.
  soldiers became almost daily, too, and U.S. adminis-
  trators were arresting political opponents.

- **Democracy for Iraq.** Would that be democracy as in
  our ally Kuwait—a country run by a single family and
  where women still could not vote—or as in the more
  egalitarian Saudi Arabia, where neither men nor
  women could vote? The Bushies neither expected nor
  intended to bring true democracy to Iraq. That would
  mean a shift in power from the Sunni minority to the
  Shiite majority (which would strengthen Iran);
  autonomous Kurdish, Sunni Arab, and Shiite regions
  (the dreaded "Lebanonization of Iraq"); and/or a government headed by the democratic Iraqi opposition
  represented by the Iraqi National Congress—all of
  which the State Department, CIA, and our Sunni allies
  in the region vehemently opposed.

- **The reform-the-Arab-world "domino theory."** A
  "liberated" Iraq would supposedly serve as the first
  "domino" in a region-wide democratization. But as

Pakistani scholar Hussain Haqqani noted, "There's a flaw in the idea that invading Iraq will lead to a new Arab dawn: for the last 700 years, Muslims have reacted to defeat not by embracing modernism but by turning inward and grasping religious fundamentalism."[172] Indeed, a secret State Department document (titled "Iraq, the Middle East and Change: No Dominoes") leaked to the press in March 2003 said that even with a new regime in Iraq, the prospects for democracy in the region remained poor. The report was dated the same day Bush made the case that ousting Saddam would promote democracy in the Middle East.

- **No quagmire.** The Bushies, famously allergic to "nation-building," deceived the country, if not themselves, about how many U.S. troops it would take to control postwar Iraq, and for how long. Army Chief of Staff General Eric Shinseki was rebuked by Rumsfeld and Deputy Secretary of Defense Wolfowitz for predicting a prolonged occupation by hundreds of thousands of troops. Postwar developments soon proved him right.

- **The cost.** Soon after Bush's economic adviser Larry Lindsey committed the sin of publicly but conservatively estimating the cost of the war at $100–200 billion, he lost his job. The White House said $50–60 billion. A month later, only days into the war, Bush asked Congress for a $75 billion down payment to cover war costs for six months. In September he requested another $87 billion—more than the combined 2004 Federal budgets for education, job training, and employment and social services. Yale economist William Nordhaus estimated the cost of war and occupation at more than $1 trillion. Yet the budget Bush sent to Congress in February 2003 included no war costs, on the preposterous pretext the White House still hoped to avoid war.

To the victors (and their corporate buddies) . . . Even before the first bomb fell on Iraq, the Bushies were busy doling out over $1.5 billion in oil and reconstruction contracts to firms closely tied to Bush, Cheney, and the GOP. Within days of the start of the war, Cheney's old firm Halliburton was at work in Iraq putting out oil-well fires. (By May, Halliburton was said to be essentially in charge of the Iraqi oil industry.) It was just the start of a bonanza of contracts for a lot of good ol' boys. Invoking "urgent circumstances" clauses, the Bushies bypassed the normal competitive bidding process and just invited a few favored companies to bid. A week after the fall of Baghdad, the construction firm Bechtel Corp., which had close ties to the Reagan and Bush I & II administrations, was awarded an open-ended contract for Iraqi reconstruction worth, just for starters, $750 million, with billions more to come. Over decades, Bechtel had "perfected the dark art of milking intimate government connections for fat, risk-free contracts,"[173] ranging from the San Francisco Bay Bridge and the Hoover Dam to Boston's notorious "Big Dig" expressway, with its staggering cost overruns, to numerous Mideast oil and infrastructure projects. Bechtel had also, according to a director of the International Forum on Globalization, "proven time and again that it has no concern for the social, environmental or human costs of its operations."[174]

Before, during, and for months after the war, top Bush officials, including Cheney, Rumsfeld and Wolfowitz, repeatedly claimed the costs would be offset by far higher Iraqi oil revenues than those estimated by a secret government task force set up in September 2002, whose existence was not disclosed publicly until October 2003.

JUDICIAL NOMINATIONS: SEEKING TOTAL RIGHT-WING CONTROL OVER THE COURTS

Perhaps nothing Bush did domestically would affect the country more profoundly and lastingly than his nominations to the federal judiciary. The goal of the right was to pack the federal courts with ideologues who were ready and eager to reverse decades of progress on civil rights, privacy rights, women's reproductive rights, religious freedom, and environmental, health, and safety protections—whose views were "out of whack with those of the vast majority of Americans," as *The New York Times* remarked. These judges, appointed for life, would leave the Bushies' far-right stamp on almost every aspect of American life for decades to come. As former Justice Department official in the Reagan administration, Clint Bolick, told *The Washington Post*, "Everyone on the right agreed in 2000 that judicial nominations were the single most important reason to be for Bush."

As of January 2002, judges appointed by Republican presidents controlled seven of the country's thirteen circuit courts of appeals, where forty-two seats were vacant.

If all of Bush's nominees as of that date were approved, Republican-nominated judges would control eleven of the thirteen appeals courts, and by the end of Bush's term, probably all thirteen. Most, if not all, of these judges would have been chosen for their commitment to right-wing judicial activism. Here, too, the campaign waged by Bush and the right was based on a monstrous lie: *They* wanted to keep politics out of the process and appoint judges that were neutral and non-ideological—"restrained" judges who would "follow the law, not make it"—while the "left" wanted "activist" judges who would use the bench to *make* law in keeping with their own "liberal" ideas and values. (Let us not dwell on the irony of the single most spectacular case of judicial activism in U.S. history—the U.S. Supreme Court decision in *Bush v. Gore*, a decision whose obvious political motivation and lack of legal precedent shocked most legal scholars. See **Election 2000**.)

Compounding this hypocrisy was the Republican canard of "obstructionism" by Democrats of Bush's nominees and of a vacancies "crisis" on the federal courts. As of November 2003, the Senate had confirmed 172 of Bush's judicial nominees in less than two years—bringing vacancies on federal courts to the lowest level in thirteen years—and Democrats had blocked only six. But that was enough for the right to keep up a nonstop "obstructionism" shriek. (An "outraged" Bush warned he "didn't like it one bit" following the rejection of PRISCILLA OWEN for the Fifth Circuit Court.)

The right carried on as though the Senate's job—in total contrast with the behavior of Senate Republicans during the Clinton years—was merely to rubber-stamp the president's judicial nominations, no questions asked. "Republican hypocrisy here is especially impressive," wrote Michael Kinsley in *Slate*. When Clinton was appointing judges, the senior Judiciary Committee Republican, Sen. Orrin Hatch, called for "more diligent and extensive . . . questioning of nominees' jurisprudential views." Under Bush, Hatch, now the committee's chairman, "says Democrats have no right to demand any such thing."[175]

Just look at MIGUEL ESTRADA, Bush's nominee for a seat on the crucially important D.C. Circuit Court (a seat open only because Republicans blocked a Clinton nominee—indeed, two Clinton nominations to the D.C. Circuit were blocked because Republicans said the circuit had too many judges already; Bush sent nominations for both those seats). Estrada's confirmation got stuck in a months-long filibuster by Democrats because neither he nor the White House would provide any information about his judicial views. Republicans, Kinsley wrote, were "hoarse with rage that Democratic senators want to know what someone thinks before making him or her a judge." Naturally, they also accused the Democrats of being anti-Hispanic. (With forty-two circuit court vacancies to fill, Estrada was, as of May 2003, Bush's only Hispanic nominee—and the major Hispanic organizations opposed him.)

The Republicans didn't just complain—they devised strategies to get around normal Senate confirmation proceedings. Bush "fired" the American Bar Association (ABA) as official auditor of judicial nominations because the ABA gave some Republican nominees a low grade. In January 2003, Hatch's Judiciary Committee began scheduling nominees' hearings in bunches, preventing senators from reviewing each nominee with any care, and "ushering in an era of conveyor-belt confirmations," *The New York Times* commented, noting that during the Clinton years, the committee took six months or more to consider the number of nominees Hatch's committee reviewed in two weeks—and these nominees' records "cry out for greater scrutiny."[176]

More disturbing still were calls by the Senate Republican leadership, backed by the White House, to change the Senate filibuster rule whereby forty-one senators could prevent debate from ending—a time-honored parliamentary tool for ensuring bipartisan consultation. Republicans—prolific filibusterers when they were in the minority—now called the filibuster unconstitutional.

Bush's Circuit Court of Appeals Nominees / Appointees.[180]

Jay Bybee, Ninth Circuit (California, Oregon, Washington, Arizona, Montana, Idaho, Nevada, Alaska, Hawaii, Guam). Critics called Bybee an extremist, hostile to **abortion** and **gay rights,** and pointed out his narrow view of individual rights and of federal power vis-à-vis the states. Bybee characterized gay rights laws as nothing more than government-sponsored "preferences" for "homosexuals,"[178] and criticized the Supreme Court's decision in a landmark equal protection case, *Romer v. Evans*, in which the court struck down Colorado's Amendment 2, which barred municipalities from enacting laws protecting gays from discrimination. He argued that U.S. senators should be elected by state legislatures, not by voters. *Confirmed.*

Deborah Cook, Sixth Circuit (Kentucky, Michigan, Ohio, Tennessee). "[R]egularly sides, as a state judge, with corporations. In one case she maintained that a worker whose employer lied to him about his exposure to dangerous chemicals should not be able to sue for his injuries."[179] Ruled that sexist workplace comments don't necessarily prove bias in discrimination cases. Anti-choice, of course. Member of the **Federalist Society**—a national network of right-wing lawyers—as were a great many of Bush's judicial nominees. *Confirmed.*

Miguel A. Estrada, D.C. Circuit, the second most important court in the country after the Supreme Court. With jurisdiction over many federal agencies, the D.C. Circuit rules on environmental, civil rights, workplace, and consumer protection statutes affecting the whole country—and on what federal agencies can and can't regulate; thus it had long been targeted by conservatives seeking to limit federal power to regulate corporations. The confirmation of Estrada, along with Bush nominee John Roberts (confirmed May 2003), would give the already conservative[180] D.C. Circuit six Republican and four Democratic appointees, with two seats still vacant, awaiting Bush nominations.

Estrada, regarded by Republicans as potentially the first Hispanic Supreme Court justice (three current Supremes—Ginsburg, Scalia, and Thomas—were promoted from the D.C. Circuit), was dubbed the "stealth candidate" because of the difficulty of getting any information out of him or the White House about his judicial views on privacy, reproductive rights and other issues. This led to a months-long filibuster by Democrats on the Senate Judiciary Committee. Estrada claimed he never read Supreme Court decisions and could not recall discussing any high-court rulings while working in the Solicitor General's office from 1992 to 1997. The White House refused to hand over recommendations Estrada wrote during that time, calling them "highly privileged." What was known about Estrada, however, made him eminently qualified, from the right's point of view: He was one of the architects of the Bush 2000 campaign's legal strategy in the Florida recount battle; and his former superior in the Solicitor General's office, Paul Bender, said he was a "right-wing ideologue" who "couldn't be trusted to state the law in a fair, neutral way."[181] *Nomination withdrawn September 2003.*

Jeffrey R. Howard, First Circuit (Maine, Massachusetts, New Hampshire, Rhode Island). Legal counsel to Bush for President (2000) campaign, New Hampshire. "Pro-life"; supported banning certain safe, common abortion procedures and requiring parental notification before young women could receive abortion services.[182] *Confirmed.*

Carolyn Kuhl, Ninth Circuit. Kuhl's appointment was opposed by environmental, labor, civil rights, and women's groups because of her record of hostility to abortion rights, privacy rights, and public access to the courts, and her slipperiness in answering senators' questions during confirmation hearings. As a lawyer in Reagan's Justice Department, Kuhl, a Federalist Society member, argued in favor of overturning *Roe v. Wade*; prohibiting federally funded family-planning clinics from even informing women that abortion is a legal option; and granting tax-exempt status to Bob Jones University, a fundamentalist Protestant school in South Carolina that promoted racial segregation and anti-Catholic bigotry. As a state judge in California, Kuhl took extreme positions friendly to corporate defendants and hostile to citizen litigants and whistle-blowers.

In her Senate hearings, *The Los Angeles Times* noted, Kuhl "tried to minimize her involvement or recast" her positions in cases involving sexual harassment, privacy claims, and labor relations. "Yet in nearly every instance, when senators pointed out the discrepancy between her testimony . . . and the written record, she recanted."[183] Kuhl "backpedaled furiously" on her prior "objectionable positions on civil rights, abortion and privacy," *The New York Times* noted. "It is also clear, given this administration's track record, that she was chosen precisely because of the actions she now seeks to distance herself from."[184]

Michael McConnell, Tenth Circuit (Colorado, Kansas, New Mexico, Oklahoma, Utah, Wyoming). Here, at least, senators knew where the nominee stood. McConnell, a Utah law professor and Federalist Society member, was a self-proclaimed "pro-life leader" who compared *Roe v. Wade* to the 1857 Dred Scott decision upholding slavery; suggested that the Constitution's equal protection clause should apply to fetuses; and argued that the federal law enacted in 1994 to prevent violence against abortion clinics and their staffs is unconstitutional.[188] McConnell also:

- Opposed the Supreme Court's view that the Constitution guarantees a right to privacy.
- Contributed to the brief supporting the Boy Scouts' discrimination against gays in *Boy Scouts of America v. Dale.*
- Severely criticized Supreme Court rulings (a)

upholding voluntary affirmative action programs; (b) holding that racial segregation in public schools in D.C. was unconstitutional; (c) holding that employers can be liable for sexual harassment committed by supervisors; and (d) recognizing "one person, one vote" ("wrong in principle and mischievous in its consequences," McConnell wrote).

- Argued that businesses should be exempt from laws against employment discrimination if they have a religious or nonreligious objection to homosexuality.
- Praised a Supreme Court ruling striking down the Violence Against Women Act, which required states to provide legal remedies for women injured by gender-motivated violence.
- Opposed the Supreme Court's landmark 8–1 ruling that the federal government had the authority to withhold tax-exempt status from Bob Jones University because of its racially discriminatory policies.
- Argued that Mormons should be exempt from laws against polygamy.

McConnell, of course, assured senators that none of these views would have the slightest prejudicial influence on his decisions as a judge. Good enough, apparently: *Confirmed.*

Priscilla Owen, Fifth Circuit (Texas, Louisiana, Mississippi). Rejected in 2002 by the then-Democratic-controlled Senate Judiciary Committee; subsequently renominated by Bush and filibustered by Democrats beginning May 2003. On the Texas Supreme Court, where she was regarded as among the most extreme right-wing judicial activists, Owen seemed "all too willing to bend the law to fit her views, rather than the reverse" and "could usually be counted upon . . . to side with business," according to the *Austin American-Statesman*.[189] The *Houston Chronicle* commented, "It's saying something that Owen is a regular dissenter on a Texas Supreme Court made up mostly of other conservative Republicans," and cited Owen's "distinct bias against consumers and in favor of large corporations."[187]

Charles W. Pickering, Sr., Fifth Circuit. The Senate Judiciary Committee rejected Pickering in 2002 over questions about his record of support for racial segregation, opposition to civil rights and voting rights, and possible links with a segregationist organization in his native Mississippi. (Karl Rove obscenely called the rejection a "judicial lynching.") Bush renominated Pickering in January 2003— just weeks after Pickering's old crony TRENT LOTT had to step down as Senate Majority Leader after carelessly getting in touch with his inner segregationist in public. Bush finally used a recess appointment to bypass Congress and put Pickering on the Circuit bench.

In 1959, Pickering published a law review article recommending ways to strengthen Mississippi's felony laws against interracial marriage. The state legislature amended the law accordingly, giving Mississippi the country's toughest criminal penalties for interracial marriage. As a state senator in the 1970s, Pickering:

• Called for a constitutional convention to ban school desegregation.

- Cast several votes to block full extension of voting rights to African-Americans as part of Mississippi's resistance to implementing the Voting Rights Act, and cosponsored a resolution calling on Congress to repeal the VRA.
- Voted twice for reapportionment plans that helped keep the State Senate entirely white.
- Voted twice to appropriate funds to the notorious Mississippi Sovereignty Commission (MSC), an agency established immediately after the Supreme Court's landmark school desegregation decision, *Brown v. Board of Education*, for the purpose of opposing integration efforts in Mississippi, and which used taxpayer dollars to help fund the racist White Citizens Council (WCC).

As a District Court judge from 1990 on, Pickering almost always dismissed claims or granted summary judgment in cases involving racial and gender discrimination. In the 1994 trial of a man who burned an 8-foot cross on the lawn of an interracial family, Pickering went to extraordinary lengths to have the sentence reduced, such as contacting the Justice Deparment—"a manifest violation"[188] of the judicial ethics code; threatening to throw out the conviction and order a new trial if prosecutors didn't drop some of the charges (they did); and calling the crime a "drunken prank." (The defendant's friend had previously fired shots into the same home.) In one voting-rights case, Pickering complained that majority-black districts would produce "polarization." In another, he called the one-person one-vote doctrine "obtrusive" and said the public is more concerned with saving tax dollars than remedying voting rights violations.

Pickering's record on women's rights was equally distinguished.

- As a Mississippi State Senator, he voted against state funding for family planning programs and for a resolution calling for a constitutional amendment banning **abortion**.
- As a District Court judge, in 99 published opinions and approximately 600 unpublished opinions, Pickering never once ruled for the plaintiff in a claim of gender discrimination.

Pickering also lectured defendants on the need to embrace religious belief, quoted from the Bible when handing down sentences, and, while president of the Mississippi Baptist Convention, declared that the Bible should be "recognized as the absolute authority by which all conduct of man is judged." Muslims, Hindus and Buddhists included, presumably.

Pickering was "not exactly known for his scholarly acumen," either, Michael Crowley noted in *The New Republic.* "He has been reversed twenty-six times—fifteen of them for rulings that departed from 'well-settled principles of law.'"[189] *Approved by Judiciary Committee Oct. 2003 by 10–9 party-line vote.*

William Pryor, Eleventh Circuit (Alabama, Florida, Georgia). Pryor, Alabama's attorney general, declared that *Roe v. Wade* "ripped the constitution and ripped out the lives of millions of unborn children." When thirty-six state attorneys general urged the Supreme Court to uphold the Violence Against Women Act, Pryor alone argued that the law was unconstitutional. He submitted a brief supporting Texas' law criminalizing gay sex. He testified in favor of repealing a key part of the Voting Rights Act. He urged the Supreme Court to take away the rights of 5 million state employees to sue under the Family and Medical Leave Act. He referred to the Court as "nine octegenarian lawyers" for deciding to delay an execution. Pryor was a founder of the Republican Attorneys General Association, which, it was revealed in July 2003 during Pryor's Senate confirmation hearings, actively solicited campaign contributions for its members from banking, insurance, HMO, and other corporate executives "in the very fields entrusted to the public officials," *The New York Times* noted. "The money was funneled to the Republican National Committee, where donors were kept secret and the committee was free, in turn, to donate $100,000 to Mr. Pryor's campaign."

Jeffrey Sutton, Sixth Circuit. As an activist and as a lawyer, Sutton argued that the courts should limit Congress's authority to enact environmental, civil rights, hate crimes, and disabilities laws. He was influential in a number of 5-4 Supreme Court rulings in such cases; for example, in 2001 he persuaded the court to rule against a nurse with breast cancer on the ground that the Americans With Disabilities Act does not apply to state employers. *Confirmed.*

Timothy Tymkovich, Tenth Circuit. As Colorado solicitor general, Tymkovich defended Amendment 2, which repealed and prohibited local laws against anti-gay discrimination.

He described gay rights laws as "special legal protections for homosexuals," and lumped homosexuality with a variety of "immoral" and harmful behaviors, including cockfighting, bestiality, suicide, drug use, and prostitution.[190] *Confirmed.*

Victor Wolski, Court of Federal Claims, which hears "takings" and other property rights claims against the federal government brought by developers and property owners affected by environmental regulations. Wolski devoted his legal career to promoting an extremist view that environmental rules amount to unconstitutional "takings" of private property. Boasted in 1999 that "every single job I've taken since college has been ideologically orientated [sic], trying to further my principles . . . "[191] *Confirmed.*

Packing the lower courts. While Democratic senators "waged a few high-profile battles over Bush's nominees to higher [appellate] courts," noted Clay Risen in *The New Republic*, there was little attention or resistance to the administration's "steady politicization" of the lower, district courts. But these, Risen pointed out, make most of the important decisions, the ones the appellate courts defer to, and serve as "farm teams" for higher courts. By May 2003, Bush had appointed 100 district court judges, who as a whole "have been at least as ideologically oriented" as the more high-profile names at the appellate level, Risen noted.[192] A few examples—all (except James Leon Holmes) confirmed by the Senate:

John Bates, D.C. District. Formerly a lawyer in KENNETH STARR'S independent counsel's office. Soon after his appointment to the D.C. District, Bates ruled against Congress's General Accounting Office in its suit for access to Dick Cheney's "energy task force" records (see **Energy policy**).

Paul Cassell, Utah District. Vigorous proponent of overturning the Supreme Court's *Miranda* ruling, the landmark 1966 decision requiring police to read suspects their rights.

Ronald H. Clark, Texas Eastern District. As a member of the Texas House of Representatives, sponsored bills to limit access to reproductive health services, e.g., placing zoning restrictions on clinics. Though confirmed in October 2002, Clark, "with Bush's blessing," refused his appointment until after he was reelected to the Texas House to ensure that the Democrat didn't win—"an unheard of step that blurs the line between the White House's political interests and its duty to promote an independent judiciary."[193]

James Leon Holmes, Arkansas Eastern District. A former president of Arkansas Right to Life, Holmes wrote articles asserting that "the woman is to place herself under the authority of the man," comparing the pro-choice movement to Nazism, and arguing that *all* abortions should be banned because "conceptions from rape occur with approximately the same frequency as snowfall in Miami." (A study published in 2000 found that about 25,000 pregnancies a year in the U.S. result from rape.[194])

Laurie Smith, Nebraska District. Testified before the judiciary committee of the Nebraska Legislature in support of a bill that would recognize an embryo at all stages of development as a separate, independent victim of a crime—effectively undermining abortion rights by granting the embryo legal status separate from and equal to that of the woman.

Jay Zainey, Louisiana Eastern District. From that bench, he ruled in April 2002 against a woman who was denied access to abortion services while in prison—something no federal court had ever done.

The Bushies also discarded traditional checks and balances in the *process* of nominating district court judges, Risen noted. A Justice staffer told him, "They have systematically ignored bipartisan commissions [and] traditions of consultation that . . . have been in place for years in order to make these ideological appointments and political rewards for jobs well done."[195]

LABOR AND WORKERS' RIGHTS: *"A MISSION TO ATTACK WORKING PEOPLE."*

As a good old-fashioned tool of corporate interests, Bush was a natural enemy of organized labor and workers' rights. The Bushies' strategy was to wage a broad war on organized labor—block strikes, prevent organizing, weaken unions— in order to weaken this traditional and vital Democratic base of support, yet at the same time, woo labor away from the Democrats. A conservative analyst called it "a sophisti- cated White House strategy to divide and conquer the labor movement."[196]

There was much glee, and exaggeration, on the right

about how Bush was cutting into labor's traditional support for the Democrats and forging alliances with major unions like the Teamsters and the AFL-CIO. But in fact, Teamsters Vice President Chuck Mack called Bush's policies "a night-mare for workers," the AFL-CIO Building Trades Department labeled them "nothing short of a declaration of war on construction workers," and an electrical workers' union leader told *The New York Times*, "He almost seems to have a mission to attack working people."

In just his first six months on the job, Bush nominated a host of anti-labor and anti–workplace safety lawyers for key government posts, directly attacked unions and labor organizing, and aggressively wiped out a decade's worth of progress on workplace safety standards with a barrage of executive orders and rule changes, which:

- Ended PROJECT LABOR AGREEMENTS, which encour-aged union contracts on federally funded construc-tion projects. (The courts later found this order illegal.)
- Abolished LABOR-MANAGEMENT PARTNERSHIPS in fed-eral agencies, a Clinton measure giving employees a voice on how to do things better, cut costs, etc. Bush was following the recommendation of the right-wing HERITAGE FOUNDATION—Labor Secretary ELAINE CHAO's previous workplace—to "reassert managerial control of government" and reduce employee and union involvement in decision-making.
- Required government contractors to post notices instructing workers on how to object to union dues—without requiring the posting of workers' rights with

respect to joining or organizing unions. (Also later found illegal by the courts.)

- Repealed Clinton's RESPONSIBLE CONTRACTOR RULES that denied government contracts to chronic corporate violators of environmental, labor, and safety laws.
- Repealed Clinton's BLACK LUNG REGULATIONS that helped miners dying from black lung to claim benefits from the mining industry. The regulations went into effect two days before Bush's inauguration, but the compassionate conservative persuaded a federal judge to suspend them.

Workplace safety: Bush's insult to injury. On an average day, seventeen Americans die from on-the-job injuries, and some 18,000 suffer occupational injuries and illnesses, a third of which—1.8 million per year—are repetitive motion injuries. The first major piece of legislation President Bush signed into law repealed ERGONOMICS REGULATIONS designed to prevent these injuries and compensate victims. The rules—enacted under Clinton—were opposed by business interests that were among the biggest GOP contributors. The workplace improvements they mandated would have cost businesses around $4 billion a year. *Not* making the improvements would cost an estimated $50 billion in lost wages, sick days, and lowered productivity—but workers themselves would shoulder much of those costs. For Bush, it was, as it were, a no-brainer.

Instead, the Bushies, as usual, proposed purely "voluntary" guidelines for businesses. To further ensure non-enforcement, the Bushies cut the Occupational Safety and Health Administration (OSHA) budget and staff, especially in the areas of enforcement, training, and outreach.

Bush v. airline workers: A Reaganesque debut for Dubya.
In March 2001, Bush blocked a strike by Northwest Airlines
mechanics, cleaners, and custodians—in order to protect
"the hardworking people of America" from travel disruption,
said Bush, the friend of the working man. He announced the
move at a rally in South Dakota to win support for his tax
cuts for the richest Americans.

With negotiations then in progress at four other major
carriers, Bush declared he would prevent any other airline
workers' strikes, thus openly putting the federal government
on the side of the airlines and undercutting the position of
the workers. For several years, the airlines, Northwest
included, had earned record profits and awarded big pay
increases to top executives, while taking a hard line on
wages, benefits, and job security.

Northwest—whose management immediately praised
Bush's action—had donated $70,000 to Bush's inaugural
committee. It was second only to American Airlines in
industry contributions to federal candidates in the 2000 election. The industry overall gave Bush $184,000—three times
more than to Gore. Before becoming Bush's labor secretary,
Elaine Chao sat on Northwest's board.

Eleven days after September 11, following intensive
industry lobbying, Bush signed a $15 billion AIRLINE BAILOUT
package. None of that money went to help laid-off airline
workers. "The only people who got bailed out were the shareholders," said Sen. Peter Fitzgerald (R-IL). "The one million
airline employees were left twisting in the wind."

Miners shafted. In August 2002, Bush met with Pennsylvania coal miners rescued from a flooded mine and praised

their and their rescuers' bravery. Meanwhile, he was seeking for a second time to cut the budget of the Mine Safety and Health Administration, which ensured that mines meet safety standards. A Labor Department inspector's report had just concluded that the mine agency lacked enough inspectors to complete legally required inspections. An Alabama mine where thirteen miners died in 2001 had thirty-one outstanding safety violations that went unchecked because of a lack of government inspectors, a Senate subcommittee was told.

War on terrorism as labor-bashing device. Throughout 2002, Bush and congressional Republicans refused to enact legislation establishing a new **Homeland Security** department unless the president was empowered to strip the department's roughly 190,000 employees of union and collective bargaining rights and job security. Employees' jobs and salaries would be safe for at least a year, Bush generously promised. Union reps and members worried that Bush would use this "flexibility" to shut down some, if not all, of the seventeen unions representing tens of thousands of employees, such as those representing Customs Service inspectors and Border Patrol agents.

Month after month, Bush promised to veto any compromise plan—such as one in which only employees primarily engaged in intelligence or terrorism investigation would lose their civil service protections. The delay enabled him to accuse Democrats during an election season of putting union "special interests" ahead of national security. Critics noted the administration could not provide any example of collective bargaining rights having impeded national security—and that some of the strongest unions in the country were at security agencies: local police and firefighter forces.

- In January 2003, the Bushies barred the 56,000 federal baggage and passenger screeners employed by the recently formed Transportation Security Administration from joining a union, saying collective bargaining was "not compatible with the flexibility required to wage the war against terrorism."[197]

Bush v. minimum wage. Business interests and their Republican servants had long dreamed of eliminating the minimum wage. (At $5.15 an hour, they felt, workers had it too good.) The Bush administration repeatedly tried to turn efforts to raise the federal minimum wage into opportunities to undermine it.

The federal minimum wage (MW) is a floor; states are permitted to enact higher MW requirements of their own—which, as of 2002, eleven states had done. The federal MW had not been raised since 1997, when it went from $4.75 to $5.15. Because of inflation, the MW would need to be raised to $8.05 to match the 1968 level in constant-dollar terms. As the chairman of President Reagan's Council of Economic Advisers, Murray Weidenbaum, told the *Wall Street Journal*, rather than undertake the "painful political process" of eliminating the MW outright, his administration had decided simply to let inflation erode it away.[198] Republicans had maintained this approach ever since.

In 2001, 2.2 million U.S. workers were paid at or below MW, while about 34 percent of women and of African-Americans, 45 percent of Hispanics, and one-quarter of the overall workforce earned less than the so-called "living wage" of $8.63—the amount officially deemed necessary to keep a family of four out of poverty.

A measure introduced by Sen. Edward Kennedy (D-MA)

in 2002 would have raised the MW by $1.50, to $6.65, by 2004. The Bushies and congressional Republicans, siding with business groups, blocked the Kennedy bill by opposing any increase in the federal MW unless individual states were allowed to opt out, and unless measures were attached gutting federal wage and hours laws, such as overtime pay, and providing huge tax breaks for businesses. Allowing states to opt out would eliminate the "floor," meaning the actual MW could go down; indeed, it might well set off a "race to the bottom" in which states, competing to attract jobs, instituted lower and lower wage MWs or eliminated them entirely.

Workfare recipients to be paid less than minimum wage. In the Bushies' March 2002 welfare overhaul proposal, they wrote that "welfare-to-work" payments were no longer to be considered wages and were therefore not entitled to be covered by minimum wage law or to any other legal benefits. "The fact that Bush thinks struggling families can pull themselves out of poverty while earning even less than minimum wage is an affront to society," said Kim Gandy, president of the National Organization for Women.

Cutting off overtime pay. In March 2003, the administration proposed new regulations that would increase by 1.3 million the number of low-wage workers who qualify for overtime pay, but cut by many more the number of higher-paid, white-collar workers who qualify—including nurses, police and military officers, and medical and computer technicians—by reclassifying them as administrative or professional personnel.

Business groups naturally preferred paying time-and-a-half to low-paid workers than to higher-paid ones. Labor advocates predicted that the number of workers cut off from overtime would far exceed the administration's estimate of 640,000—the Economic Policy Institute estimated 8 million—and that many would be given bogus managerial job titles just to disqualify them from overtime pay. "It's an absolute disaster for white-collar workers," a union spokesman told *The New York Times*.[199]

The Bush labor-fighting team.

Michael Bartlett and William Cowen, National Labor Relations Board. With these two (recess) appointments, Bush put GOP appointees in the majority on the five-member NLRB, whose job is (or was) to enforce labor relations laws and investigate and remedy unfair labor practices. Bartlett previously headed labor policy at the U.S. Chamber of Commerce, a business lobby group; Cowen headed a notoriously anti-union management relations firm.

Elaine Chao, (Anti-)Labor Secretary was previously a policy analyst with the Heritage Foundation, where she attacked affirmative action programs and minimum wage laws as undermining "free enterprise." She served on the boards of Northwest Airlines, Clorox, C.R. Bard, Dole Foods, Bank of America, and hospital chain HCA. Her husband, Sen. Mitch McConnell (R-KY.), accepted nearly $6 million in political contributions from 1997 to 2002, 88 percent of which came from business, 0.4 percent from labor. **Linda Chavez,** Bush's *first* choice for labor secretary, met with a firestorm of protest and was withdrawn. As Chavez boasted in a fundraising letter soon afterward,

"[T]he media were calling me 'Big Labor's Worst Nightmare.' . . . *And they were right!*" She went on to say, "We can cripple liberal politics in this country by passing the Workers' Freedom of Choice Act"——a Republican bill attacking labor's right to contribute to political causes—as corporate interests do on a vastly larger scale. "If we stop now," Chavez added, "the terrorists win."

Becky Norton Dunlop, Federal Services Impasses Panel. In January 2002, in a historically unprecedented move, Bush fired all seven members of the FSIP, which handled disputes between federal agencies and employees' unions over work conditions. A few days later, Bush nominated Dunlop, a vice president at the right-wing Heritage Foundation, as FSIP chair.

John Henshaw, Occupational Safety and Health Administrator. The least bad of Bush's labor appointments, Henshaw nonetheless said he would emphasize "flexibility" (that all-purpose Bushie argument for killing regulations opposed by business) and "voluntary" compliance programs; actual enforcement of workplace safety rules would be used only against "the worst lawbreakers."[200]

"Scary" Eugene Scalia, Labor Department Solicitor. This choice for the department's top lawyer provoked such outrage that Bush used a recess appointment to put him in office. In ten years as a "labor lawyer," Scalia, the son of Supreme Court Justice Antonin Scalia, represented workers only twice; his practice was representing large corporations in fights *against* workers' rights. He fought against workplace safety and ergonomics rules in court and on op-ed pages. A union official called Scalia's appointment "scary."

MEDIA, MANIPULATION OF: *CRAFTING BUSH'S IMAGE*

In March 2003, Bush told reporters that they could help him "explain to people why I make the decisions I make"—a casual-enough comment that nonetheless summed up Bush's view of the press's purpose: Not to serve the public as a check on government and other powerful institutions, not to investigate, criticize, and tell the truth, but to serve him and his political agenda, spread his "message"—be his propaganda outlet—or be shunned, left out of the loop, or intimidated by subtle threats (see **Free speech**).

Consider a report in *USA Today* about a Bush news conference on the eve of the Iraq war. The White House press corps, rather than filing in as usual, "were summoned into the East Room in pairs, 'as if we were in grammar school' [CBS' Bill Plante told the paper] . . . .Veterans say they hadn't seen such a stifling atmosphere since the 1980s . . . All in all, Plante says, Thursday's event was designed to control the media and make Bush look strong . . . " Bush called on reporters from a predetermined list prepared by Press Secretary Ari Fleischer. No reporter known to ask hard or critical questions was called, Bush refused to answer questions about the cost of the war, and for the first time, no follow-up questions were taken. "What you saw was political media control at a high level," Tom Rosensteil of the Project for Excellence in Journalism told *USA Today*.[201]

Every administration tries to use the media to its advantage—though perhaps none so aggressively as this. Even more disturbing and depressing was the media's compliance. The TV networks' general suspension of criticism—Bush's free ride—began in earnest, if not on **election** night

2000 (when Fox News—where Bush's first cousin headed the election team—was the first to declare Bush the winner), then during the Florida recount battle, when most of the media fell in with the Bushies' insistence that the trivial issue of who really won the election be put behind us as quickly as possible "for the good of the country." Media acquiescence and sycophancy remained the pattern thereafter, particularly on the TV and radio networks and after 9/11.

Mythologizing the leader. The networks' fawning coverage of the president at times approached the leader-worship of departed totalitarian states. Contributing mightily to this effect was the White House's management—"direction" is more apt—of Bush's televised public appearances. The flag-festooned settings, wildly cheering crowds, Norman-Rockwellian ranks of schoolchildren and crisply uniformed soldiers, slogan-emblazoned backdrops and martial music—such political pageantry hadn't been seen since, well, the work of Leni Riefenstahl.

In an article headed "Keepers of Bush Image Lift Stagecraft to New Heights,"[202] *The New York Times* described how the Bush team, "going far beyond the foundations in stagecraft set by the Reagan White House, is using the powers of television and technology to promote a presidency like never before." Officials of past administrations "marvel at how the White House does not seem to miss an opportunity to showcase Mr. Bush in dramatic and perfectly lighted settings." The White House communications department was stocked with veteran network TV experts in sets, lighting, camera angles. A "small army," headed by a former Fox News producer, moved days in advance of Bush to set up the staging of his appearances.

His image makers posed him in front of Mount Rushmore,

shamelessly aligning his face with the other four presidents';
in front of the Statue of Liberty, specially lit up for the occasion by barges full of giant stadium lights; and most famously,
landing on the aircraft carrier *Abraham Lincoln* in a Navy jet,
wearing a flight suit, to proclaim his victory over Iraq, in front
of ranks of crew members and a banner reading "Mission
Accomplished": "one of the most audacious moments of presidential theater in American history," the *Times* story
remarked. The speech was timed for late-afternoon "magic
hour light," which "cast a golden glow on Mr. Bush."

Few expenses were spared in these productions, no details
were left to chance—and no deception was too brazen. In
answer to critics of the jet landing on the Abraham Lincoln—
which cost taxpayers $1 million—the White House had said it
was the only way the president could reach the ship on time.
(In fact, it was an easy helicopter hop from shore.) So, the ship
was turned around so viewers wouldn't see the California
coastline and would think the ship was far out at sea. For a
speech promoting his economic plan, the people standing
behind Bush were asked to take off their ties "so they would
look more like the ordinary folk the president said would benefit from his tax cut," the *Times* reported. "[T]hey've taken it to
an art form," said an awestruck Michael Deaver, Reagan's communications director.

The sound-bite president. Bush's Communications
Director Dan Bartlett summed up his team's regard for the
public's intelligence and attention span. The goal, he told the
Times, was to give Americans "an instant understanding of
what the president is talking about by seeing 60 seconds of television . . . " Or just a couple of words—the Orwellian "message
of the day" stenciled on the ubiquitous backdrops placed

behind Bush: "Economic growth," "Jobs," "Protecting the Homeland." (The trickery could get pretty embarrassing, as when Bush touted his "economic plan" in front of a backdrop of boxes stamped "Made in U.S.A." and it was learned that his aides had covered up the actual "Made in China" stamps.) Indeed, Karl Rove once decreed that every Bush TV appearance should be designed as though viewers have the sound turned off.

Such comparisons are *verboten*, so I will not identify the writer of the following (look it up on Goebbels—I mean, Google): "The receptivity of the great masses is very limited, their intelligence is small, but their power of forgetting is enormous. [Therefore], all effective propaganda must be limited to a very few points and must harp on these in slogans [which] should be persistently repeated over and over."

"Militainment." In May 2002, *Variety* reported that the military was teaming with Jerry Bruckheimer, the producer of the movies *Top Gun*, *Black Hawk Down*, and *Pearl Harbor*, to make a thirteen-part ABC docudrama following U.S. troops as they hunted Al Qaeda in Afghanistan. The Pentagon also planned to cooperate with a VH1 show called the *Military Diaries Project*, in which soldiers would create and star in their own "reality" series. The shows were reportedly signed off personally by Rumsfeld and Cheney. To critics, these were poor substitutes for giving real journalists access to battlefield reporting. "I'm outraged about the Hollywoodization of the military," Dan Rather told the *Santa Monica Mirror*. "The Pentagon would rather make troops available as props in gung-ho videos than explain how the commanders let Osama bin Laden and al-Qaida leaders escape or target the wrong villages."

"Black propaganda": The OSI. In February 2002, a new department was set up in the Pentagon called the OFFICE OF STRATEGIC INFLUENCE (OSI). Its purpose was to influence public opinion abroad, among other ways by planting false information in foreign media in order to damage governments unfriendly to the U.S.—a process known as "black propaganda." Pentagon "psyops"—psychological operations, such as dropping leaflets and broadcasting radio propaganda—had previously been confined to war zones.

MEDIA OWNERSHIP

Of all the areas in which the Bushies, at the behest of a powerful and deep-pocketed industry, dismantled rules designed to protect the public interest, their rollback of media ownership rules aroused the most opposition, and probably posed the greatest threat to American democracy, by allowing a handful of giant media conglomerates more and more control over the ideas and information on which a democracy depends.

The previous decade had already seen vast consolidations of media ownership—from local newspapers and radio stations to cable and satellite TV and the Internet—into the hands of a few conglomerates possessed of enormous political influence and concerned mainly with expanding their reach, keeping their programming cheap, entertaining, and profitable, and their news coverage conservative and corporate-friendly. By one reckoning, the number of companies owning a "controlling interest" in the major media had already declined from fifty in 1984 to a mere six in 2002.[203] With the TELECOMMUNICATIONS ACT OF 1996—which was virtually dictated by the media lobby—Congress raised the cap on how many TV stations one company could own nationwide, removed the limit on nationwide ownership of radio stations, and raised the limit on ownership of radio stations in a single community from two to eight. Within a few years, the number of TV station owners in the U.S. fell by half—just six owned more than 75 percent of the local TV markets. And around two-thirds of U.S. radio stations had been sold, mostly to giant chains like Texas-based Clear Channel Communications—a close Bush ally—which often owned all the stations in a single "market" and typically replaced live, local programming with homogenized, prerecorded product. The resulting loss of local news coverage was dramatized in 2002 when authorities in Minot, North Dakota were unable to warn residents about a dangerous toxic spill because all six radio stations had been bought by Clear Channel, and there was no one on hand to answer the phone or make an on-air announcement.

This was the business model which would quickly spread from radio to the other media under the more sweeping deregulation the media lobby would seek and get from the Bushies—natural allies, fanatical deregulators, indeed, little more than industry lobbyists themselves, whose political interests aligned well with the media lobby's agenda. Deregulation benefited both: It would allow the media giants to swallow up or shut out competitors (for example, after acquiring majority control of the DirectTV satellite service, the Fox network's owner, News Corp., threatened to drop its main rival, CNN, from the service); use their own channels to distribute their own content; gain audience share; and "service" all the media outlets they owned in a given "market" with a single newsroom. The more independent outlets that disappeared, the more the conglomerates could control the news and squelch criticism of corporate or Republican policies. (Clear Channel helped organize pro-Iraq war demonstrations and protests against the Dixie Chicks after a member of the singing group said she was ashamed Bush was a fellow Texan.) And the more money they made, the more they could contribute to industry-friendly political coffers—to buy more industry-friendly policy. As Robert Kuttner summarized it, "More concentration suits the Bush era perfectly: more blurring of commerce and news, more opportunities for a few right-wing insiders to get very rich and dictate news coverage—and fewer dissenting voices."[204]

The Powell FCC and the "empty vessel" of public interest. Bush's appointed Federal Communications Commissioner, Michael Powell, the son of Secretary of State Colin Powell, was probably the most aggressive supporter of the media lobby's agenda ever to sit on the FCC. Two other Bush appointments gave Republicans a 3–2 majority on the five-member FCC board.

Powell viewed the press not as the founding fathers did, as the oxygen of a free society, but as just another profit-making industry (much as Reagan FCC Commissioner Mark Fowler had famously opposed regulation by referring to television as "just another appliance . . . a toaster with pictures"). Powell referred to regulation per se as "the oppressor" and said, "The market is my religion." Before the House telecommunications subcommittee, Powell referred to broadcast corporations as "our clients."

Far from believing that, in exchange for the privilege of using the publicly owned airwaves, broadcasters had an obligation to serve the public interest, Powell, when asked at his first press conference as FCC chairman what he thought "public interest" meant, blithely admitted, "I have no idea . . . It's an empty vessel in which people pour in whatever their preconceived views or biases are." "The night after I was sworn in [as an FCC commissioner]," Powell said on another occasion, "I waited for a visit from the angel of the public interest. I waited all night, but she did not come."

Powell—the angel of the private interests—argued that the proliferation of cable and satellite TV channels and websites provided plenty of media diversity and competition. Never mind that, with the help of his own FCC's policies (such as its approval of the AOL-Comcast merger, creating the nation's largest cable company), fewer and fewer companies owned all these outlets, particularly the TV and radio stations from which most Americans got their news; never mind how similar were the programming and viewpoints they presented. The Republican FCC members explicitly endorsed the media giants' contention that First Amendment free speech rights were at stake—meaning, of course, *their* right to own as many outlets as they wanted, not the public's right to hear a diversity of viewpoints.

Congress, the courts, and relentless industry pressure and litigation played their parts. For example, in 2001, the notoriously conservative D.C. Circuit Court told the FCC to drop its long-standing rule preventing any one company from serving more than 30 percent of U.S. cable subscribers. But instead of appealing the order, Powell launched a study to see if any cap at all was justified. The court also ruled that the FCC must show "empirical evidence" that its rules are necessary, or revoke them. And the Telecom Act had mandated that the FCC review its rules every two years. The Powellies were only too happy to oblige.

D-(Dereg) Day. On September 12, 2001—while most Americans' thoughts were elsewhere—the Republican FCC commissioners stayed focused and carried a 3–2 vote to "review" the remaining media ownership rules. As Powell said, "I *start* with the proposition that the rules are no longer necessary" [emphasis added]. According to both sides, it was probably the FCC's most important decision ever—yet Powell held just one public hearing on it, and that one only on the insistence of the FCC's two Democrats. The latter were reduced to holding public hearings on their own—which Powell mocked as a "nineteenth-century whistle-stop tour."

D-Day was June 2, 2003, when, by the same partisan 3–2 vote, and with the White House's endorsement, the FCC swept aside checks and balances developed over six decades and changed the rules to permit a single company to own up to three TV stations, eight radio stations, a daily newspaper and a cable TV operator in one city, and to own more stations nationwide—"a huge giveaway of public resources and political power to a tiny few," in the words of the Center for Digital Democracy. The rule changes were as follows:

Broadcast-Newspaper Cross-Ownership Rule (1975):
Banned ownership of both a daily newspaper and a local television or radio station in the same market. **New rule:**

Restriction lifted altogether in markets with nine or more TV stations and eased in those with more than three.

Local Television Ownership Rule (1964): A broadcaster could own no more than two stations in a single market, but only if neither was among the top four and if eight independent outlets remained. **New rule:** One company could own three stations in the largest markets and two in markets with five or more stations.

Television-Radio Cross-Ownership Rule (1970): A company could own up to two TV and seven radio stations in a single large market and one TV and four radio stations in a smaller market, provided specified numbers of independent outlets remained. **New Rule:** Lifted all restrictions in large markets.

Local Radio Ownership Rule (1941): Permitted one company to own no more than eight stations in large cities. **New Rule:** Market maps redrawn in a way that critics said loosened the rule and proponents said tightened it.

Dual Network Rule (1946): No entity could own more than one of the four major TV networks—ABC, CBS, NBC, and Fox. No change in 2003, but Powell's FCC had already loosened the rule in 2001 to permit buyouts of smaller networks, such as CBS owner Viacom's purchase of UPN.

National Television Ownership Rule (1941/1996): After the rule was loosened by the 1996 Telecom Act, a single network could own local TV stations that collectively reached no more than 35 percent of the national viewership. **New Rule:** Cap raised to 45 percent, but effectively 90 percent.[205] In July 2003, the House of Representatives voted 400–21 to reverse this change. The White House responded by saying it would veto the appropriations bill the House provision was attached to—which would block funding of the Commerce, State, and Justice Departments and the federal judiciary. "And to what end?" asked conservative columnist William Safire. "To turn what we used to call 'public airwaves' into private fiefs, to undermine diversity of opinion and—in its anti-federalist homogenization of our varied culture—to sweep aside local interests and community standards of taste."[206]

What the new rules portended:

The informational "company town." Most business analysts predicted a wave of media mergers that would dwarf the merger mania of the 1990s. The large newspaper chains—which had lobbied heavily for broadcast-newspaper cross-ownership—would likely partner or merge with network owners; independent papers would go the way of radio stations and get swallowed up too. "America's cities could turn into informational 'company towns,' with one behemoth owning all the local print organs . . . as well as the TV and radio stations, the multiplexes and the cable system," wrote media critic Mark Crispin Miller. "[This] has no place in a democracy, where the people have to know more than their masters want to tell them."[207]

The decline of local programming. A 2002 study by Columbia University's Project for Excellence in Journalism found that TV stations owned by smaller media firms generally produced better local reporting and newscasts and did longer stories and fewer "softball" celebrity features, and concluded that ownership of local TV by a few large corporations "will erode the quality of news Americans receive."[208]

Less news, more trash. The media giants preferred to fill endless hours and weeks with a "story" like Gary Condit's sex life—"the sort of lurid fare that can drive endless hours of agitated jabbering," as media critic Robert McChesney put it—than invest in international coverage and investigative reporting that costs more and may ruffle advertisers' and government's feathers. "It's so much cheaper to have a couple of blowhards exchange insults." The takeover of every remaining corner of the media universe by corporate bottom-line values portended an accelerated slide into inanity, more and more advertising, and more "commercial"—sensationalistic, sex-driven, or just plain moronic—programming, with immeasurable but surely corrosive effects on the entire culture.

Loss of objective political coverage. Media corporations that are regularly seeking deregulation, tax relief, and other favors from the government are unlikely to provide reliable and objective coverage *of* the government. The loss of journalistic objectivity is especially worrisome when the government is trying to sell the public on going to war. During the Iraq war, the *New York Times*' Paul Krugman noted, many Americans turned to the BBC for their news because of the way the U.S. networks, as the BBC's director general put it, "substituted patriotism for impartiality." "The BBC is owned by the British government," Krugman observed. Yet "it tried hard—too hard, its critics say—to stay impartial. America's TV networks are privately owned, yet they behaved like state-run media."[209]

Or as Mark Crispin Miller put it, "U.S. coverage of this government is just a bit more edifying than the local newscasts in Riyadh."

Loss of objective election coverage. With the bottom line as the top priority, the amount of election campaign coverage had already plummeted while the amount of campaign advertising had risen dramatically. Moreover, election coverage was increasingly slanted in favor of the corporate owners' preferred party. In 2000, first Fox, then NBC—at the personal insistence of Jack Welch, CEO of GE, NBC's owner—helped subvert the election by prematurely declaring Bush the winner. Throughout the election recount fight, Fox and other networks served as a full-time, powerful PR machine working, subtly or not so subtly, on Bush's behalf.

Industry lobbying and donations. Media lobbyists contributed around $75 million to Congressional candidates between 1993 and 2000. The Bush 2000 campaign received $1,070,728 from media companies—more than any other politician except Gore received from 1993 through 2000 combined. From 1997 to 2000, media corporations and lobbyists paid for 315 junkets for members of Congress and senior staffers, and provided 1,460 all-expense-paid trips for FCC personnel, according to the Center for Public Integrity.

No one left to monitor the conglomerates themselves. Media-owning corporations like Disney and GE are huge economic, political and social forces, whose business and political activities demand public scrutiny. But with their news divisions unwilling or unable to report objectively on their parent companies—and with these swallowing up more and more independent media outlets—fewer and fewer ways remain for the public to learn what they're up to. One story the corporate media notably failed to cover, not surprisingly, was media consolidation itself. In February 2003, a survey found that 72 percent of Americans had never heard about the proposed changes.

MEDICAID

Most advanced countries accept the principle that basic health care is a right, not a privilege only for those who can afford it. Even in the U.S., as *The New York Times*'s Paul Krugman put it, "There are limits to how much inequality the public is prepared to tolerate. . . . a society in which rich people get their medical problems solved, while ordinary people die from them, is too harsh even for us." [210] But perhaps not for all of us. To the Bushies, even our limited government health insurance programs, Medicaid and **Medicare**, were too generous, while not doing enough to benefit big business—specifically, the private insurance/HMO industry.

Medicaid, funded jointly by the federal and state governments, covered 42 million poor, disabled, and elderly Americans;[211] not exactly a constituency whose wealth and influence translated into political clout. For the Bushies, a crisis in Medicaid funding was, only naturally, an opportunity to try to strangle the program.

In 2002, a bill to help states with their Medicaid costs was approved in the then-Democratic-controlled Senate but didn't make it through the Republican-controlled House. By 2003, facing budget crises and rising medical costs, every state except Alabama had made Medicaid cuts: forty-five states reduced payments for prescription drugs; thirty-seven reduced or froze payments to doctors and hospitals; twenty-seven restricted eligibility for the program; twenty-five cut benefits such as dental and vision care, and seventeen increased the co-payments beneficiaries must pay. Because of how the program was co-financed by state and federal government, every Medicaid dollar cut from state budgets meant less federal money as well.

The Bush block-grant/time-bomb scheme. It was the states' desperate straits that gave the Bushies their chance. A Bush plan to radically restructure Medicaid and SCHIP (STATE CHILDREN'S HEALTH INSURANCE PROGRAM)—to do away with them, truth be told—was announced in January 2003. The plan was a Faustian bargain. States that accepted the deal (and only those) would receive a total of $12.7 billion in additional funds from 2004 to 2010. After that, however, federal aid would be reduced below current levels by the same amount; the states would, in effect, pay back all the earlier aid. By 2013, they would receive $8.8 billion less than they would under existing law—and not enough to keep up with increasing costs. (By that time, of course, the Bushies would be long out of office.)

States that accepted the deal would also agree to convert their Medicaid and SCHIP funds to a capped "block grant": The Feds would no longer match states' Medicaid contributions dollar for dollar, and would thus no longer help states cope with the increased Medicaid enrollments that occur when the economy weakens and people lose jobs and health insurance. Just when the need is greatest, states would have less money to spend per enrollee. This, noted the National Health Law Program (NHeLP), an advocacy group, would deny beneficiaries the right to obtain needed services in a timely manner and thus destroy Medicaid as an entitlement program—as *insurance*.[212] As Al Hunt put it, "Here's the deal: Give them some crumbs now to quell the protests . . . and then later force a reduction either in services offered or poor people covered. Conveniently," he added, "this budgetary savings kicks in when the massive tax cuts for the wealthy start draining the federal budget even more."[213]

The Bush plan also made it easier for states to cut benefits, increase "cost-sharing" (co-payments, deductibles, and premiums paid by patients), and limit Medicaid enrollment for "optional beneficiaries," who were mostly people with disabilities and the elderly. Over 56 percent of elderly Medicaid patients, such as those residing in nursing homes and the medically needy, were "optional." But many "optional" services, particularly nursing home care, were generally not covered by private insurers or **Medicare**.[214]

Allowing unlimited increases in "cost-sharing" was, for the poor, an especially ominous change. It would allow states to price coverage above the means of low-income people, and would likely lead to a Medicaid system that many of the most needy cannot afford.

Bush's plan also proposed "saving" $9 billion over five years by reducing Medicaid payments to public hospitals in at least thirty-one states. Those cuts would hurt the only facilities that serve the poor in most communities.

NHeLP's analysis of the Bush plan concluded that, contrary to the Bushies' claim, it would allow states to cover *fewer* people and swell the fast-growing numbers of the uninsured, which already exceeded 41 million.

MEDICARE

Medicare, the government-funded health insurance program that covers the elderly, was in the Bushies' crosshairs from the start. After all, this was publicly funded health care. Socialized medicine. Great Society. Liberal. Moreover, its expenditures were rising quickly due to spiraling medical costs and an aging population. But politically, how do you kill such a popular and vital program? Or—better—how might public Medicare funds be funneled into the hands of the private insurance and pharmaceutical industries, which the GOP could then count on for fat contributions? And how do you neutralize a potent Democratic issue—the push to *expand* Medicare by adding prescription drug coverage? To consider the latter first:

Bush's placebo prescription drug plan. Bush promised in his 2000 election campaign to provide a prescription-drug–coverage plan for seniors. Instead, he first tried to get away with a plan that not only failed to keep up with rising drug prices but ate into other Medicare funding, leaving seniors with less medical care overall than before. In March 2002,

Bush proposed a Discount Drug Card that the administration estimated would save seniors around 15 percent off retail prices. Only problem was, in 2000, drug prices rose 17.3 percent on average—and that was the sixth straight year of double-digit increases. Many seniors found themselves hundreds of dollars short every month for needed drugs.

Bush claimed the drug card was just an interim step toward a more comprehensive drug benefit—for which he budgeted $77 billion over the next 10 years. Even Republican House Majority Leader Dennis Hastert had proposed *$300* billion. The National Committee to Preserve Social Security and Medicare estimated it would cost at least $450 billion. Moreover:

- Bush's $77 billion over ten years was to come out of the $190 billion he budgeted for Medicare reform—which was $300 billion less than the nonpartisan Congressional Budget Office (CBO) said would be needed even to maintain *current* benefits, without drug coverage.
- In order to participate in Bush's drug discount plan, states would be required to expand drug coverage for **Medicaid** recipients—at the states' own expense, naturally, and at a time when were already facing drastic budget cuts (see **State and local governments**). This was consistent with Bush's overall approach to funding health and social services: Shift more and more of the burden to the states, knowing full well they cannot handle them. Make phony promises, then pass the buck.

Stealth privatization. As for their dream of privatizing

Medicare, the Republicans' inspired idea was to attack it *through* the prescription drug benefit. In early 2003, the White House floated a proposal to offer drug coverage only to seniors who were willing to move from Medicare into private "managed care," such as HMOs. That didn't fly, so Republicans came up with a more diabolically clever version, contained in a House bill in July 2003, which attached the drug provision to a broader "reform" plan aimed at destroying traditional, "fee-for-service" Medicare by driving up premiums and pushing people into private insurance. First, Medicare would stop covering the cost of medical services and instead only subsidize a portion of beneficiaries' health-care premiums. In any area where traditional Medicare costs were higher than average medical costs, Medicare beneficiaries would be hit with premium increases—or they could move to a private plan.

As *The New York Times* observed, a little competition is fine, "but this game is too easy to rig." Medicare, with low overhead and no need to generate profits, basically operated more economically than private insurance; but Medicare "cannot 'cherry-pick' the population to enroll only the healthiest beneficiaries, as many private plans routinely do."[215] Under the GOP plan, Medicare would increasingly get stuck with the oldest, sickest, most expensive patients, thus raising Medicare costs. This, in turn, would raise beneficiaries' premiums and drive still more of them into private plans—and ultimately, to paraphrase Grover Norquist,[216] shrink Medicare to a size where it could be drowned in the bathtub.

Meanwhile, the Bush administration lost no time attacking Medicare in other ways. It had already:

- Cut the Medicare reimbursement rate for physicians by 5.4 percent, even though reimbursements had already been squeezed to the point where more and more doctors were refusing to accept Medicare patients.

- Cut off advice and assistance services to Medicare beneficiaries—ordering the contractors that handled Medicare claims to stop providing beneficiaries with information about their rights, how to deal with overcharges by doctors or hospitals, report Medicare fraud, appeal the denial of a claim, obtain benefits, select a nursing home, get discounts on prescription drugs, etc.

- Proposed legislation and rule changes that made it harder for beneficiaries to appeal the denial of benefits by turning many such decisions over to lawyers or hearing officers at Health and Human Services instead of independent, impartial judges. "This puts beneficiaries at a disadvantage, with unequal bargaining power and inadequate expertise to do battle with the Medicare agency," noted the director of the Center for Medicare Advocacy.[217] In more than half of the approximately 350,000 such cases in the previous five years, federal judges had ruled that frail elderly people with severe illnesses were improperly denied coverage. In addition, administrative law judges would be required to "give deference" to administration policies. The Association of Administrative Law Judges called Bush's proposals "a stealth attack on the rights of citizens to fair, impartial hearings" and "a serious assault" on the 1946 law that guaranteed the fairness of government proceedings.[218] As usual when doing down the little guy, the Bushies touted these proposals as "reform" and as providing "flexibility."

MISSILE DEFENSE AND THE ABM TREATY: *"AN ARMS RACE AGAINST OURSELVES"*

In December 2001, Bush announced that the U.S. would withdraw from the 1972 Anti-Ballistic Missile (ABM) Treaty, which limited testing and prohibited deployment of any national missile defense system by the U.S. and Russia. At the same time, Bush committed new funds for the development of such a system—a holy grail of Republicans and defense contractors since Ronald Reagan's Strategic Defense Initiative (SDI)—a.k.a. "Star Wars"—proposal of 1983.

This issue might well prove more important to U.S. and world security in the long run than anything to do with Islamic radicalism or the Middle East. In abandoning the ABM treaty—while reviving the development and expanding the potential uses of nuclear weapons—Bush, in one swoop, unilaterally threw out what had been the key weapons treaty between the superpowers; committed billions to developing a missile "shield" that could probably never work to defend against attackers that probably didn't exist; and alarmed and antagonized not only Russia[219] and China, which had reasons to feel threatened by the move, but also our European allies and most other nations as well. Indeed, the move risked provoking a new arms race and launching a new era of nuclear proliferation, leaving America not more secure but far less.[220]

The Federation of American Scientists responded with a statement titled "ABM Treaty Withdrawal an Attack on American Security," calling the decision "both unnecessary and unwise. It is ironic that as we rediscover the need for international cooperation, we are taking an action almost universally opposed by our allies....*Scientists are nearly unanimous in calling national missile defense unworkable*" [emphasis added].[221] The same opinions were stated by fifty-one American Nobel-laureate scientists in a letter to Congress.

Learning nothing from 9/11. On that day, the deadliest attack ever on U.S. soil was carried out by nineteen men armed with box cutters. Then came effective nationwide terror by anthrax-filled letters. In 2000, the Navy destroyer USS *Cole* was crippled by four men in an explosive-packed rowboat. A truck bomb was used in an attempt to destroy the World Trade Center in 1993, and one had destroyed the Murrah Federal Building in Oklahoma City in 1995. In 1997, Russia's former national security chief claimed more than 100 of Russia's "suitcase" nuclear bombs were missing. Osama bin Laden was rumored to have acquired a number of them.

But up until 9/11, the Bushies were calling not for better defense against terrorism, but for the building of an awesomely expensive ($230 billion was the Congressional Budget Office's estimate) system to shoot down intercontinental ballistic missiles (ICBMs)—one of the *least* likely forms of attack on the U.S., according to a CIA report, because it is one of the most expensive and least reliable, and cannot be delivered anonymously. *Whose* missiles, exactly? None of the nations designated by the U.S. as state sponsors of terrorism—Iran, Iraq, Syria, Libya, Cuba, North Korea, and Sudan—possessed missiles capable of reaching the U.S.

In April 2001, former UN ambassador Richard Holbrooke called Bush's passion for missile defense "almost a religious matter," and warned that the threat from Al Qaeda was more serious. Bin Laden, he noted, had no ICBMs.

Yet even after 9/11—far from doing the unthinkable and admitting to a misplaced priority—the Bushies insisted we needed missile defenses more than ever.

Back to the future: Star Wars II. Bush called for increasing spending on missile defense by 44 percent in 2002 and expanded the scope to include possible airborne or space-based lasers. Like the Bush cabinet, the Bush missile defense vision was a Reagan/Bush I déjà vu. It called for accelerated development of chemical lasers to be fired from space or high in the atmosphere, as in President Ray-gun's "Star Wars," and renewed research on the abandoned, Bush I–era "Brilliant Pebbles" scheme of launching thousands of interceptors into space.

Easy to foil. Experts, such as Nobel physicist Steven Weinberg,[222] said any missile "shield" would be easy to penetrate. The enemy could deploy large numbers of cheap decoys that the "kill vehicle" would be unable to distinguish from the actual warheads. Alternately, the attacker's missile could launch hundreds of "bomblets" carrying biological weapons, such as anthrax spores. These would be immune to any missile defense envisioned.

Meanwhile, hitting even *one* incoming missile remained, well, hit and miss. In five Pentagon tests from 1999 to 2001, the much-touted success of the first was, according to Congress's General Accounting Office, fabricated; the "kill vehicle" only found the target because a large decoy balloon was deployed nearby. A second and third test failed, a fourth and fifth succeeded. A June 2003 test failed. Did we really want to rely on such a system to shoot down real, incoming nuclear missiles—especially if the system's very existence made such an attack more likely—and when only one missile would have to get through to destroy New York or Washington?

More security, or just more weapons everywhere?
According to Weinberg, the real question was how best to minimize the likelihood of such attacks in the first place. Given the possibilities of accidental or unauthorized launch or theft of any of Russia's nearly 4,000 nuclear warheads, he argued, nothing was more important to American security than reducing nuclear forces on both sides. But a U.S. missile defense system would only discourage Russia from reducing its nukes—"the sole remnant of its status as a superpower."[223] Moreover, a National Intelligence Estimate said that if the U.S. developed missile defenses, China would increase its force of nuclear-armed ICBMs from the current twenty or so to about 200. Countries that could feel threatened by China—such as India—would likely follow suit. Pakistan would then have to match India's buildup—and so on. Meanwhile, our missile defenses would take years to develop before they had any protective value against this proliferation.

Indeed, Weinberg explained, our missile shield might induce a rival power to use its nuclear weapons first—if they thought that *we* thought our defenses could stop their missiles, and that we could therefore strike first with impunity. Missile defense thus undermined the deterrence function of nuclear weapons, which, under the ABM Treaty, had kept the peace between the superpowers for decades.

NEPOTISM

They say a fish rots from the head. From the head down, the Bush administration embodied the political value of family connections. "In some ways the Bush administration has become a family affair, reeking of nepotism," wrote columnist Helen Thomas. "A staggering number of relatives of high administration officials have been appointed to government jobs, giving new meaning to 'family values.'"[224]

A little gossip-column style seems in order. In February 2002, the State Department appointed **Elizabeth Cheney**, VP **Dick Cheney**'s daughter, deputy assistant secretary of state for Near East affairs. (State Department officials, speaking anonymously, said the post was created especially for her, *The Washington Times* reported.[225]) The week before, Ms. Cheney's husband, **Philip Perry**, left the Justice Department to become chief counsel for the Office of Management and Budget. OMB spokesman **Chris Ullman**'s wife, Kris, was a Justice Department official—as was Assistant Attorney General **Deborah Daniels**, the sister of OMB director **Mitch Daniels**. Also at justice was **Chuck James**, whose mother, **Kay Coles James**, was director of the Office of Personnel Management, and whose father, **Charles James Sr.**, was a top Labor Department official. Labor Secretary **Elaine Chao** was married to Sen. **Mitch McConnell** (R-KY). Her department's top lawyer, Labor Solicitor **Eugene Scalia**, is the son of Supreme Court Justice **Antonin Scalia**—and represented the president-select before the Supreme Court in *Bush v. Gore*. **Janet Rehnquist**, daughter of Chief Justice **William Rehnquist**, became inspector general of Health and Human Services. Bush appointed **David Bunning** as a federal judge for the Eastern District of Kentucky; his father was Sen. **Jim Bunning** (R-KY). Bush appellate judge nominee **Charles W. Pickering** was the father of Rep. **Charles W. "Chip" Pickering Jr.** (R-MS). Out of law school only three years, S**trom Thurmond Jr**., son of the legendary, 6,443-year-old South Carolina Republican senator, was named the new U.S. attorney in South Carolina, heading a sixty-person office. ("It's only nepotism when you hire your kin," Strom Sr. said. "I'm not employing Strom Jr. I am recommending him for a position.")

Bush appointed **Michael Powell**, son of Secretary of State **Colin Powell**, as FCC chairman. FCC commissioner **Kevin Martin** was married to Cheney aide **Cathie Martin**. Cheney aide **Nina Rees**'s husband was White House speechwriter **Matthew Rees**. White House political director **Ken Mehlman**'s younger brother **Bruce Mehlman** was an assistant commerce secretary. White House press secretary **Scott McClellan**'s brother **Mark McClellan** was on the president's Council of Economic Advisers and later named as FDA commissioner. The FTC's director of policy planning, **Ted Cruz**, was married to a senior official in the U.S.

Help for Jeb. Florida governor Jeb Bush faced a tough challenge in his November 2002 reelection bid from his Democratic opponent, Bill McBride. But the governor had an ace up his sleeve: His brother was *George* Bush, the president of the United States.

George did more than attend fundraisers with Jeb that raised millions for his campaign. "From health care to education to the environment," *The New York Times* reported, "the White House has showered projects and money on Florida, a state that [is also] vital for the president's reelection prospects in 2004."[226]

- The Bush administration gave federal help for a Florida prescription drug program highlighted in GOP ads promoting the governor.
- The Bushies agreed in May 2002 to buy drilling rights to prevent oil exploration in Florida's Big Cypress National Preserve, pleasing Florida environmentalists. This benefited not only Jeb: The Bush Interior Department agreed to pay the Collier family—which donated more than $50,000 to the Florida Republican Party in 2002—$120 million for the rights. The market value was only $5–20 million, according to a National Park Service study. Indeed, the deal specified that the Colliers could claim the value at

Trade Representative's office, **Heidi Cruz**. National Economic Council staffer **John Ackerly**'s brother was on the Council of Economic Advisers. It was all enough to make Kevin Bacon's head spin.

"There have never been so many family combos in an administration at the same time," *Business Week* noted.

much *more* than $120 million and claim the difference as a charitable deduction.

- The Bushies agreed to buy back more than $115 million worth of offshore drilling rights sought by Florida, but not those sought by California. (In fact, the administration appealed a court ruling won by California that strengthened its power to block offshore drilling.)
- The governor scored big against his opponent by saying the latter's proposal to de-emphasize standardized testing in Florida schools would cost the state $2.5 billion in federal aid. As proof, Bush cited a letter he happened to have just received from the federal under secretary of education, threatening to cut off Florida's Title I federal education funds if the state didn't comply with federal testing requirements.

Republicans made no bones about Florida being specially favored. "Karl Rove probably wakes up every morning and says, 'What have we done for Florida lately?'" Rep. Mark Foley (R-FL) told *The New York Times*. The Florida Democratic chairman, on the other hand, said of Jeb's campaign, "They've used the [federal] treasury as their own political piggy bank."

"These appointments are not illegal," Helen Thomas commented. "But they reveal an arrogant administration that apparently feels there is nothing strange about hiring so many sisters, brothers, nieces and nephews of government bigwigs. . . . Those appointed by virtue of their relationship to other top members of the administration obviously will carry a lot of extra weight and power in any agency where they operate." The editor of *The Washington Spectator* remarked, "If President Clinton had done this, there would have been a congressional investigation."

NUCLEAR WEAPONS

The Bushies were all for nuclear disarmament—of other countries, of course. As for the U.S., the decade-long shrinking of our nuclear weapon "enterprise"—a good thing, some might think—was, like so many other areas of progress, to be reversed. While demanding the disarmament of Iraq, Iran, North Korea, etc., the Bushies—exercising their prerogative as the world's *good* guys—moved toward the development of a new generation of nuclear weapons intended not for deterrence but for actual, battlefield use, and toward rejection of the Comprehensive Test Ban Treaty and resumption of nuclear testing after a more than ten-year moratorium. This was in conjunction with their abandonment of the Anti-Ballistic Missile Treaty (which had already undermined the deterrence function of nuclear weapons—see **Missile Defense**) and their assumption of a right to "preemptively" attack any country deemed a threat. It was all part of the Bushies' vision of a new world order maintained not by international agreements and multilateral disarmament but by the threat and use of overwhelming U.S. military force—and a big step toward the old Republican dream of the "winnable nuclear war"—as George Bush Sr. called it in 1980.

A policy paper Secretary of Defense Rumsfeld delivered

to Congress in 2002, the "Nuclear Posture Review," called for a "new triad" of smaller nuclear weapons to attack hard and deeply buried targets such as underground bunkers, mobile targets, and chemical and biological weapons sites.[227] Existing U.S. nuclear weapons could do all this, but only at the cost of unacceptably huge "collateral" civilian damage. The whole point of creating smaller weapons was that they would be *usable*. The report listed Iraq, Iran, Libya, North Korea, Syria, Russia, and China as potential targets.

In May 2003, Congress approved the White House's requests to abandon a ten-year-old ban on development of such "battle-field" nukes, provide $50 million for producing them, and cut the lead time for conducting nuclear tests. Bush's 2004 defense budget requested $6.4 billion for maintaining and developing nuclear weapons—a 15 percent increase over 2002 and 50 percent more than the average amount the U.S. spent on its nuclear arsenal during the Cold War.

At a secret meeting in August 2003 (the plans were leaked to the Los Alamos Study Group, a nuclear watchdog group), administration and military officials were to decide on a resumption of nuclear testing and discuss the "future [nuclear] arsenal."[228] Non-proliferation groups said these moves put the U.S. in clear violation of the Nuclear Non-Proliferation Treaty, which called on states possessing nuclear weapons to stop acquiring more and to reduce their existing arsenals.

"We're moving away from more than five decades of efforts to delegitimize the use of nuclear weapons," warned Sen. Jack Reed (D-RI), a member of the Senate Armed Services Committee. Every U.S. president since World War II had pursued a policy of nuclear arms control, Robert Scheer noted. "Every administration, that is, until this one."[229] Although the nuclear threat from Iraq "proved to be nonexistent," he wrote, "the United States' threat to use nuclear weapons and make a shambles of nuclear arms control is alarmingly vibrant."[230] Instead of disarming, critics asked, why shouldn't other countries, such as India and Pakistan, follow our lead and develop battlefield nukes?

OIL, APPEASEMENT, THE SAUDIS, AND THE WAR ON TERRORISM

From the Bushies' apparently little-diminished friendship with the rulers of Saudi Arabia, you wouldn't have known the Saudis ran one of the most repressive regimes on earth, where women were beaten for failing to cover their heads properly and could be put to death for adultery; where no religious expression but Islam was tolerated; where there were no independent newspapers or political parties. You wouldn't know the Saudis sponsored telethons to support suicide bombers who targeted Israeli school buses; that they financed and armed Islamic Jihad; that they spread the extreme Wahhabi Islam that had bred a generation of fanatical haters of America, the West, and non-Muslims in general (who for them included the Shiites); that their country produced Osama bin Laden and fifteen of the nineteen **September 11** hijackers; and that even afterward, the Saudis denied U.S. requests to turn over information about Saudi links to terrorism, and refused to let U.S. planes targeting the Taliban (who they sponsored) take off from Saudi soil.

Yet, as Christopher Hitchens wrote in June 2002, "This high-level collusion still goes on . . . Bush continues to fawn on this disgusting dynasty."[231]

It was widely alleged that before 9/11, FBI investigations of Al Qaeda were hobbled by U.S. officials and oil interests who did not want to offend, embarrass, or undermine the Saudi regime. Former FBI Deputy Director John O'Neill, who was in charge of the investigations into the bin Laden–connected bombings of the World Trade Center in 1993, the destruction of an American troop barracks in Saudi Arabia in 1996, the African embassy bombings in 1998, and the attack upon the USS *Cole* in 2000, told two French researchers in the summer of 2001, "The main obstacles to investigate [*sic*] Islamic terrorism were U.S. oil corporate interests, and the role played by Saudi Arabia in it. . . . All the answers, everything needed to dismantle Osama bin Laden's organisation, can be found in Saudi Arabia."[232] In a tragic irony, O'Neill quit the FBI two weeks before 9/11 in disgust over the Bush administration's refusal to investigate Saudi ties to Al Qaeda and went to work as head of security at the World Trade Center, where he was killed in the attack.

The French intelligence analysts who interviewed O'Neill also charged that shortly after taking office the Bushies slowed down FBI investigations of Al Qaeda activities in Afghanistan as they sought a deal with the Taliban for construction of an oil pipeline across the country by U.S. oil companies to access the vast Central Asian reserves—a project in which Cheney's firm HALLIBURTON and Bush's buddies at **Enron** had interests. The Taliban was in fact receiving financial aid from the Bush administration up until 9/11. After that, the U.S. secured the pipeline deal by other means.

Bush-Saudi ties went back decades—as did U.S. willing-
ness to turn a blind eye to "evil," as W. might say, for the sake
of oil. The first Bush White House was dominated by corporate executives who had made millions from oil and arms
deals with the Saudi rulers. At the time, the CIA was helping
to arm and train Osama bin Laden's largely Saudi mujahiddin
to fight the Soviets (who were also after the oil route) in
Afghanistan. (Our other erstwhile protégé, Saddam Hussein—
an ally when he was all that stood between Iran and the
Saudi oil fields—had just become an enemy for threatening
those oil fields himself.)

Throughout the 1990s, even after the 1993 Al Qaeda
attack on the World Trade Center and the 1996 attack on
Khobar Towers, the FBI, when offered evidence of Saudi-Al
Qaeda links, was "told to 'see no evil,'" according to journalist Greg Palast. "[The] State [Department] wanted to keep
the pro-American Saudi royal family in control of the world's
biggest oil spigot, even at the price of turning a blind eye to
any terrorist connection . . . " But, Palast said, a "high-placed
member of a U.S. intelligence agency" told him that "while
there's always been constraints on investigating Saudis,
under George [W.] Bush it's gotten much worse. After the
[2000] elections, the agencies were told to 'back off' investigating the Bin Ladens and Saudi royals."[233]

The censored 9/11 report. The Bush administration continued covering for the Saudis after 9/11. According to ABC
News, to avoid embarrassing the Saudi rulers, the Bushies
edited out of an Osama videotape released in December
2001 a portion showing a Saudi visitor assuring bin Laden of
continued support by Saudi clerics on the Saudi government

payroll.[234] In July 2003, a joint House-Senate intelligence panel released its long-awaited report on pre-9/11 intelligence failures. On the White House's insistence, most of a section dealing with the role of the Saudis was censored out of the version released to the public. Sen. Bob Graham (D-FL), who helped write the report, said, "It is my conclusion that officials of a foreign government aided and abetted the terrorists attacks on our country." (Graham was barred from identifying the country, but everyone knew.) The White House had withheld additional information even from the intelligence panel, Graham complained. "There seems to be a systematic strategy of coddling and cover-up when it comes to the Saudis," said Sen. Charles Schumer (D-NY).[235]

The Carlyle Group. On 9/11, when all commercial flights were grounded, the only flight permitted was one evacuating bin Laden family members from the U.S. back to Saudi Arabia—arranged by Saudi Ambassador Prince Bandar with the help of the FBI and with top White House officials' approval, according to then-White House aide Richard Clarke. That morning, as it happened, bin Laden family investors had been meeting in Washington with fellow principals in the CARLYLE GROUP, an investment firm with major Bush/GOP connections and major stakes in U.S. defense firms that equipped and trained the Saudi military. Carlyle Chairman FRANK CARLUCCI had been Reagan's defense secretary. After leaving the White House, GEORGE BUSH SR. had became Senior Adviser to Carlyle specializing in attracting Saudi investors—including the bin Ladens. "The idea of the President's father, an ex-president himself, doing business with a company [Saudi Binladin Group, the bin Ladens' construction firm] under investigation by the FBI [in connection with 9/11] is horrible," commented Larry Klayman of Judicial Watch.[236] Carlyle board member and Senior Counsel JAMES A. BAKER III was Bush I's secretary of state and counsel to the Bush 2000 campaign. In 2002, Baker's law firm was busy defending the Saudi defense minister against a lawsuit brought by the families of 9/11 victims and helping Texas oil companies seeking to build the pipeline through Afghanistan. In the early 1990s, Dubya was himself a director and shareholder in a Carlyle division, and his oil company received investments from the U.S. business representatives of Osama's father and brother-in-law (see **Bush's business career**).

The Saudi Binladin Group was also a joint venture partner with a division of HALLIBURTON under then-CEO **Cheney** in 1996. As Cheney once said, "You've got to go where the oil is"—Bush-Cheney foreign policy in a nutshell. As good as his word, from 1998 to 2000, on Cheney's watch, Halliburton sold $73 million in oilfield equipment to Saddam Hussein's Iraq—more than any other U.S. company. Halliburton also sold equipment to, maintained an office in, and lobbied against sanctions on Iran—long number one on the U.S. list of states sponsoring terrorism. Other countries that had abundant oil, scarce human rights, and business deals with Halliburton while Cheney was in charge included Azerbaijan, Indonesia, Libya, and Nigeria.

The giant U.S. construction company BECHTEL CORP., which was closely tied to the Reagan and Bush administrations (I and II), had long partnered with the Saudi Binladin Group to build oil refineries, pipelines, factories, and ports in Saudi Arabia and around the Gulf. In 1983, Donald

Rumsfeld, then Reagan's special envoy to make nice to Saddam Hussein, tried to sell Saddam on a Bechtel project to build an oil pipeline across Iraq. After Gulf War I, the Bush I administration awarded Bechtel contracts to extinguish oil fires in Kuwait. The company scored even bigger after Gulf War II (see **Iraq:** *To the victors*).

PATIENTS' RIGHTS, BUSH STYLE *(PROTECTION FOR HMOS AND INSURANCE COMPANIES)*

In 1995, Governor Bush vetoed a Patient Protection Act in Texas that spelled out hospitals' obligations toward patients and required health maintenance organizations (HMOs) to let patients see doctors outside their own networks. Critics said Bush was protecting Columbia/HCA, the giant hospital chain founded and part-owned by his top contributor and business partner, real estate tycoon Richard Rainwater (see **Bush's business career**).

In 2001, the White House sabotaged a bipartisan patients' bill of rights that would allow patients to seek redress in court against health insurance companies and HMOs. Under a 1974 law, these companies, unlike any other businesses, could not be held liable for their actions or decisions—for example, if a patient suffered injury or death as a result of being denied treatment.

In July 2001, The Senate had passed the McCain-Edwards-Kennedy patients' rights bill, which contained guarantees that patients could not be denied medical care by their insurance company and gave patients the right to sue these companies for decisions that resulted in injury or death. It also contained strong protections for employers against lawsuits blaming them for the actions of the health insurance companies they contract with. Nine Republican senators voted for the bill. Bush threatened to veto it. Naturally, the insurance industry claimed the bill was designed to promote reckless lawsuits that would drive up the cost of health insurance. And—just as naturally—it was the industry's problems that concerned the Bush White House.

As a nearly identical, bipartisan bill took shape in the House, the White House cut a private, overnight deal with one of its sponsors, Charlie Norwood (R-GA), who got an amendment passed next day that gutted the House and Senate bills. "The House actually passed a health maintenance organization and insurance company protection act that would leave patients with even fewer options for legal recourse than they have now," said Rep. Marion Berry (D-AR).[237] It gave the HMOs special protections—such as federal limits on damages—that no other industry had; made it harder for a plaintiff against an HMO to prove liability; and voided existing patients' rights laws in various states. It was a bill the Democratic-majority Senate could never agree to—and as a result, there was still no patients' bill of rights as of 2003 .

PHARMACEUTICAL INDUSTRY AND THE FDA

From 1997 through 2002, the drug industry spent around $500 million on lobbying and maintained an army of more than 600 Washington lobbyists (including some two dozen former Congress members)—more than one for every member of Congress. In 2000 and 2002 drug companies gave more than $30 million to Congressional candidates, three-quarters of it to Republicans, and helped underwrite another $15 million of TV ads supporting Republican candidates. Bush received $466,000 from the industry in 2000, topping all other candidates.

The industry's legislative priorities were to ensure that any **Medicare** prescription drug benefit would not involve price controls; to block legislation easing the approval and marketing of generic drugs; block imports of lower-priced drugs from Canada; fight Congressional efforts to limit "direct-to-consumer" drug advertising on TV and in newspapers; and limit damages in lawsuits over harm caused by their products. Quite a shopping list—but the Bushies were there to help.

Drug advertising as "free speech." The Food and Drug Administration (FDA) is responsible for ensuring both the safety and efficacy of drugs and the accuracy of drug advertising and labeling. The Bush FDA seemed to have different priorities. In October 2002, it invited the industry to point out any FDA regulations regarding drug advertising that the industry felt infringed on its First Amendment rights to free speech.

The FDA's general counsel and chief drug marketing "regulator," Bush appointee DANIEL TROY, previously represented the right-wing Washington Legal Foundation in a successful legal challenge to the FDA's power to regulate drug marketing. As a trade magazine reported, "The case stood for the dramatic proposition that . . . First Amendment free speech rights are the primary consideration."[238]

On Troy's watch, FDA enforcement actions against drug companies for questionable advertising fell from around ninety a year to less than thirty. Some staffers blamed a new policy under which all enforcement letters were reviewed by Troy's office, which they said had an intimidating effect. Troy and FDA Commissioner Mark McClellan insisted they were merely ensuring that their enforcement actions would stand up in the courts, where, they said, the FDA had been losing on First Amendment issues. *Astounding* hypocrisy; no one had done more to bring about those losses than Troy himself. His efforts to limit the FDA's ability to restrict tobacco advertising in the 1990s led the Supreme Court to rule in 2001 that such advertising was protected by the First Amendment.

Fighting the FDA from *inside*. Troy, a **Federalist Society** member who once clerked for Judge Robert Bork, converted the general counsel's office "from a legal office to an activist [anti-regulation] policy office," and had "an open-door policy" with industry, a former FDA official said. For more than a year while he was the de facto FDA head, Troy held at least fifty private meetings with drug manufacturers and others regulated by the FDA. *U.S. News and World Report* sought records of those meetings under the Freedom of Information Act but was told by Troy's office that there are "no minutes, no memos, no nothing." However, the magazine reported several instances in which Troy, shortly after such meetings, agreed to manufacturers' requests for regulatory changes that could raise serious health and safety risks. In July 2002, *U.S. News* reported, Troy "stalled efforts to investigate complaints about ephedra, an herb used in a dietary supplement suspected as a factor in at least 100 deaths . . . When a top regulatory official at the FDA's Washington headquarters opposed Troy's decision, he was transferred to Texas."[239]

Immunizing vaccine makers from lawsuits: "The Lilly rider," SARS, and the good Dr. Frist. The Homeland Security Act of November 2002 contained a provision—smuggled in by Republicans the night before the final House vote—whose relevance to homeland security escaped some Americans. It protected the drug maker Eli Lilly from current and future lawsuits over a vaccine it manufactured containing a mercury-based preservative, thimerosal, which allegedly caused autism. The FDA had asked in 1999 that thimerosal be removed from vaccines. Thousands of lawsuits had already been filed against Lilly by parents of autistic kids. Under the new provision, a federal fund—i.e., taxpayers—not Lilly, would compensate such plaintiffs.

Though he denied it, the "Lilly rider"—which Lilly, a large GOP contributor, had lobbied for—proved to be the work of SEN. BILL FRIST (R-TN), who had earlier sponsored a nearly identical measure that lawmakers rebuffed. The Homeland bill was passed only on a promise to members of Congress that the measure would be amended so it did not apply to lawsuits already filed. But right after the 2002 election, Republican leaders reneged, and Frist went on pushing his original bill. Better yet, Frist was soon using SARS—severe acute respiratory syndrome, the terrifying ailment that spread in early 2003—as a new rationale for the "Lilly rider":

Fear of "frivolous lawsuits," he claimed, would prevent companies from manufacturing SARS vaccines.

Frist, a physician whose family founded one of the country's biggest hospital chains, was the Republicans' health-care point man, soon to be Bush's hand-picked Senate majority leader, and a major raiser of health-care-industry contributions to the GOP (Frist himself received $258,000 from the industry between 1997 and 2000). In June 2002, while Congress debated a Medicare prescription drug bill, Frist helped to organize a dinner, sponsored by Glaxo-SmithKline and other large drug makers, that raised more than $20 million for GOP Congressional campaigns. Frist's letter to potential donors said the goal was to return the Senate to GOP control so as to "relax the stranglehold of rules, regulations, and restrictions on American business."[240]

Blocking lower-cost imports. In March 2003, the FDA warned health insurers that they faced civil and criminal liability if they paid for prescription drugs imported from Canada, and "reserved the right" to prosecute individuals who import medicines. Drug companies had lobbied vigorously for the new policy. Americans were buying between $500 million and $1 billion worth of drugs from Canada, where they cost on average 43 percent less than in the U.S.—whose consumers paid by far the highest drug prices in the industrialized world. Despite FDA warnings that imported drugs might not be safe, Rep. Bernard Sanders (I-VT) said, "There hasn't been one problem" and added that at least seven out of the eleven FDA commissioners who cited safety risks "have strong financial ties to the pharmaceutical and medical equipment industry."

AID to U.S. drug companies. Bush's January 2003 announcement of a $15 billion AIDS relief package for Africa, which included AIDS drugs, was much praised. Yet even the pro-business cable channel CNBC described the move to provide AIDS drugs at taxpayers' expense as one that took the heat off the drug industry, which was under international pressure to provide the medicines at low cost to poor countries. The Bushies managed at once to create a new taxpayer subsidy to a favored big business while presenting Bush as "compassionate."

Prescription drug testing for children suspended. In March 2002, the Bush administration suspended a rule enacted by Clinton that required drug companies to test their products to ensure they are safe and effective for children. Around 75 percent of all drugs in America had never been tested for children. (The move was prompted in part by a lawsuit brought two years earlier by the drug industry challenging the FDA's authority to order pediatric drug trials. The lead attorney for the plaintiffs was Daniel Troy.)

The American Academy of Pediatrics (AAP) and other medical experts said voluntary testing would once again leave doctors guessing about whether medicines are safe for children. A spokesman recalled infant deaths resulting from inadequately tested dosages of a hypertension drug in the days before the Clinton rule. "The FDA's action today is five steps backward," said a former FDA commissioner.

Helping the drug giants fend off generics. By 2002, there was growing pressure to stop brand-name drug makers from blocking rival generic drugs—which cost up to 80 percent less—from coming to market. A 1984 law gave drug makers an automatic thirty-month extension on their expiring patents if they sued a generic competitor for infringement of patents on packaging or some such nonsense—a loophole through which they had learned to fend off competition for years with frivolous and repeated lawsuits.

Bush proposed rules in October 2002 to make lower-cost generic drugs available more quickly by allowing drug companies only one thirty-month extension per drug, and not granting patent extensions merely for packaging. But that fell far short of a Senate bill already passed months before, by a 78-21 vote, which Bush rejected. By eliminating the automatic thirty-day extension and allowing re-importation of drugs from Canada, that bill would have saved consumers twice as much as Bush's proposal—$60 billion versus $30 billion over ten years.

SCIENCE POLICY: *GETTING THE ANSWERS THEY WANT*

> *"Bush's quarrel is not simply with the Democrats, the liberals, or even the scientists; his quarrel is with nature itself."*
> —Ernest Partridge, "The Gadfly Online"

"Here are the conclusions upon which my facts shall be based." Adlai Stevenson once witticized. While Bush never said, or could say, anything like that, that was the Bushies' approach to science and its uses in shaping policy: Bush officials repeatedly rejected the findings and recommendations of leading experts on **health and safety**, the **environment**,

global warming, **energy**, and other issues because their findings were politically unwelcome. The director of the program on science, technology, and public policy at the Kennedy School of Government at Harvard said scientists were seeing "a pattern of government agencies' shaping the composition of panels advising them."[241]

- In March 2002, the Department of Defense (DOD) terminated its contract with PROJECT JASON, an influential panel of around 50 elite scientists that had advised the DOD on projects involving advanced technology since 1959. Panel members said they were terminated because they objected to a Bush administration attempt to place on the panel three "political appointees" who lacked scientific expertise (two of the three did not even have PhDs). The panel had always had final say over its membership. After a struggle, the contract was renewed. Still, researchers and policy analysts said the affair pointed up, as one said, "a general trend in the [DOD] to reduce the possibility that someone may come up with the wrong answer or produce inconvenient conclusions."[242]
- The Bushies didn't merely ignore critics of their **missile defense** plans—they retaliated. Public opposition by Dr. Theodore Postal of MIT cost him federal research grants and brought threats of research cutbacks to MIT.
- The Intergovernmental Panel on Climate Change (IPCC)—the world's 2000 top climate scientists—concluded in 1995, and reaffirmed in 2000, that fossil fuel use was causing **global warming**. Bush asked the

National Academy of Sciences (NAS) to review the IPCC findings. No luck: "The [NAS] committee generally agrees" with the IPCC report, came the answer. Never daunted, Bush then orchestrated the ouster of the IPCC chair, an eminent atmospheric scientist, and his replacement by an economist.

- In September 2002, the Environmental Protection Agency (EPA) released its annual federal report on air pollution, and with White House "approval," the section on global warming was deleted for the first time in six years.

- In April 2002, the U.S. Geological Survey, an agency of the Interior Department, submitted the results of a twelve-year study concluding that oil exploration in the Arctic National Wildlife Refuge would adversely affect the region's wildlife. Interior Secretary GAIL NORTON ordered a reassessment—and, a mere week later, got a report that concluded there would be *no* harm to wildlife.

- In August 2001, Bush, pandering to abortion opponents, put crippling restrictions on funding for human embryonic STEM CELL RESEARCH, which could lead to treatments for many diseases but involves the destruction of embryonic cell samples, which are discarded anyway.

- Bush said "the jury is still out" on evolution, and favored equal time for teaching creationism in schools.

- While ignoring *actual* scientific findings it found inconvenient, the Bushies adopted what they called a "SCI-ENCE-BASED" approach to regulation—typically using

"SOUND SCIENCE" to "prove" that the "economic costs"—i.e., the short-term effect on corporate profits—of health, safety, and environmental regulations outweigh the benefits to the public. (See **Deregulation**.)

- At Health and Human Services (HHS), expert committees were "retired" before they could present data that might contradict the Bushies' views on medical matters (see **Health and safety regulations**).

SECRECY AND "EXECUTIVE PRIVILEGE"

As a Yale student, George W. Bush became a member of the most secret of the student societies, the SKULL AND BONES—following in the footsteps of his father and grandfather. Some thirty-five years later, the Bush administration quickly established a record on secrecy "that makes Richard Nixon . . . look like a boy scout," Russ Baker of *The Nation* wrote.[243] From day one, the Bushies showed a passion for keeping their employers, the American public, out of their affairs. Soon the Bushies were invoking "executive privilege" liberally, as it were, to cover up embarrassing conflicts of interest—angering even conservative Republicans who had attacked President Clinton for the same thing. Rep. Dan Burton (R-IN) (an inveterate Clinton hounder) called the Bushies' obsession with secrecy "dictatorial." Then-Judiciary Committee Chairman Patrick Leahy (D-VT) said in the twenty-eight years he had been in the Senate, "I have never known an administration that is more difficult to get information from that the oversight committees are entitled to."

Gutting the Presidential Records Act. One of Bush's first acts as president was to block the release in January 2001 of Ronald Reagan's White House papers as scheduled under the Presidential Records Act, which required all but the most "sensitive" documents to be made public twelve years after a president leaves office. The law allowed the current president a thirty-day delay. But more than a year later, Bush had released less than 10 percent of the Reagan papers. The reason, it was widely assumed, was that many current Bush officials, including Dick Cheney and Donald Rumsfeld, were among their authors.

After 9/11, the White House accorded itself almost unlimited powers of secrecy. In November 2001, a Bush executive order declared that a sitting president could block the release of the papers of a predecessor even if the latter had approved their release. And—most alarmingly—former presidents or vice presidents or their families or appointed representatives could block release of documents against the will of a sitting president, including those related to "military, diplomatic or national security secrets." In the all-purpose name of the **war on terrorism,** Bush had effectively turned public records into private, family affairs, and given himself and Cheney control over the records of Cheney, Rumsfeld, and Bush Sr.'s actions going back to the beginning of the Reagan administration—likely including such embarrassing matters as past support for Saddam Hussein and Osama bin Laden.

"Executive privilege" and Cheney's energy task force. Since the Supreme Court first recognized a president's right to withhold certain information from Congress in 1974, courts had consistently interpreted "executive privilege" to apply only to a narrowly defined range of high-level deliberations involving the president and his closest advisers. The Bush White House interpreted it a little differently. From the time it became known that Cheney had invited energy industry insiders to closed-door meetings to tailor national **energy policy** to their liking, Congress was locked in a struggle with the White House for the release of names of those with whom Cheney and his aides met. Repeated requests and formal demands by Congress's General Accounting Office (GAO) were rebuffed. According to GAO Comptroller David Walker, no prior administration had ever challenged the GAO's authority in such requests. In January 2002, the GAO sued the White House to obtain the information. The suit was dismissed eleven months later by U.S. District Judge JOHN BATES, a recent Bush appointee (see **Judicial nominees**).

Selective **privilege.** Even while blocking release of Cheney's energy task force records, the Bushies released thousands of Clinton White House documents to Congressional committees on at least seven occasions (so much for their claim to be preserving the sacred principle of keeping executive branch discussions confidential)—but only those most embarrassing to Clinton. For example, they released only an out-of-context portion of a Clinton transcript dealing with his pardon of financier Marc Rich. It was, they said, simply a part of their long-standing effort to make more information available to Congress, and they were actually *assisting* the former president! (When Clinton aides asked that the rest be released, the White House said *that* was classified.)[244]

Open government rules subverted. Following the same

pattern set by Cheney's energy task force, Bush established a "Commission to Strengthen **Social Security**," which he stocked with supporters of privatization from right-wing think tanks and with executives of companies that would reap huge profits from it. They met behind closed doors, beginning in August 2001. A legal expert on open-government rules told *The New York Times* that federal statutes clearly required such meetings to be open, and that a new Bush rule that supposedly permitted such closed-door meetings "subverts not only the plain language but [the] overriding open-government purpose" of the statute and "makes a farce" of the process.

Ashcroft v. Freedom of Information Act. In October 2001, Attorney General John Ashcroft sent out a memo saying Justice Department policy should be, whenever possible, *not* to give out information requested under the Freedom of Information Act. This reversed the Clinton policy that documents should be withheld only when disclosure would cause harm—a policy the Clinton White House honored by handing over to the House Government and Oversight Committee over a million pages of documents.

Classified adds. In March 2003, the Bush administration revoked Clinton rules that said information should not be classified "if there is significant doubt" that releasing it would harm national security. The new Bush policy also:

- Allowed documents to be kept classified for up to twenty-five years without a specific reason, instead of 10 years, normally, under the Clinton rule.
- Postponed automatic declassification of documents

twenty-five or more years old, as was required under a Clinton rule that was about to go into effect.

- Permitted *re*classification of documents that have already been made public.
- Gave the CIA special authority to reject decisions of an interagency panel that handles declassification requests from researchers.

SEPTEMBER 11:
WARNINGS DISCOUNTED, PRECAUTIONS NOT TAKEN, FAILURES COVERED UP

Throughout the summer of 2001, even as U.S. embassies buzzed with word of an impending attack, the Bushies remained focused on such ancient obsessions as ousting Saddam Hussein from **Iraq** and building a **missile defense** shield against long-range missiles that no terrorists or rogue states possessed—instead of thinking about, say, men armed with box cutters boarding commercial planes, the sort of scenario of which there was truly an embarrassment of warnings. On taking office, the Bushies had abandoned a Clinton plan to attack Al Qaeda, and instead chose to develop their own anti-terrorist strategy from scratch, which had still not landed on Bush's desk by 9/11.

During their eight months in office prior to 9/11, the Bushies failed to act on repeated warnings that the U.S. counterterrorism and **homeland security** apparatus was urgently in need of reorganization and reinforcement. They discounted or failed to "connect the dots" in a rapid accumulation of warnings of major attacks on U.S. soil—some of them remarkably specific, such as warnings in late summer of impending attacks on U.S. landmarks using aircraft. Despite repeated, even frantic warnings from CIA Director George Tenet and others in U.S. and foreign intelligence, Bush went on vacation for the entire month of August, and admitted later, "I didn't feel that sense of urgency." Talk about intelligence failures. Months later, when the public learned of the extent of the warnings the intelligence services *and* the White House had received, the Bushies tried to cover up.

Even *after* 9/11, Bush, while declaring his presidency to now be all about protecting America and defeating terrorism, remained astoundingly stingy with funding for homeland security. Meanwhile, the Bushies exploited the "war" footing to justify their entire pre-9/11 agenda, from rolling back environmental protections and weakening civil liberties to doling out huge tax breaks to corporations and the wealthy (as House Majority Leader Tom DeLay said, "Nothing is more important in the face of a war than cutting taxes"). It was the first "wartime" period in U.S. history when *that* had happened; generally, taxes are raised to pay for wars. For the Bushies' political benefit, *this* war was to be billed to future generations. (See **War on terrorism: Bush's political WMD**.)

During the eight months prior to 9/11, the Bushies:

- Ignored the HART-RUDMAN COMMISSION (see **Homeland security**).
- Ignored warnings in January 2001 from the outgoing Clinton national security team that Al Qaeda and its sleeper cells in the U.S. were *the* major security threat facing the U.S.
- Abandoned the Clinton plan to attack Al Qaeda,

which was presented to the incoming Bush administration in January 2001, in favor of developing their
own. Bush's Cabinet-rank advisers held their first
meeting on terrorism on September 4.

- Failed to take action against the Taliban regime in
Afghanistan even after determining in February 2001
that Al Qaeda was responsible for the October 2000
attack on the USS *Cole*.

- Gave the Taliban $43 million in aid in April 2001—
largely as a reward for the regime's outlawing opium
growing as "against the will of God." (Wrote Robert
Scheer, "The war on **drugs** has become our own
fanatics' obsession and easily trumps all other concerns."[245]) The funding—which was also connected
with the hopes of U.S. energy companies to build an
oil pipeline across Afghanistan—made the U.S. the
Taliban's leading sponsor. The "irrelevant" UN was at
the time imposing sanctions on the Taliban regime for
refusing to turn over bin Laden.

- Prevented FBI terrorism experts from investigating
Saudi ties to Al Qaeda (see **Oil**).

- Fought *against* international anti–money laundering
accords that would have helped track down Al Qaeda
financial assets, because they involved empowering
governments to investigate rich folks' financial
affairs—and because they were, well, international
accords. The Bushies continued to obstruct anti-
money laundering efforts after 9/11.

- Attorney General Ashcroft rejected the FBI's request
for $57.8 million for more counter-terrorism agents
and researchers. While no counterterrorism add-ones

were included in his funding-request letter to budget director Mitch Daniels—on September 10, 2001—it did include a *reduction* in anti-terrorism grants to state and local governments.[246]

Reporter to White House Press Secretary Ari Fleischer on September 11: "Had there been any warnings that the President knew of?" Fleischer: "No warnings."

- In June 2001, the National Security Agency (NSA)'s ECHELON electronic spy network gave warning that Mideast terrorists were planning to hijack commercial aircraft to use as weapons to attack important symbols of American culture; and a CIA summary for National Security Adviser Condoleezza Rice said, "It is highly likely that a significant Al Qaeda attack is in the near future, within several weeks." CIA Director George Tenet was said to be "nearly frantic," and by late summer, a senior political appointee said, Tenet had "repeated [the warning] so often that people got tired of hearing it."

- On July 5, NSA Counter-terrorism Chief Richard Clarke, a Clinton holdover, told representatives of a dozen federal agencies meeting in the White House situation room, "Something really spectacular is going to happen here, and it's going to happen soon." Every agency was put on highest alert, but began to stand down after several weeks.

- On July 10, an FBI agent in Phoenix, Kenneth Johnson, reported to headquarters that Arabs with a "strong connection" to Al Qaeda were training in a local flight school. He suspected a hijacking plot organized by bin Laden, and urged a nationwide investigation. The FBI failed to share the warning with any other agency. Ashcroft and FBI Director Robert Mueller both learned of all this in the days following 9/11,[247] but kept it to themselves, not telling any congressional investigators or legislators or even, apparently, Bush until it came to light in May 2002. Three of the 9/11 hijackers received flight training in the U.S.

- On August 6, CIA staff personally warned Bush that Al Qaeda planned to hijack U.S. planes and attack targets within the U.S. The White House kept the briefing secret until CBS broke the story eight months later. Administration officials then tried to downplay the briefing, calling it "general" and "historic and analytic in nature" and said intelligence officials in the months before 9/11 had been focused primarily on threats to U.S. interests *overseas*. Ari Fleischer even lied to reporters about the briefing memo's title: He said it was, "Bin Laden Determined to Strike the United States." In fact, it was called "Bin Laden Determined to Strike *in* U.S. [emphasis added]"—and the briefing itself emphasized Al Qaeda plans to "bring the fight to America" and suggested they might hijack U.S. airliners. Cheney dismissed the briefing memo as merely a "rehash" that "didn't give us anything new or precise or specific." Then why wasn't it turned over to Congress, he was asked a moment later? Because, he now claimed, it contained "the most sensitive sources and methods . . . it's the family jewels"![248]

- In the weeks before 9/11, Russian, Israeli, Jordanian, Egyptian, and Moroccan intelligence warned U.S.

intelligence of imminent, large-scale terrorist attacks on targets in the U.S., including warning of attacks using aircraft and attacks in New York that summer or fall.[249]

- Shortly before 9/11, the NSA intercepted or detected multiple phone calls from bin Laden's chief of operations, Abu Zubaida, to the U.S.

- According to an October 2001 NBC report, on September 9 bin Laden phoned his mother and told her something big was to happen in two days and that she wouldn't hear from him for a while. A foreign intelligence service recorded the call and relayed the information to U.S. intelligence.

Despite all those warnings:

- Bush went on vacation in Crawford, Texas, for the entire month of August (after six months on the job). "The alerts of the early and mid-summer—described by two career counter-terrorist officials as the most urgent in decades—had faded to secondary concern," *The Washington Post* reported.[250]

- The Federal Aviation Administration (FAA), which knew by August of hijacking warnings, failed to warn the airlines or order increased airline security, such as assigning more sky marshals or securing cockpit doors.

- In July, without explanation, the administration changed FAA policy to prohibit pilots from carrying guns.

- The administration failed to increase the Air Defense readiness levels. The nearest of the twenty or so U.S.

fighter planes on permanent full alert within the U.S. remained deployed at bases several hundred miles from New York or Washington—positioned against attacks from the former Soviet Union. When the second plane hit the World Trade Center, the nearest approaching fighter plane was seventy miles away.

- A few weeks before 9/11, top Justice and FBI officials denied a request by agents in Minneapolis for a warrant to search the computer of ZACARIAS MOUSSAOUI— the alleged "twentieth hijacker." The agents had been tipped that Moussaoui had sought lessons in flying but not taking off or landing aircraft; had specifically inquired about flying over New York City air space; and had radical Islamic affiliations. One of them had speculated Moussaoui might be planning to fly an airliner into the World Trade Center. The computer proved to contain a flight simulation program, information about crop dusters, and the phone number of a roommate of Mohammed Atta. In May 2002, FBI Director Mueller stamped "classified" on a memo he received from agent COLEEN ROWLEY, a twenty-one-year veteran, which detailed how FBI headquarters had "consistently, almost deliberately thwart[ed]" her and other agents' efforts to investigate Moussaoui. Rowley disputed Mueller's assertion that a fuller investigation could not have averted 9/11.

- On September 10, the NSA intercepted two messages in Arabic warning that something was about to happen—"Tomorrow is zero hour," and "The match begins tomorrow." The messages were not translated until September 12.

"I don't think anybody could have predicted that these people would take an airplane and slam it into the World Trade Center."—Condoleezza Rice

Oh, really?

- In 1993 the Pentagon commissioned a study called "Terrorism 2000," which predicted the use of planes as weapons in multiple, simultaneous attacks targeting large landmarks, financial centers, etc.
- In April 1994, a FedEx employee tried to crash a DC-10 into FedEx headquarters in Memphis, Tennessee, but was apprehended.
- In September 1994, an apparently deranged man crashed a small plane onto the White House grounds, just short of the president's bedroom.
- In December 1994, members of the Al Qaeda–linked Armed Islamic Group hijacked an Air France flight in Algeria, aiming to crash it into the Eiffel Tower. French special forces stormed the plane on the ground and killed the hijackers.
- In 1995, Philippines police uncovered, and informed the U.S. of, Al Qaeda plans to blow up U.S. airliners in flight over the Pacific and/or hijack planes and fly them into targets in the U.S., including CIA headquarters, the Pentagon, and the World Trade Center. One of the two planners was apparently Ramsi Yousef, who boasted of the plan after he was later arrested and convicted for planning the 1993 World Trade Center bombing.
- In 1998, terrorism analysts briefed FAA security officials on scenarios in which terrorists crashed planes

into U.S. nuclear plants, the World Trade Center, the Pentagon, and other targets.

- In 1999, a report prepared for the CIA-affiliated National Intelligence Council warned that terrorists associated with bin Laden might hijack a plane and crash it into the Pentagon, the White House, or CIA headquarters.
- In December 2000 the Pentagon conducted a drill to respond to an airline crashing into the Pentagon building.

Conservative columnist Robert Novak concluded, "From the moment of the September 11 attacks, high-ranking federal officials insisted that the terrorists' method of operation surprised them. . . . Actually, elements of the hijacking plan were known to the FBI as early as 1995 and, if coupled with current information, might have uncovered the plot."[251]

"A veil of silence." One might have expected heads to roll at the FBI and the rest of the intelligence system. But it was as though the Bushies decided they must not admit such bungling was committed on their watch (let alone own up to any responsibility). The U.S. "has drawn a veil of silence" over the intelligence failures, a Canadian intelligence consultant wrote.[252]

The Bushies opposed any investigation—even by the House and Senate intelligence committees, which traditionally maintained cozy relations with the intelligence services. First, they delayed this; after it got under way in February 2002, according to then-Senate Majority Leader Tom Daschle, Cheney pressured him at least twice to shut it down. "Press the issue, Cheney implied, and you risk being accused of interfering with the mission," *Newsweek* reported.[253] Then news leaked that the Justice Department and CIA weren't fully cooperating. "The administration's actions suggest a cover-up," wrote Al Hunt in *The Wall Street Journal*.

As more and more was learned about the intelligence failures, the administration opposed bipartisan Congressional demands for an independent investigation, saying open hearings would divert attention from the **war on terrorism,** unnecessarily embarrass government officials, and, of course, compromise national security. "The administration knows that inevitably such [an investigation] will provide a road map to what has not been fixed in the nine months since," wrote Frank Rich in *The New York Times*.

Investigate the investigators instead. Indeed, the Bushies seemed more angered by *criticism of* the intelligence failures, and by calls for an investigation, than by the failures themselves. In June 2002, when the media reported that the National Security Agency had intercepted two warnings in Arabic on September 10 that something was about to happen, the White House went ballistic and ordered the FBI to investigate—not the intelligence lapse, but who among the members of the Senate and House Intelligence Committees had leaked this classified information to the press. Almost all the members of the committees responsible for investigating the FBI found themselves being grilled *by* the FBI and being asked to subject themselves to lie detector tests.

The White House finally switched course in September 2002 and agreed to the commission of inquiry, but continued to oppose an investigation of intelligence failures. As of August 2003, there had still been no public hearings into the events of, and preceding, 9/11.

SOCIAL SECURITY "REFORM"

That's **BushSpeak** for *privatizating* the Social Security system—turning it into a profit-making industry for financial services corporations. Bush wanted workers' payroll taxes to go into private accounts that could be invested in, for example, **Enron** stock, or its future equivalent, instead of into the Social Security trust fund; this would supposedly give workers bigger nest eggs and monthly incomes when they retire. This claim was much debated. Infinitely more certain was that Bush's plan would benefit corporations by vastly expanding the market for their stocks, and enrich the financial firms that would market the shares and receive tens of millions of new retirement accounts. Equally certain was that Bush misled the public about the benefits—and risks—to retirees.

A bogus crisis . . . The Bushies' plan was premised largely on the idea that the Social Security system was in a financial crisis that called for drastic restructuring. Actually, the Social Security and Medicare Trustees Report of March 2002 said Social Security benefits were guaranteed until 2041— twelve years longer than predicted in 1997. Hardly the gloom-and-doom scenario that supporters of the Bush plan described. Mind you, Bush had only just begun spending the Social Security trust fund—which he had vowed not to touch—on his tax cuts and military buildup.

. . . and bogus benefits. Talk about fraudulent insurance claims. Bush's advertising of his "reform" plan's benefits was as phony as the crisis that supposedly necessitated it. According to the Privatizer-in-Chief, a person who worked forty-five years and invested his payroll taxes in the stock market would after retirement have three times the monthly income he would have received from Social Security.[254] Bush forgot to mention that to get that result, this person would have to invest *every penny of these savings in the stock market throughout his entire working life* (a strategy no sane and responsible money manager would follow) and luck into the best period in history for stock market returns—and never get nervous and sell stock during market downturns.

Even the president's so-called Commission to Strengthen Social Security—though packed with supporters of privatization from right-wing think tanks and with executives from companies that stood to reap a fortune from privatization—did not use such crazy assumptions in the proposals it released in December 2002—according to which the worker's retirement benefits would be around half the amount in Bush's example (which, a White House spokeswoman later said, was just "for the purpose of example").

Sound political accounting. As Paul Krugman noted in *The New York Times*, Bush forgot to mention something else: the system's existing obligations—the debt it owed to older Americans. Social Security, Krugman wrote, is "really a social contract: each generation pays taxes that support the previous generation's retirement, and expects to receive the same treatment from the next generation."[255] If, as Bush proposed, younger workers' payroll taxes went into private accounts instead of Social Security, who would pay for their parents' benefits—the masses of baby boomers approaching retirement? There were only two possibilities. One was default—break the contract, slash the benefits. The other was to use money from other sources to replace the diverted funds. Either way—as even the president's commission apparently ended up realizing—private accounts wouldn't "save" Social Security but only create a financing crisis.

STATE AND LOCAL GOVERNMENTS' FINANCIAL CRISIS

While Bush lavished trillions on tax cuts for the justly infamous richest 1 percent and on a hypertrophied military buildup, state governments across the land were struggling with a growing share of the burdens of government, shrinking revenues, and reduced federal help. Bush didn't just fail to come to the states' aid; his fiscal policies and tax cuts aggravated their problems, as did the recession he presided over.

The recession cost states revenue from income and sales taxes. As unemployment rose and people lost job-related health coverage, more were thrown onto **Medicaid**, increasing the states' burden when they could least afford it. By the end of 2002, state budget deficits nationwide totaled $100 billion. Under a president who had loudly and often declared his commitment to improve **education**, a number of states had been forced to cut the length of the school year and school week. Drastic cuts were under way in state funding for everything from health care and social services to roads and prisons.

Bush's one-two punch to states. Economic aid to the states was expected to be included in Bush's January 2003 "economic stimulus/growth" plan, but was quietly dropped. In fact, the plan, which centered on cutting taxes on stock dividends, would actually worsen the states' fiscal crisis by depriving them of a collective $4 billion a year in dividend tax revenue.

States faced an additional potential loss of $50 to $100 billion over ten years because of Bush's repeal in 2001 of the federal estate tax, to which the states tied their own estate and inheritance taxes. To preserve those revenues, state governments would have to take the unpopular step of creating new estate and inheritance taxes.[256] Indeed, because of a complicated formula, the *feds* would get the estimated $36 billion in estate/inheritance tax revenues that the states would have received from 2006 to 2011. The states would thus bear a quarter of the $138 billion ten-year cost of repealing the *federal* estate tax. Even Republican state governors and legislators who had supported the repeal were furious when they realized this, especially as the repeal was decided by Washington after little or no consultation with state leaders. Florida governor Jeb Bush complained to Florida legislators, "Shifting the burden merely allows Washington to spend more, while requiring us to spend less." (See **Estate tax.**)

TAX EVASION:
EASING UP ON THE RICH WHILE CRACKING DOWN ON THE POOR

Big-time tax evaders never had it so good as under Bush. In what was aptly called the tax cheaters' lobby, the Bush administration, congressional Republicans, and a gaggle of right-wing pressure groups opposed efforts to stop rich

Americans from evading taxes by banking their money in Caribbean tax havens like the Cayman Islands; sought to shelter foreign depositors in U.S. banks from IRS scrutiny; and gave winks, nods, or all-out lobbying support to U.S. corporations which, with a bit of paperwork, became Bermuda corporations, in order to avoid U.S. taxes.

The Bermuda loophole: "Profits over patriotism." In 1998, corporations avoided as much as $54 billion in taxes by hiding profits in tax shelters. Under Bush, the ascendancy of radical anti-tax leaders and lobby groups gave the cleared-for-takeoff signal to dozens of corporations to "move" (on paper) to offshore tax havens like Bermuda and the Cayman Islands to avoid up to hundreds of millions of dollars per year each in taxes—this while the country was supposedly at war, while taxpayers were footing the bills for huge defense and homeland spending increases, and amid federal deficits and domestic spending cuts, massive corporate layoffs, and rising unemployment and hardship. As this corporate patriotism drew criticism, the White House "called for further study, which may take several years,"[257] while their allies in Congress worked to *expand* the tax loopholes that permitted it.

Little or nothing about these companies' operations changed when they "moved" offshore. The chief financial officer of New Jersey–based Ingersoll-Rand told *The New York Times* his company wouldn't even have to set up an office in Bermuda. "We just pay a service organization" to accept mail. The big accounting firms encouraged this behavior. As Ernst & Young told its clients, it might look bad but "the improvement on earnings is powerful enough that maybe the patriotism issue needs to take a back seat."

These sleazy corporations hired a slew of prominent

Republicans to lobby for them, including Bob Dole, Bush family
confidant and consultant Charles Black, former Rep. Bob Liv-
ingston (R-LA), and Ken Duberstein, chief of staff of the
Reagan White House. In August 2002, thirty Republican
groups—including the Heritage Foundation, the Cato Institute, Grover Norquist's Americans for Tax Reform, and the
Christian-right Coalitions for America—sent a letter of praise
to House Ways and Means Chairman Bill Thomas (R-CA) for
introducing legislation making it even easier for companies
to exploit offshore tax havens. These same groups also joined
the Bushies in opposing efforts to stop rich individual Americans from evading taxes by moving their money to Caribbean
tax havens like the Cayman Islands.

But in the wake of **corporate scandals** such as **Enron**,
which built a vast tax-avoidance mechanism involving
around 400 offshore subsidiaries, even some Republicans
called for reform. "There is no business reason for [corpora-
tions to move offshore], other than to escape U.S. taxation,"
said Charles Grassley (R-IA), the ranking Republican on the
Senate Finance Committee. "It's not illegal, but it is
immoral." Companies shouldn't be allowed to "choose
profits over patriotism," said Rep. Charles Rangel (D-NY).

Even the White House felt compelled to condemn the
tactic. "The President is concerned," spokesman Ari Fleischer assured us in July 2002. He had good reason to be: It
had come to light that very day that the oil company in which
he was a partner, Harken Energy, set up an offshore subsidiary in the Cayman Islands tax haven in 1989, while Bush
sat on Harken's board of directors (see **Bush's business
career**). It was also reported that Halliburton registered as
many as forty-four offshore subsidiaries while **Cheney** was
CEO.

Shielding millionaires, foreign and domestic. As Robert McIntyre reported in *The American Prospect*,[258] toward the end of the Clinton administration, the IRS proposed requiring U.S. banks to report the interest they paid to foreign investors, who were exempt from U.S. taxes. The purpose was to curb tax cheating by foreigners in their home countries and by Americans pretending to be foreigners to evade U.S. taxes.

"The banking industry [was] apoplectic," McIntyre wrote. "So was Florida Gov. Jeb Bush, whose no-income-tax state harbors a large share of the [federal] tax-free deposits." Joined by the usual right-wing anti-tax groups and House Republicans, banking lobbyists prevailed on the Bush White House to kill the proposal—which it did in August 2002, replacing it with one that exempted the majority of foreign depositors. McIntyre called it so limited that it is almost meaningless.

Meanwhile, a crackdown on the poor. Compare and contrast this Bushite aid and comfort for tax evasion by the rich with this: "The Internal Revenue Service is planning to ask more than four million of the working poor who now claim a special tax credit to *provide the most exhaustive proof of eligibility ever demanded of any class of taxpayers* [emphasis added]" (*The New York Times*, April 25, 2003).

The EARNED INCOME TAX CREDIT (EITC) was widely praised—even by George Bush—for helping to lift countless families out of poverty. Out of the other side of his mouth, Bush singled out the program for criticism that it was plagued with fraud, and asked Congress for $100 million and 650 new IRS employees to examine claims.

The new standard of proof was set so high, critics said, that even honest taxpayers wouldn't be able to meet it; some who were entitled to the credit would no longer receive it; and those seeking it would almost certainly have to pay commercial tax preparers more to do the extra paperwork. Meanwhile,

- Government reports found that the Treasury was losing roughly $6–8 billion per year by paying undue EITCs, whereas, according to a Harvard economist's study, corporations avoided as much as $54 billion in taxes in 1998 by hiding about $155 billion in profits in tax shelters.
- An IRS study said the biggest tax dodgers by far

A reward for corporate tax avoiders and job exporters. In October 2003, the White House made clear that Bush would sign a bill providing a huge windfall to U.S. corporations that had "deferred" taxes for years on as much as $400 billion in foreign profits by sheltering them overseas. The bill would give these companies a one-time, six-month tax holiday, during which those that brought their foreign profits "home" would pay a tax rate of 5 1/4%. As Sen. John Breaux (D-LA) noted, "The company that left Louisiana is going to pay a 5 percent tax on the widgets they make overseas, and the company that stayed in Louisiana is going to pay a 35 percent tax." Even Assistant treasury Secretary Pamela Olsen said the bill could "undermine taxpayers' perception of the fairness of the tax system." But the White House was more concerned with passing the legislative package containing the measure, which, *The New York Times* reported, was "packed with items that benefit farmers and agribusinesses, oil and gas pipeline companies, and even movie producers."

were people running their own businesses, not the working poor.

- In 2002, about one in every sixty-four filers receiving the EITC was audited, while only one of every 120 taxpayers with annual incomes over $100,000 was audited, as were about one in 400 partnerships, which are primarily owned by the wealthy.

Let 'em go barefoot! A Treasury official characterized the EITC crackdown as a *benefit* to the poor, because it would reject their claims for credit *before* they received it, so they wouldn't have to be audited and to pay the money back with interest after they had already spent it! ("These people didn't invest [that money]," the official explained to the *Times*. "They went out and bought their kids sneakers.") The Bushies really were too kind.

TOBACCO INDUSTRY, FAVORS FOR

In the late 1990s, Big Tobacco had big political and legal problems. But after Bush's election, the industry had big allies in the White House, friendly new "regulators," and the friendliest attorney general ever in John **Ashcroft**—a ferocious defender of Christian family values and clean living, if not of clean lungs. (The industry already had a largely friendly Congress, thanks to more than $25 million in campaign contributions over the previous six years, chiefly to Republicans.) A few leading Bush administration FOTs (Friends Of Tobacco):

- As a Missouri senator, ASHCROFT had an extensive track

record of tobacco-friendly maneuvers, including casting
the sole dissenting vote in a 1998 Senate committee decision to approve debate on a tobacco settlement bill.

- Bush political adviser KARL ROVE was a lobbyist and
  political consultant for Philip Morris from 1991 to 1996.
- Bush's liaison to the business community, KIRK BLALOCK,
  was a former Philip Morris public relations official.
- A Philip Morris lobbyist, CHARLES BLACK, was a Bush
  family confidante and adviser to the Bush 2000 campaign.
- When he was governor of Wisconsin (1993–2000),
  Secretary of Health and Human Services TOMMY
  THOMPSON accepted more than $72,000 from Philip
  Morris, which also bankrolled some of his overseas
  trips to promote free trade.
- Heading the consumer protection bureau at the Federal Trade Commission was HOWARD BEALES, a former
  professor and consultant to RJ Reynolds Tobacco,
  who wrote an article saying the Joe Camel ads were
  not aimed at teenagers. (Maybe he meant they were
  aimed at *younger* kids.)
- Bush's deregulation czar, JOHN D. GRAHAM, was a
  former head of the Harvard Center for Risk Analysis,
  where he solicited tobacco industry money and wrote
  letters to the government disparaging the risks of secondhand smoke.

With a pack of résumés like those, these Bush administration favors for Big Tobacco came as little surprise:

- In 2001, Ashcroft's Justice Department tried to undermine its own lawsuit against the tobacco companies

(initiated under Clinton) for "false and deceptive" statements and practices and the health damage they had caused over the years. The budget for the suit was cut, questionable stories about what a weak case it was were leaked, and the department tried to cut a sweetheart deal with the companies.

- The Bush trade office reversed Clinton's opposition to tobacco companies expanding their international markets. Thus, when South Korea imposed tariffs on cigarette imports, the trade office complained; they just wanted "fair treatment" for Philip Morris and RJ Reynolds.

At the World Health Organization's convention on tobacco control in spring 2001, the U.S. delegation:

- Objected to a requirement that cigarette warnings be written in the principle language of the country where they are sold. Such a proposal might not "work best for its own population," our delegates warned. ("In other words," Al Hunt commented, "perhaps it might be better to publish warnings in Swahili for cigarettes sold in Italy."[260])
- Opposed licensing of retailers, a provision aimed against smuggling.
- Backtracked on cracking down on cigarette advertising aimed at children.
- Backtracked on mandating tobacco taxes.
- Reversed course on curbing the effects of passive smoking, also in opposition to most other countries.

According to the executive vice-president of the

Campaign for Tobacco-Free Kids, "On the No. 1 cause of preventable death in America, President Bush is providing absolutely no leadership. He acts as if the problem doesn't exist. It is a complete abdication." (See **Tort reform.**)

TORT REFORM

"Tort reform" is conservative-speak for protecting corporate wrongdoers from lawsuits brought by the citizens they harm. The fabulously well-financed tort-reform lobby was a major contributor to Bush's gubernatorial and presidential campaigns—and Bush was without doubt the most aggressively pro–"tort reform" governor *and* president ever.

These folks argued that punitive-damages awards were too onerous to business and that "frivolous" lawsuits were clogging the courts. (The right swears by harsh punishment, unto the death penalty, as a deterrent to crime—except, of course, when the wrong-doers are corporations and their executives.) The tort reform lobby claimed it was mainly trial lawyers who got rich bringing such suits while their clients ended up receiving relatively little. The culprit was supposedly contingency fees, in which trial lawyers take cases for no fee but are guaranteed a percentage of a final judgment. But that was the only way many people could afford legal representation; and such an arrangement was hardly likely to encourage frivolous suits.

As Joe Conason noted in *Salon*, litigation was perhaps the most effective, if not the only, way of discouraging corporations from selling faulty or dangerous products, polluting the environment, or otherwise endangering public health and safety. "By depriving citizens of the means to redress their grievances against powerful corporations in court, tort reform threatens to render meaningless our constitutional guarantee of equality before the law."[260]

Rise of the tort reform lobbyist-in-chief. Protecting businesses from lawsuits may have been Bush's single highest priority as Texas governor, and indeed the key to his rise in politics.

In 1994, Bush political adviser Karl Rove—who was also a lobbyist/consultant for **tobacco** giant Philip Morris—persuaded gubernatorial candidate Bush to make tort reform a priority.[261] Money promptly began to pour in from Texas' main tort reform lobby groups (essentially a couple of dozen tycoons and corporations, including **Enron**), which eventually contributed more than $4 million to Bush's two gubernatorial campaigns. "Business groups flocked to us," Rove boasted.

"Three days after taking office . . . [Gov. Bush] proclaimed an emergency situation demanding the Legislature's immediate attention," *The Washington Post* recalled. "The issue was not education, welfare or the state's juvenile justice system, all of which Bush had vowed to tackle, but . . . curtailing what he called 'the junk lawsuits that clog our courts.'"[262]

Opponents said the supposed "litigation explosion" was nonexistent. In the preceding year, said the president of the Texas Trial Lawyers Association, "more people froze to death in Texas than actually collected punitive damages." Some said Bush had a personal motive—a lawsuit pending against himself. In any case, Bush quickly signed seven bills that made it harder to win damages against businesses, doctors, hospitals and insurers—"more tort reform in one session than any state in the country in the last fifteen to twenty years," said a delighted lobbyist. The "reforms" included narrower definitions of "gross negligence";

tougher standards of proof for plaintiffs; and lower limits on the liability of the wealthiest defendants and on punitive damage awards, even to people horribly injured by negligent companies. Following Bush's "reform" of the state's Deceptive Trade Practices Act, "you could more easily prove negligent homicide," said the former chief of the state attorney general's consumer protection division.

The malpractice "crisis" (and $250,000-per-life solution). As president, Bush put special emphasis on the supposed explosion in medical malpractice suits, and their supposed blame for driving up health care and insurance costs. But a study published by *USA Today* in March 2003 found that while some doctors had been hit hard by rising malpractice premiums, most "are minimally affected." Premiums were not rising any more rapidly than other health care costs and, on average, physicians spent more on rent than on insurance.

Bush and his congressional allies' proposed solution for this "crisis" was to cap malpractice awards at $250,000. That would be the maximum award for someone whom a doctor's or hospital's mistake had killed or left crippled, paralyzed, or comatose for life.

The Bushies singled out Democratic presidential contender John Edwards, a former trial lawyer, as their poster boy for greedy trial lawyers, and one of his cases in particular as their pet case study: As a result of a negligent obstetrician, an infant girl, Bailey Griffin, had been born severely brain-damaged, was confined to a wheelchair, and died at age six. A Health and Human Services report labeled the $23 million jury award excessive; Bush termed such suits "a legal lottery." As Al Hunt asked in *The Wall Street Journal*, "Did the Griffins hit the jackpot?"

There are abuses in the legal system, and some changes are needed, Hunt added. "But the White House egregiously distorts the case. . . . what the current advocates desire is not real tort reform but to immunize powerful interests from the consequences of irresponsible civil behavior. They would create a caste system for litigation: Those with resources would have easy access, those without would not."[263]

TRADE AND TARIFFS

Like a true, conservative, free-trade fundamentalist, Bush called free trade a "moral imperative." His *actions* on trade and tariffs were consistently dictated by political expediency and the wishes of powerful interest groups.

The paradigmatic example was steel. It was a shock to conservative free-traders when Bush appeared with union workers in March 2002 to announce he was slapping a 30 percent tariff on imported steel—supposedly to protect steel jobs. Of course, his tariff move had nothing to do with the fact that steel-producing Pennsylvania, Ohio, West Virginia, and Michigan were important election swing states—or that Florida, a state Bush "won" by a hair, was home to 300,000 retired steelworkers. That would amount to positively Clintonian "triangulation." (Actually, Clinton had the courage to tell steelworkers that free trade was the greater good.)

Meanwhile, the higher cost of steel would hurt steel-consuming U.S. industries, like auto manufacturing, *and* their workers, and lower U.S. GDP by up to $1.4 billion. For every steel job saved as a result of the tariff, according to one study, eight would be lost in other sectors, and higher prices for products like cars would cost consumers around $450,000. With the tariff, Bush had in fact imposed a tax on consumers.[264] At least *that* was consistent—with Bush's goal of shifting the tax burden from the rich to middle- and lower-income Americans.

In March 2003 the World Trade Organization (WTO) ruled that Bush's steel tariffs were illegal, which permitted other countries to retaliate with trade sanctions against U.S. exports, hurting U.S. workers in an even wider range of industries. Under Bush, the U.S. lost thirteen out of fifteen cases brought against it by the WTO. In August 2002, the WTO ruled that the European Union was entitled to impose $4 billion in trade sanctions against the U.S.—by far the biggest trade penalty ever imposed—for violating trade agreements by subsidizing U.S. exporters through special tax breaks. *The New York Times* called the decision "a rebuke that was all the more stinging because it was aimed at a country that routinely lectures the rest of the world on the need to open its markets."

Other Bush violations of free trade principles included $100 billion in farm subsidies awarded in August 2002; stiff tariffs on Canadian lumber, wheat, and energy—hurting Canadian producers and U.S. consumers; and protection for the **pharmaceutical industry** from reimportation of cheaper drugs from Canada and from other countries' exports of generics. Annual U.S. subsidies to a relative handful of large cotton growers exceeded the entire gross national product of several poor cotton-producing countries in Africa, whose farmers, unable to compete with subsidized Western crops, were condemned to poverty.

VETERANS' RIGHTS

"Promises made to our veterans will be promises kept."
—George W. Bush, January 2000

No president ever praised and posed with veterans and service men and woman more than Bush. Meanwhile:

- In 2002, the White House threatened to veto a bill to allow vets disabled in service to collect disability pay without forfeiting an equal amount of their retirement pay.
- Bush's 2003 budget proposal provided $2 billion less for veterans' health care than vets groups said was needed. Moreover, $400 million the administration called a funding increase was to come out of vets' own pockets, mostly in the form of increased co-payments. "The President promised an historic increase in the veterans budget in his State of the Union address," noted Rep. John Dingell (D-MI). "Today, we see only smoke and mirrors, and accounting gimmicks."
- The administration refused to reverse a 1995 government decision to rescind a promise of free lifetime health care to veterans who had served twenty or more years. Vets could still be treated at VA hospitals— where, a 2002 report said, more than 300,000 veterans nationwide were waiting for primary care appointments. (In August 2003, the Veterans Affairs Department proposed closing seven VA hospitals across the country and reducing services at dozens of others.)
- Bush's 2004 budget proposal disqualified veterans making more than $24,000 a year—an estimated 173,000 vets nationwide—from enrolling for health care benefits.

You didn't have to wait to leave the service to be stiffed by the Bushies. By August 2003, there were widespread reports of bad living conditions among U.S. forces in Iraq, including bad food and insufficient water rations, leading to a rash of illnesses and heat stroke. Col. David Hackworth, a decorated veteran and Pentagon critic, blamed administration officials who "thought they could run a war and an occupation on the cheap." Others pointed to the dismal performance of private firms (like **Cheney's Halliburton**) to which the privatization-happy Bushies were "outsourcing" military logistics, support and any other functions that weren't nailed down.

Secretary of Defense Rumsfeld insulted thousands of Vietnam vets at a press briefing in January 2003 when, asked about reinstating the draft, he said Vietnam-era draftees were people "without choices" in the civilian job market who added "no value, no advantage, really" to the armed services.[265]

WAR ON TERRORISM: BUSH'S POLITICAL WMD

"But all in all, it's been a fabulous year for Laura and me."
　　　　　—George W. Bush, White House press release,
　　　　　　　　　　　　　　　　　December 21, 2001

By July 2001, his fifth month in office, Bush's approval rating had fallen below 50 percent—a five-year presidential low. He was viewed, strangely enough, as favoring the rich over ordinary Americans and the energy industry over the environment—and as none too bright, or hard-working, or even interested in his job; the running joke was that Cheney was in charge.

Two months later—after **September 11**—Bush's job approval was up to 84 percent and he had been recast as a war leader of Churchillian stature. It didn't take a Karl Rove to see that politically, the war on terrorism was going to work big-time for the Bushies. And they were going to work *it* for all it was worth to further every aspect of their political agenda, however absurdly unrelated. It worked so well, no wonder they wanted to extend the war to **Iraq**.

"For Bush, leveraging the war on terrorism knows no bounds," Ryan Lizza observed in *The New Republic.* "He has repackaged his entire domestic agenda in the garb of 'security.'"[266] Moreover, as Paul Starr pointed out in *The American Prospect*, the war on terrorism had no end in sight—and thus provided "an indefinite warrant for intensified security measures" and for whatever else the Republicans have wanted to do—"and they plan to use it to create a new Republican era in American politics."[267]

The war on terrorism naturally forced Bush to freeze or cut back broadly on domestic spending while accelerating the biggest military spending spree since Reagan (as though 9/11 resulted from a shortage of fighter jets or nuclear subs). More remarkably, it made it necessary to pass a huge new round of tax cuts for fat cats, in the guise of "economic security" (see **Budget and taxes**). After 9/11, Bush exulted in public about his new excuse for turning a $5.6 trillion surplus into a $4 trillion deficit: Claiming he had promised not to run deficits except in the event of recession, war, or national emergency, he joked, "Lucky me—I hit the trifecta."

The war on terrorism gave the Bushies cover for a massive attack on Americans' **civil liberties and privacy**—and for appropriating unprecedented powers of **secrecy**. Weeks after 9/11, Bush issued an executive order giving him the power to seal White House records forever (including, perhaps, records of U.S. support for Saddam Hussein *and* Osama bin Laden under Reagan and Bush I officials such as Cheney, Rumsfeld, and Bush I). War gave Cheney the right—no, the duty—to refuse to turn over the records of his closed-door energy-policy meetings with **Enron** and other **energy** company executives to Congressional investigators. On the day he announced his decision not to cooperate, he said, "Can you imagine an FDR or Teddy Roosevelt, in the midst of a grave national crisis . . . as a matter of political expediency, trading away a very important fundamental principle of the presidency?" (The hard thing to imagine was the Bushies doing anything *not* for political expediency.) The whole Bush-Cheney drill-and-pollute energy policy was likewise repackaged and sold as vital to national security. The war on terrorism fed into Bush's war on the environment in other ways. The Environmental Protection Agency pulled information about pollution problems at chemical plants off the Internet, ostensibly because terrorists might use it. Soon after 9/11, the chief of the Army Corps of Engineers Regulatory Branch emailed his staff, "The harder we work to expedite issuance of [wetlands development] permits, the more we serve the nation by moving the economy forward." War meant the military—the nation's biggest polluter—should be exempted from key environmental laws on 25 million acres of military bases, ports and airfields.

War gave the Bushies an excuse to strip union rights from some 200,000 federal employees shifted to the new **Homeland Security** department (also see **Labor**). And war obviously obligated the Senate to approve swiftly and without fuss Bush's **judicial nominees**: As Press Secretary Ari Fleischer shamelessly said, "The president deserves to have his team in place, particularly during a time of war."

Even Bush's "Faith-based Initiative" was now always referred to as the "armies of compassion" bill by Bush's army of deception—i.e., White House spokespersons.

Best of all, Republicans could use the war to attack Democrats who dared oppose them on virtually anything—even smearing the mild-mannered Senator Tom Daschle by running attack ads linking him to Saddam Hussein. And while they warned *Democrats* not to try "politicizing" the war, "General" Karl Rove urged Republicans to use the war on terrorism to take back the Senate in 2002 and reelect Bush in 2004.

WATER POLLUTION AND WETLANDS

Having attacked and eviscerated the Clean Air Act (see **Air pollution**), what *would* be next on the Bushies' agenda?

The CLEAN WATER ACT (CWA) of 1972 had resulted in the restoration of numerous rivers, lakes, and wetlands, but 45 percent of U.S. waters remained unsafe for drinking, swimming, fishing and aquatic life, according to a 2002 Environmental Protection Agency (EPA) report. But the Bushies had a solution: If polluters were violating regulations, get rid of the regulations. In just their first year and a half, they:

- Removed thirty-year-old CWA protection from large numbers of streams and wetlands.
- Abandoned the national "no net loss of wetlands" goal, established under Bush Sr.
- Gutted the program for cleaning up polluted waters.
- Eliminated a twenty-five-year-old ban on dumping mining and other industrial wastes into wetlands and streams.

Wetlands protection attacked. By 2001, nationwide, pollution and development were destroying 58,500 acres a year of wetlands—the marshes, swamps, and bogs that filter and cleanse water, help retain floodwaters, and provide critical wildlife habitats. Regulations drafted under Clinton and due to go into effect in February 2001 would have expanded protections by, among other measures, requiring acre-for-acre replacement of destroyed wetlands.

Then the Bushies came to town. A Bush pledge to protect wetlands—made on Earth Day, 2001—proved to be the usual Bush BS (bait-and-switch). In August 2001, the U.S. Army Corps of Engineers—by law the nation's primary protector of wetlands—set new rules that allowed individual Corps officials to waive the Clinton requirements and that made it easier for developers, mining companies, and other industries to destroy wetlands or streams without public review. According to the National Resources Defense Council (NRDC), "If these decisions are made at the whim of an individual Corps official, wetlands will disappear rapidly in many parts of the country."[268] Bush signed off on the new rules in January 2002.

"No net loss" lost. The requirement for replacing destroyed wetlands acre-for-acre was one of the few clear standards for measuring the Corps' performance in preserving wetlands—which by all accounts was miserable. In the past, the Corps had often let developers destroy wetlands on a mere promise that they would replace them. Under their new "mitigation" policy, they didn't even ask that much; instead, they would allow the preservation or enhancement of *existing* wetlands to count as mitigation. In other words, henceforth, every acre lost was simply lost.

In January 2002, it was reported that arch-anti-environmentalist Interior Secretary Gail Norton had suppressed criticism of the new policies by her own agency's Fish and Wildlife Service, which had drafted comments saying the policies had "no scientific basis" and would result in "tremendous destruction of aquatic and terrestrial habitats."

Wiping wetlands off the map. The Bushies used every possible excuse to remove wetlands from federal protection. In September 2002, they proposed new rules whereby streams that dry up periodically and wetlands next to them—some 20 percent of the nation's remaining wetlands—would no longer be protected from dumping and filling by developers, mining companies, etc. At the site of a new container port under construction near Galveston, Texas, the Corps of Engineers counted more than 100 acres of wetlands that would be lost. On a second count, they came up with a figure of less than three acres. The Corps had simply reduced the wetlands area over which it claimed authority—citing as justification a narrow loophole created by a sharply divided Supreme Court ruling in 2001. And so the Bushies had won another recount battle.

The same thing was happening all over the country. In the two years since Bush Corp. took over the country, the total wetlands area over which the Corps claimed jurisdiction shrank by at least 40 percent.

Mountaintop removal mining legalized. In April 2002, the Bushies, responding to coal lobbying, proposed a new rule allowing industrial wastes used to fill, bury and destroy U.S. waters. The rule was intended to legalize the practice of "mountaintop removal" coal mining, in which the entire tops are blasted off of mountains and huge amounts of waste are dumped into nearby valleys, burying streams and wetlands and killing all aquatic life. (See **Environment**.)

WELFARE "REFORM": *THE POOR STILL HAVE IT TOO GOOD*

With Clinton's landmark 1996 welfare reform law set to expire in 2002, there came a new debate on welfare—and new GOP/Bush demands for getting tougher on the poor (in case the Bush recession wasn't already accomplishing that).

The 1996 law replaced entitlements for cash assistance for poor families with block grants to states and with work requirements; it required at least 50 percent of all families on welfare and 90 percent of two-parent families to be working. In February 2002, with the economy sagging and unemployment way up, the National Governors Association urged that work requirements for welfare recipients be relaxed, saying they were unrealistic and that welfare recipients needed more education and training to secure jobs. The governors also opposed a Bush proposal to take $300 million out of welfare funds and spend it on programs aimed at "encouraging healthy, stable marriages."

Two days later, Bush proposed *increasing* the work requirements and pushing the states harder to meet them. He called for raising the 50-percent requirement to 70 percent and the weekly work requirement from thirty hours (including up to ten hours of job training or education) to forty, and for closing "loopholes" in the work requirements, lest any of those lazy bums try to sneak through. Bush announced the welfare plan at a church in Washington, standing before a backdrop emblazoned with BS (see **BushSpeak**) slogans like "Opportunity," "Work," "Family," "Responsibility," and "Working toward independence." "We must never be content with islands of despair in the midst of a nation of promise," Bush preached. "We want all Americans to believe in the potential of their own lives and the promise of their own country." Meanwhile, his just-released 2003 budget plan reduced funding for job training.

The tougher requirements were not a response to increasing welfare dependency; the number of welfare recipients had dropped from 12.2 million in 1996 to 5.3 million in September 2001. The Bushies disputed the view of welfare experts that the most important factor in that drop was the booming economy of the '90s—a view that implied that (a) it was not principally the work requirements that had got people off welfare, and (b) in the slower economy under Bush, increased workfare requirements were little more than a cruel joke.

ZINNI, ANTHONY

Retired Marine Corps general, former chief of U.S. Central Command, commander of a successful 1992 operation in northern Iraq, and an opponent of Bush's war in **Iraq**, who predicted that long-term, it would foment civil war and chaos. "Our relationships in the region are in major disrepair," Zinni said in an August 2002 speech. "[W]e need to quit making enemies . . . There's a deep chasm growing between that part of the world and our part of the world." Among his greatest contributions was a name that fulfilled this book's A-to-Z promise.

ENDNOTES

1 Asjylyn Loder, "Bush's Anti-Choice Policies Felt Around the World," *Women's eNews*, 1/20/03.

2 "'Mexico City' Policy," Democratic Office Foreign Policy Briefs, January 2001.

3 Nicholas Kristof, "Mr. Bush's Liberal Problem," *The New York Times*, 2/18/03.

4 Center on Budget and Policy Priorities press release, 10/4/02.

5 Karen Tumulty, "Jesus and the FDA," *Time*, 10/5/02.

6 The drug companies (echoed by the Bushies) claimed generics would undermine their ability to fund research and development. Actually, the industry spent more than twice as much on marketing as on R&D; much of the R&D for AIDS drugs had been paid for by U.S. taxpayers, through funding for the National Institutes of Health and its various divisions; and Africa accounted for only 1.3 percent of the industry's revenues.

7 "The Bush Administration's Air Pollution Plan," Natural Resources Defense Council fact sheet, February 2003.

8 Ben Ehrenreich, "Roe v. Wade v. Ashcroft," *LA Weekly*, 4/30/02.

9 Quoted in "Ashcroft Whistles Dixie," *Salon*.com, 1/3/01, among other places.

10 Other leading Republicans who found this magazine appropriate to give interviews to included Trent Lott, Jesse Helms, Dick Armey and Patrick Buchanan.

11 Bush, despite his admiration for Ashcroft—whom, God help us, he referred to as a potential Supreme Court justice—preferred former Montana governor Marc Racicot, his point man in the Florida recount battle, for AG. But the far right saw Racicot as insufficiently anti-abortion and anti-gay. (Bush made Racicot Republican National Committee chairman instead.)

12 Lee Cokorinos, "John Ashcroft: An Asset of the Far Right," Institute for Democratic Studies.

13 Jessica Portner, "Ashcroft's Desegregation Record Questioned," *Education Week*, 1/24/01; Alicia Montgomery, "Ashcroft Whistles Dixie," *Salon*, 1/3/01.

14 Peter Schrag, "Ashcroft's hypocrisy," *The American Prospect*, 1/1/02.

15 Robert Scheer, "An Orgy of Defense Spending," Los Angeles Times, 2/5/02.

16 The huge deficit Bush racked up "raises long [interest] rates and stifles investment, reducing productivity and economic growth," according to a *Business Week* article, "The Heavy Long-Term Toll of the Bush Tax Cuts" (6/9/03).

17 Lars Erik Nelson, "Bush And Cheney Self-Made Men?: They've Got To Be Kidding" *New York Daily News*, 10/11/00.

18 Economic Policy Institute press conference on Bush plan, C-SPAN, 2/10/03

19 Bush claimed the richest 1 percent would get "only" 22 percent of the tax cut and that he was cutting taxes more at the bottom than the top. But this ignored (a) payroll taxes, the biggest burden on low-income working people; (b) the cut in

estate taxes, paid primarily by the rich; and (c) the benefits for the wealthy that kicked in after the first few years.

20 "51 Million Taxpayers Won't Get Full Rebates from 2001 Tax Bill," Citizens for Tax Justice, 6/1/01.

21 Peter G. Peterson, "Deficits and Dysfunction," *The New York Times Magazine*, 6/8/03.

22 Jonathan Chait, "Another Bush Scandal: The Budget," *The New Republic*, 7/29/02.

23 At the same time, Bush's budget was phasing out payments to the states to help cover unemployment insurance.

24 The situation, wrote Molly Ivins, "has an eerie familiarity to Texas, where [Bush] pushed through not one but two tax cuts that left the cupboard so bare that . . . [w]ith an estimated $5 billion deficit, Texas will probably have to follow the lead of Gov. Jeb Bush in Florida" (who had just slashed $600 million from education).

25 Economic Policy Institute press conference on Bush plan, C-SPAN, 2/10/03.

26 Ibid.

27 BCCI was also involved in money laundering, tax evasion, bribery, arms trafficking, and nuclear technology sales. BCCI "clients" included the Medellin drug cartel, Manuel Noriega, and Saddam Hussein.

28 Charles Lewis, *The Buying of the President 2000*, Center for Public Integrity, 2000.

29 Quoted by Wayne Madsen, "Questionable Ties: Tracking bin Laden's money flow leads back to Midland, Texas," *In These Times*, 12/11/01.

30 Steven J. Hedges, "The Color of Money," *U.S. News and World Report*, 3/16/92.

31 Joe Conason, "Notes on a Native Son," *Harper's Magazine*, February 2000.

32 Lars Erik Nelson, "Bush And Cheney Self-Made Men? They've Got To Be Kidding," *New York Daily News*, 10/11/00.

33 Gene Lyons, "A Bush family tradition," *Arkansas Democrat-Gazette*, 1/12/00.

34 Robert Parry, "Bush Family Politics," Consortiumnews.com, 10/5/99.

35 Bush was trying to make light of a remark he had made a few years earlier; as he related in a 1994 interview, while visiting his parents at the White House in January 1993, he told his mother the New Testament said "only Christians have a place in heaven." (Mrs. Bush disagreed, and phoned Billy Graham, who agreed with George.) [Source: Eric Fingerhut, *Jewish World Review*, 12/23/98].

36 Tucker Carlson, "Devil May Care," *Talk*, September 1999.

37 Dave Shiflett, "A Noble Hypocrisy," *Salon*, 8/24/99.

38 Richard Brookhiser, "Boy Bush," *National Review*, 9/13/99.

39 George F. Will, "Bush has some growing up to do," *The Washington Post*, 8/14/99.

40 Joan Walsh, "Bushed!" *Salon*, 2/21/02.

41 "Notes on a national disorder: An interview with Mark Crispin Miller," *LiP* magazine, 6/25/01.

42 Gary Kamiya, "Did I Watch the Wrong Channel?" *Salon*, 1/31/02.

43 Paul Krugman, "See No Evil," *The New York Times*, 9/24/02.

44 David Lazarus, "White House Connections to Energy Giants Under Investigation Emerge," *The San Francisco Chronicle*, 11/22/02.

45 Arianna Huffington, "Good-Bye, Soft Money; Hello, Hard Choices," 3/7/02.

46 Meanwhile, two other commissioners with expired terms awaited replacement by Bush. (Paging Katherine Harris . . .) Another sitting member, Bradley Smith, picked by Senate Republicans in 1998, had called for the FEC and all campaign finance laws to be abolished.

47 John Bonifaz, "Lawsuit Unearths New Details About Bush Campaign's Fundraising Practices," National Voting Rights Institute news release.

48 Lawrence Noble and Paul Sanford, "Undermining the New Campaign Law," *The New York Times*, 3/29/02.

49 "Rescuing Campaign Reform," editorial, *The New York Times*, 6/27/02.

50 Andrew Wheat, "George W. Bush, Corporate Candidate: How Money Grows on the 'Shrub,'" *Multinational Monitor*, March 2000.

51 Texas rules (if there were any) did not limit how much money individuals and political action committees (PACs) could give candidates.

52 Richard A. Oppel Jr., "Campaign Documents Show Depth of Bush Fund-Raising," *The New York Times*, 5/5/03.

53 S.C. Gwynne, "Did Dick Cheney Sink Halliburton?" *Texas Monthly*, 10/01/02.

54 Michelle Cottle, "Funny Business," *The New Republic Online*, 7/17/02.

55 The unit included in its ranks sons of former governor John Conally and of senators Lloyd Bentson and John Tower; seven Dallas Cowboys; and two sons of the family friend who pulled the strings for Bush.

56 Walter V. Robinson, "One-year gap in Bush's National Guard duty," *The Boston Globe*, 5/23/00.

57 Pat Dawson, "Of Deregulation, Enron and Chickenhawks," *Billings [Montana] Outpost*, 11/23/02.

58 Ibn Warraq, *Why I Am Not a Muslim*, Prometheus Books, Amherst, New York, 1995.

59 Bush's flaunting of his faith made excellent political sense. In a December 2001 Gallup poll, 46 percent of Americans described themselves as evangelical or born-again Christians.

60 Eric Fingerhut, "Bush clarifies his stand on Jews, heaven," *Jewish World Review*, 12/23/98.

61 Jeffrey S. Siker, "President Bush, Biblical Faith, and the Politics of Religion," *Religious Studies News*, April 2003.

62 Interview with David Frum, "The Real George Bush," *The Atlantic*, 2/12/03.

63 Americans United for Separation of Church and State press release, 7/19/01

64 Marvin Olasky, "Rolling the Dice," *World*, 8/4/01.

65 "Bush's Own Denomination Opposes White House 'Faith-Based Initiative,'" Americans United for Separation of Church and State press release, 6/14/01.

66 Rev. Wanda Henry at the National Press Club, 1/30/01, quoted in Americans United for Separation of Church and State press release, 2/20/01.

67 Texas Freedom Network press release, 10/10/02.

68 Ron Suskind, "Why Are These Men Laughing?" *Esquire*, January 2003.

69 Lee Cokorinos, "John Ashcroft: An Asset of the Far Right," Institute for Democratic Studies.

70 Ashcroft said on another occasion, "Islam is a religion in which God requires you

to send your son to die for him. Christianity is a faith in which God sends his son to die for you."

71 Christopher Hitchens, *The Nation*, 12/17/01.

72 American Civil Liberties Union, "Surveillance Under the USA Patriot Act," 4/3/03

73 Ibid.

74 Jeffrey Rosen, "Civil Right: Thank goodness for Dick Armey," *The New Republic*, 10/21/02.

75 Ibid.

76 "Urge Congress to Protect Against Domestic Spying!" ACLU press release, October 3, 2002.

77 Michelle Delio, "Privacy Activist Takes on Delta," Wired.com, 3/5/03.

78 Matthew Brzezinski, "Fortress America," *The New York Times Magazine*, 2/23/03.

79 "A Chilly Response to 'Patriot II,'" *Wired*, 2/12/03.

80 Bob Herbert, "Beware Mr. Bush's 'compassion,'" *The New York Times*, 2/14/03.

81 Quoted in "Ex-Aide Insists White House Puts Politics Ahead of Policy," *New York Times*, 12/2/02.

82 Jonathan Chait, "Special K: Why The Bush Administration Is Worse Than DiIulio Said," *The New Republic*, 12/30/02.

83 Billy Ray Kidwell, "The Bush Administration has Quietly Declared War Against America's Veterans," Vets for Justice.com, 2002.

84 "Possible Ashcroft Campaign Violation," *The Washington Post*, 2/1/01.

85 Kristen Sykes of Friends of the Earth, on *Now with Bill Moyers*, 5/30/03.

86 "Executive Summary: Norton's Fringe Benefits," National Resources Defense Council.

87 Robert Kuttner, "Mr. Corporate Reform?" *The American Prospect*, 8/5/02.

88 Arianna Huffington, "The Enron Scandal," 12/19/01.

89 "Senate Passses Corporate Reform Bill," CNN.com 7/16/02.

90 "SEC Weakens Auditor Independence Rules," *Fulcrum Financial Inquiry*, 1/27/03.

91 Andy Serwer, *Fortune*, 1/30/03.

92 Kevin Drawbaugh, "Bush's SEC Budget Stance Draws Fire from Congress," Reuters, 12/5/02.

93 Michael L. Radelet et al., *In Spite of Innocence*, Northeastern U. Press, 1994.

94 Over 90 percent of defendants charged with capital crimes in the U.S. cannot afford to hire an experienced criminal defense attorney, and are forced to use inexperienced, underpaid court-appointed attorneys.

95 Op-ed, *New York Daily News*, 10/12/00.

96 Adam Liptak, "Puerto Ricans Angry That U.S. Overrode Death Penalty Ban," *The New York Times*, 7/15/03.

97 Robert Scheer, "An Orgy of Defense Spending," *The Los Angeles Times*, 2/5/02.

98 Al Hunt, "The Bush Budget: Guns and Champagne," *The Wall Street Journal*, 2/14/02.

99 Jason Vest, "Costs a Bundle and Can't Fly," *The American Prospect*, 3/11/02.

100 "Fill 'Er Up: Back-Door Deal for Boeing Will Leave the Taxpayer on Empty," Project on Government Oversight report, 2002.

332 *Endnotes*

101 "Concern Over Rumsfeld Transformation Grows," Project on Government Oversight, 5/13/03.

102 "Rumsfeld Agenda Would Gut U.S. Democracy," Green Party media release, 5/13/03.

103 Arianna Huffington, "Compassionate Conservative vs. Enron Conservatives," 1/10/02.

104 Molly Ivins, "What's the policy today?" *Fort Worth Star-Telegram*, 2/5/02.

105 Robert Kuttner, "The Road to Enron," *The American Prospect*, 3/25/02.

106 Robert Kuttner, "University for Rent," *The American Prospect*, 5/7/01.

107 Ellen Nakashima, "Chief Plans Overhaul of Regulatory Process, Report: 'Science-Based' Approach Sought," *The Washington Post*, 3/20/02.

108 Diana R. Gordon, "Ashcroft Justice," *The Nation*, 7/23/01.

109 "Unemployment Rate Rises to a 9-Year High," *New York Times*, 6/6/03.

110 In March 2002, Bush generously signed into law a measure allowing teachers a tax deduction of up to $250 for money they spend on supplies.

111 "Reform without resources isn't realistic," New Jersey Education Association report, 2/23/03.

112 An Arizona State University study released in March 2002—the largest to date on the subject—concluded that such "high-stakes" tests had little or no effect on true student performance. Students weren't necessarily learning more—just focusing on what would be on the test. The tests "create the impression of accountability without the substance," one critic said.

113 Bob Herbert, "Heavy Lifting," *The New York Times*, 2/13/03.

114 "Reform without resources isn't realistic," New Jersey Education Association report, 2/23/03.

115 Timothy Egan, "Failures Raise Questions for Charter Schools," *The New York Times*, 4/5/02.

116 Elisabeth Bumiller, "Bush Seeks Big Changes in Head Start, Drawing Criticism From Program's Supporters," *The New York Times*, 7/8/03.

117 The media encouraged this. "How many people still care about the election deadlock that last fall felt like the story of the century—and now faintly echoes like some distant Civil War battle?" wrote Howard Kurtz in *The Washington Post*.

118 Joe Conason, "A Year Later, It's Still a Sham," *New York Observer*, 11/26/01.

119 John W. Dean, "Vote of no confidence: A self-described 'election junkie' surveys dozens of books about the 2000 presidential contest and arrives at some troubling conclusions," *Salon*, 1/30/02.

120 Arthur Schlesinger Jr., "Not the People's Choice," *The American Prospect*, 3/25/02.

121 "Executive Order Followed Energy Industry Recommendation, Documents Show," *The New York Times*, 4/4/02.

122 Cheney co-sponsored a bill for this purpose in 1987 as a Wyoming congressman.

123 Paul Krugman, "2000 Acres," *The New York Times*, 3/1/02.

124 *Los Angeles Times*, 4/8/02.

125 Common Assets Defense Fund fact sheet, May 2003.

126 Arianna Huffington, "Got Oil?" 10/21/02.

127 Richard Simon, "Bush energy bill passes House," *Los Angeles Times*, 4/12/03.

128 American Council for an Energy-Efficient Economy press brief, 4/9/01.

129 Arianna Huffington, "Will Saddam's Oily Scheme Help Save Bush's ANWR Dream?" April 11, 2002.

130 Friends of the Earth, Fact Sheet on James E. Cason.

131 Joe Stephens, "Bush 2000 Adviser Offered To Use Clout to Help Enron," *The Washington Post*, 2/17/02.

132 David Corn, "W.'s First Enron Connection," *The Nation*, 3/4/02.

133 "Bush-Lay letters suggest close relationship," CNN.com, 2/17/02.

134 Josh Gerstein, "Friends in High Places: Bankrupt Enron Held Sway With Current Bush Administration," ABCNews.com, 12/10/01; David Corn, "'Enronitis' Ravishing the GOP!," AlterNet, 1/25/02.

135 Pat Dawson, "Of Deregulation, Enron and Chickenhawks," *The Billings Outpost*, 11/23/02.

136 Molly Ivins, "Photo-op Alert," *Fort Worth Star-Ledger*, 12/21/01.

137 Ibid.

138 "U.S. Acts to Shrink Endangered Species Habitat," *The New York Times*, 3/20/02.

139 Minority staff, Committee on Government Reform fact sheet, 6/21/02.

140 Michael Kinsley, "Dead Wrong," *The Washington Post*, 4/6/01.

141 Julie R.F. Gerchik, "Slouching Towards Extremism," *IDS Insights*, November 2000.

142 Fareed Zakaria, "Our Way: The trouble with being the world's only superpower," *The New Yorker*, 10/14/02

143 George Monbiot, "The Logic of Empire," *The Guardian*, 8/6/02.

144 Hendrik Herzberg, *The New Yorker*, 10/14/02.

145 Peter Johnson, "Bush Has Media Walking a Fine Line," *USA Today*, 3/9/03.

146 ACLU report, "Freedom Under Fire: Dissent in Post-9/11 America."

147 Dana Milbank, "Charity Cites Bush Help in Fight Against Hiring Gays," *The Washington Post*, 7/10/01.

148 Richard Goldstein, "Bush's Gay Gambit: Does Silence = Support for Gay Rights?" *The Village Voice*, July 17–23, 2002.

149 John Mason, "US pressure forces removal of climate change chief," *Financial Times*, 4/19/02.

150 Jessica Tuchman Matthews, *Foreign Policy*, January 2002.

151 Said to televangelist James Robison; quoted by Tony Carnes, "A Presidential Hopeful's Progress," *Christianity Today*, 10/2/00.

152 Arianna Huffington, "The Evildoers and the Misled," 12/6/01.

153 Jeffrey S. Siker, "President Bush, Biblical Faith, and the Politics of Religion," *Religious Studies News*, April 2003.

154 "Issues 2000," *The Economist*, 9/30/00.

155 Paul Duggan, "Gun-Friendly Record Expected to Be Issue: '95 Law Lets 200,000 Conceal Arms," *The Washington Post*, 3/16/00.

156 Deborah Amos, "Gun Land," *Now, with Bill Moyers*, PBS, 11/15/02.

157 A U.N. document blamed small arms for 4 million deaths in forty-six conflicts since 1990—about 90 percent of them civilians and 80 percent women and children.

158 Robert Pear, "After Decline, the Number of Uninsured Rose in 2001," *The New York Times*, 9/30/02.

159 Frank Rich, "The Jack Welch War Plan," *New York Times*, 9/28/02.

160 Rick Weiss, "HHS Seeks Science Advice to Match Bush Views," *The Washington Post*, 9/17/02.

161 Harold Evans, "What We Knew," *Columbia Journalism Review*, Nov.–Dec. 2001.

162 Rep. David Obey, National Press Club speech, 12/18/02.

163 Jonathan Chait, "The 9/10 President," *The New Republic*, 3/10/03.

164 Matthew L. Wald, "White House Cut 93% of Funds Sought to Guard Atomic Arms," *The New York Times*, 4/23/02.

165 Raymond Hernandez, "New York Officials Complain of Unfair Share of Security Money," *The New York Times*, 3/30/03.

166 Dana Milbank, "For Bush, Facts Are Malleable," *The Washington Post*, 10/22/02.

167 Al Hunt, "What They Say and What They Do," *The Wall Street Journal*, 2/6/03.

168 Paul Begala, *Crossfire*, CNN, 2/10/03

169 Molly Ivins, "Photo-Op Alert," *Fort Worth Star-Telegram*, 12/15/01.

170 Bruce B. Auster et al., "Truth and Consequences," *U.S. News and World Report*, 6/9/03.

171 Douglas Jehl, "Iraqi Trailers Said to Make Hydrogen, Not Biological Arms," *The New York Times*, 8/9/03.

172 Nicholas Kristof, "After War, Let Iraqis Triumph," *The New York Times*, 3/21/03

173 Chris Floyd, "Group Therapy: Bush, Bin Laden, Bechtel and Baghdad," *Counterpunch*, 5/12/03.

174 Aaron Davis and Dana Hull, "Bechtel to Get Richer in Post-War Iraq," *San Jose Mercury News*, 3/25/03.

175 Michael Kinsley, "Estrada's *Omertà*," *Slate*, 2/13/03.

176 Editorial, "Steamrolling Judicial Nominees," *The New York Times*, 2/6/03.

177 The federal judiciary consists of the Supreme Court, appeals courts, and trial courts. Appeals courts are organized into twelve regional "circuits" plus one federal circuit with nationwide jurisdiction for specialized cases involving, for example, trade and patent laws. Trial courts include ninety-four district courts, the bankruptcy courts, Court of Federal Claims, and Court of International Trade.

178 Human Rights Campaign news release, 2/12/03.

179 Editorial, "Steamrolling Judicial Nominees," *The New York Times*, 2/6/03.

180 In 1999 the court rolled back EPA Clean Air Act standards in a decision so radical in its limiting of federal regulatory powers, the Supreme Court reversed it unanimously.

181 "PFAW Concerns About Miguel Estrada Detailed in Letter To Senate Judiciary Committee," People for the American Way, PFAW.org, 9/25/02.

182 NARAL Pro-Choice America information sheet, April 2002.

183 Editorial, "Haunted by Her Record," *Los Angeles Times*, 5/8/03.

184 Editorial, "Another Unworthy Judicial Nominee," *The New York Times*, 4/24/03.

185 In the preceding 16 years, more than 1,000 acts of violence against providers of reproductive health services were reported, including at least 1 murder, 36 bombings, 81

arsons, 131 death threats, 84 assaults, 2 kidnappings, 327 clinic invasions, 71 chemical attacks, plus more than 6,000 blockades and related disruptions.

186 Editorial, "Owen Deserves A Vote But Not A Confirmation," *Austin American-Statesman*, 4/29/03.

187 Editorial, "An Activist: Owen's Record Gives Reason For Pause On Judicial Post," *Houston Chronicle*, 5/11/03.

188 Steven Lubet, Northwestern University legal ethicist, quoted by Michael Crowley, "Judgment Day," *The New Republic*, 3/5/02.

189 Ibid.

190 Human Rights Campaign, 2/12/03.

191 "Sen. Leahy, Environmentalists Fight Bush Nominee To Claims Court," InsideEPA.com, 3/24/03.

192 Clay Risen, "Understudies," *The New Republic*, 5/26/03.

193 Ibid.

194 Jillian Jonas, "New Federal Judges Likely to Curtail Women's Rights," *Women's Enews*, 5/14/03.

195 Clay Risen, op. cit.

196 Marshall Wittmann, quoted in "Bush's steel tariff is an early bit of politicking," *Philadelphia Inquirer*, 3/13/02.

197 Matthew Weinstock, "Transportation security chief says no to collective bargaining," GovExec.com, 1/9/03.

198 Quoted in "Bush Placing Roadblocks in Front of Minimum Wage Hike," Labor Research Association Online, 7/30/01.

199 Washington State Labor Council/AFL-CIO press release, 3/28/03.

200 Nathan Newman, "Bush's Assault on Workers Rights," Americans for Democratic Action (ADA) Workers Rights Forum, May 13, 2002.

201 Peter Johnson, "Bush Has Media Walking a Fine Line," *USA Today*, 3/9/03.

202 Elisabeth Bumiller, *The New York Times*, 5/16/03.

203 *Now with Bill Moyers*, PBS, 4/4/03. Counting the movie industry, some nine corporations now ruled the media universe: AOL Time Warner, Disney, General Electric, News Corp., Viacom, Vivendi, Sony, Bertelsmann, and Liberty Media.

204 Robert Kuttner, "Diversity is Squashed in FCC Rules Change," *The Boston Globe*, 5/28/03.

205 Because of a formula that discounted UHF stations.

206 William Safire, "Bush's Four Horsemen," *The New York Times*, 7/24/03.

207 Mark Crispin Miller, "What's Wrong With This Picture?," *The Nation*, 12/20/01.

208 "Does Ownership Matter in Local Television News?" Journalism.org, 4/29/03.

209 Paul Krugman, "The China Syndrome," *The New York Times*, 5/13/03.

210 Paul Krugman, "Bad Medicine," *The New York Times*, 3/19/02.

211 The program covered 30 million low-income Americans, including one in five children; provided health and nursing home payments for 7 million people with disabilities; and supplemented Medicare for 6 million elderly living in poverty.

212 National Health Law Program (NheLP), "The Administration's Proposal for Medicaid," 2/5/03.

213 Al Hunt, "What They Say and What They Do," *The Wall Street Journal*, 2/6/03.

214 National Health Law Program (NheLP), op cit.

215 Editorial, "A Fair Medicare Competition," *The New York Times*, 7/17/03.

216 The GOP adviser/activist who said, "My goal is to get [government] down to the size where we can drown it in the bathtub."

217 Robert Pear, "Bush Pushes Plan to Curb Medicare Appeals," *The New York Times*, 3/16/03.

218 Ibid.

219 Russia's opposition to Bush's war in Iraq was probably, in part, payback for his abrogation of ABM.

220 When Reagan announced his SDI plan, he said it was intended to make nuclear weapons "impotent and obsolete." But the Bushies were pushing for missile defense and a new generation of nuclear weapons. What would Russia, China, or other potential rivals make of this, and how would they respond?

221 Statement by the Federation of American Scientists, 12/13/01.

222 Steven Weinberg, "Can Missile Defense Work?" *The New York Review of Books*, 2/14/02.

223 Russia had already said it would not go through with implementing the START II treaty, by which both sides were to eliminate all land-based MIRVs (multiple-warhead missiles), if the U.S. abrogated the ABM treaty.

224 Helen Thomas, "Bush keeps it all in the family," syndicated column, 8/17/01.

225 "Cheney's daughter offered State Dept. job," *The Washington Times*, 2/28/02.

226 Richard A. Oppel Jr., "President's Help for His Governor Brother Includes More than Campaign Stops," *The New York Times*, 10/18/02.

227 In a letter to *The New York Times*, Michael May, emeritus professor of engineering at Stanford and emeritus director of the Lawrence Livermore National Laboratory, said a "significant fraction" of targeted bioweapons "would be vented into the atmosphere along with the radioactivity from the nuclear explosion."

228 Julian Borger, "US plan for new nuclear arsenal," *The Guardian*, 2/19/03.

229 Robert Scheer, "A Nuclear Road of No Return," *Los Angeles Times*, 5/13/03.

230 Robert Scheer, op. cit.

231 Christopher Hitchens, "Knowledge (and Power)," *The Nation*, 6/10/02.

232 Jean-Charles Brisard and Guillaume Dasquie, *Forbidden Truth: U.S.-Taliban Secret Oil Diplomacy and the Failed Hunt for Bin Laden*, Thunder's Mouth Press/Nation Books, July 2002.

233 *Newsnight*, BBC News, 11/6/01.

234 John Miller, "Tape Missing Subtleties: Bin Laden Translation Omitted Sections," ABCNews.com, 12/21/01.

235 Thomas Ferraro, "Democrats Question Blank Pages in 9/11 Report," Reuters, 7/24/03.

236 Judicial Watch press release, 9/28/01.

237 Editorial, "How Patients' Rights Became a Fight," *The New York Times*, 9/1/01.

238 Eric F. Greenberg, "Happy New Year for FDA," *Packaging Digest*, January 2002.

239 Stacey Schultz, "Mr. Outside moves inside: Daniel Troy fought the FDA for years; now he's helping to run it," *U.S. News and World Report*, 3/24/03.

240 Richard Oppel, "Drug Makers Sponsor Event For GOP as Bill is Debated," *New York Times*, 6/19/02.

241 Ron Southwick, "Elite Panel of Academics Wins Fight to Continue Advising Military," *The Chronicle of Higher Education*, 6/7/02.

242 Ibid.

243 Russ Baker, "What Are They Hiding?" *The Nation*, 2/25/02.

244 Joshua Micah Marshall, "Bush's executive-privilege two-step," *Salon*, 2/7/02.

245 Robert Scheer, "Bush's Faustian Deal With the Taliban," *Los Angeles Times*, 5/22/01.

246 Al Hunt, "The Unaccountable Attorney General," *The Wall Street Journal*, 6/6/02.

247 By July, Ashcroft had switched from taking commercial flights to private jets, apparently because of terrorism warnings, or as his department said, an FBI "threat assessment."

248 *Fox News Sunday*, 5/19/02.

249 John Cooley, "The U.S. ignored foreign warnings, too," *International Herald Tribune*, 5/21/02.

250 Barton Gellman, "Before Sept. 11, Unshared Clues and Unshaped Policy," *The Washington Post*, 5/17/02.

251 Robert Novak, *Chicago Sun-Times*, September 27, 2001.

252 Wesley Wark, *Globe and Mail*, 12/18/01.

253 Howard Fineman, "The Battle Back Home," *Newsweek*, 2/4/02.

254 Edward Wyatt, "Bush Uses Own Brand of Math on Social Security," *The New York Times*, 3/2/02.

255 Paul Krugman, "Breaking the Contract," *The New York Times*, 3/5/02.

256 Bush's policies seemed designed to accelerate an already well-advanced trend toward more regressive state tax policies, as a result of which, in 2000, families earning $30,000 a year paid considerably more in state taxes than in 1990, while those earning $600,000 paid considerably less.

257 David Cay Johnston, "G.O.P. Is Moving to Slow Action on Tax Loophole," *The New York Times*, 6/18/02.

258 Robert S. McIntyre, "The Tax Cheaters Lobby," *The American Prospect*, 11/18/01.

259 Al Hunt, "Going Into the Tank for Tobacco," *The Wall Street Journal*, 8/2/01.

260 Joe Conason, "Lessons from Erin Brokovich," *Salon*, 3/28/00.

261 James Moore, Wayne Slater, *Bush's Brain*, John Wiley & Sons, 2003.

262 George Lardner Jr., "Texas 'Tort Reform' Aided Business—and Bush," *The Washington Post*, 2/10/00.

263 Al Hunt, "The Bogus Tort-Reform Case," *The Wall Street Journal*, 3/6/03.

264 Michael LaFaive, "New Steel Tariffs Will Kill Jobs," Mackinac Center for Public Policy, 3/8/02.

265 "Rumsfeld Not Speaking Softly," CBSNews.com, 1/23/03.

266 Ryan Lizza, "Divide and Conquer," *The New Republic*, 2/11/02.

267 Paul Starr, "The Democrats' Energy Problem," *The American Prospect*, 3/11/02.

268 National Resources Defense Council press release, 8/8/01

ACKNOWLEDGMENTS

I most gratefully thank Renée Sicalides for her companion-ship, love, support, careful reading, and wise suggestions; William Clark, for his enthusiasm, calm, and expertise; Hillary Frey, for her skillful, patient, and invaluable editing and guid-ance; and all the friends and relatives who lent encourage-ment, including Brenda Chabon, Marco Persichetti, Jami Stutz, Barbara Olson, Joel Feiner, Gordon Sander, Barbara Zemsky, Carmen Michaud, Hawthorn Smith, Yinka Akinsu-lure-Smith, Kathleen Lehey, Elliot Majerczyk, Marvin Huberman, and my mother, Ruth Huberman. I am indebted to David Corn, Maureen Dowd, Bob Herbert, Arianna Huffin-gton, Al Hunt, Molly Ivins, Paul Krugman, Robert Kuttner, Bill Moyers, Frank Rich, Robert Scheer, Paul Starr, and Joan Walsh, among others whose columns and commentaries were bountiful sources of information, indignation, and acerbic quotes; and to the many publications, organizations, and fellow writers and malcontents whose websites aided my research. Finally, I thank the Bush administration, for helping me know more clearly where I stand and who I am.